· WHERE ·
MERCY
IS SHOWN —
MERCY
· IS GIVEN ·

· WHERE ·
MERCY
— IS SHOWN —
MERCY
· IS GIVEN ·

DUANE "DOG" CHAPMAN

with Laura Morton

ⒽⓎⓅⒺⓇⒾⓄⓃ

NEW YORK

Photo credits, appearing on page 335, constitute a continuation of the copyright page.

Copyright © 2010 Dog TBH, Corporation

Library of Congress Cataloging-in-Publication Data has been applied for.

Mass market ISBN: 978-0-7868-9135-1

Hyperion books are available for special promotions and premiums. For details contact the HarperCollins Special Markets Department in the New York office at 212-207-7528, fax 212-207-7222, or e-mail spsales@harpercollins.com.

Design by Renato Stanisic

FIRST MASS MARKET EDITION

10 9 8 7 6 5 4 3 2 1

TO ANYONE I OFFENDED WITH MY MOUTH

"We make a living by what we get.
We make a life by what we give."

—Winston Churchill

· WHERE ·

MERCY

IS SHOWN—

MERCY

· IS GIVEN ·

INTRODUCTION

July 17, 1971

It was an unusually hot summer day in Colorado. I tried to beat the heat by taking a ride on my Harley from Denver up to Boulder. I roared along the interstate for thirty minutes, and as I rolled over the last ridge before the exit, the majestic foothills of the great Rocky Mountains came into sight. The flatirons are breathtaking, especially when the summer haze beats down on their jagged copper-colored edges.

Life was good. I was in the Devil's Disciples, had money in my pocket and my chopped Harley under me. When I pulled into town, my engine rumbled loudly as I slowly cruised along Broadway, Boulder's main strip. I couldn't help but notice people turning their heads to check me out. I stopped at a red light, placed my feet on the pavement to balance my machine, and then looked to my right. I recognized the guy on the bike next to me. It was Magic, a member of a rival gang, the Husky Hustlers. I was in no mood for trouble. It was too hot, and even though I never backed down from someone like Magic, I didn't have the fight in me that day. At least, that's what I was thinking when I opened my leather vest to show Magic my .45 automatic. He saw the gun and looked me right in the eyes as if to say, "Yeah, so what?" Magic was tough like that.

When the light turned green, I took off, but not before pulling the hammer back on my .45.

Blam.

I shot him.

I didn't feel a thing as I watched the bullet pierce his chest. It appeared to be moving in slow motion as I pulled away. I kept riding as Magic fell to the street, splattering his bike and brains all over the pavement.

It was an unwritten rule in our gang that if you pulled a gun, you'd better shoot. What's the point of shooting to wound? There is none. You had to aim to kill or be prepared to take a bullet for your hesitation.

I knew I'd killed him. I punched the throttle so that the sound of my engine would drown out the thoughts of prison racing through my head.

Police cars sped past me as I made my way out of town. The last image of Boulder I recall that day was the spinning red lights of an ambulance in my rearview mirrors.

I made my way back to Denver in less than twenty minutes. I was flying down the highway. I spent the entire ride figuring out what I would do, where I could hide, who I could tell, and what I would say if I got pulled over.

I wasn't worried about being popped. I had been pulling off robberies for years and never got caught. I rolled hippies in Washington Park in Denver for their drugs and cash. I had battled and survived the infamous shoot-out on Mission Hill. After that incident, I had convinced myself I was invincible. And for a time, I was. Nothing could stop me or take me down, especially a dead biker hood from a rival gang. Who would give a damn about him anyway? At least, that's what I kept telling myself all the way back to Denver.

When I got home, I hid my bike in a neighbor's garage. I wanted to be careful not to give the cops a reason to come knocking on my door. If they showed up, I'd have to run. If I headed back to Phoenix, they'd probably find me there. I could go to New Mexico or Texas. I had been thinking of getting out of the Disciples anyway. Maybe this was the right time. I had to think, clear my head. I took a couple of Valium and slammed an ice-cold beer to help calm my nerves. My anxiety was growing with each passing minute. I jumped every time I heard a car outside, thinking it might be the cops.

I was tired—mentally exhausted—so I lay down on my old worn couch. I kept my heavy black boots on just in case I had to run. It didn't take long for the Valium to kick in. Soon I was out cold. It seemed like I had been sleeping for only a few minutes before I heard a loud pounding on the door.

"Open up. It's the police. We know you're in there. Come out with your hands up and no one will get hurt."

I immediately jumped into action. I thought that if I got a running start out the door I could make it over the hedges in the backyard. I checked for my wallet and a picture of my mom. I was making a run for it. I wasn't about to go down without a fight. Hell, at the very least, I'd give them a good run.

I bolted through the door and leapt across the yard in two giant steps. I put my entire body into it. I was up and over the hedges like an Olympic high jumper. I hit the ground hard, so hard I momentarily lost my breath. I rolled out of my fall and made it to my feet in one fast motion. My legs were moving as fast as they could run. I was in a full sprint. Sweat from my brow stung my eyes. I turned the corner onto Sixteenth Street to find it barricaded with cops and patrol cars. The police had formed a human chain so I couldn't bust through. I scanned the perimeter to see if I could take a chance. But it was clear I had nowhere to run, nowhere to hide. I threw my hands up in the air.

"You got me." I began to laugh, but it wasn't funny. No, there wasn't anything funny about what was happening. I was screwed and everyone knew it.

As I stood in front of the judge on my day of reckoning, I heard him say, "Duane Lee Chapman, you have been found guilty of murder in the first degree. I hereby sentence you to death. You will suffer as your victim did. I sentence you to the gas chamber." The judge slammed his gavel down like he was hammering nails. And he was—the nails to my coffin.

The next thing I knew, a guard held each of my arms as two of them led me to the chamber where I was set to die. I sat straight up, scared and confused as they strapped me in so tight that I was unable to move. I could barely see the bucket underneath me, but I knew it was there because I could hear the bubbling sound of toxic substances as the guard slowly switched on the gas.

"Breathe in, Chapman. Long, deep breaths." The officer was instructing me on how to die. I closed my eyes, squeezing them tight.

I didn't want to be there. "Please God. Make this stop," I pleaded.

Suddenly I heard a voice I'll never forget. It was the voice of the Almighty.

"There's a thin line between success and failure, Duane. You have crossed that line one too many times. I have waited for you to find your way, but you failed me, and now, you will be eternally lost, my son."

Suddenly images began flashing in my head. My mind became cluttered but my heart was strangely calm. I saw myself thirty-five years older. I had a family. Children, grandchildren, and a beautiful buxom blonde I didn't recognize by my side. The Lord was showing me a television show. *My* show. How could that be? I looked exactly the same, only older.

"Take another deep breath, Chapman," the guard demanded.

"Wait!" I screamed. "Stop! This can't be happening. I'm too young to die. I want to live. I'll do better. I promise." I was pleading for my life.

"Ain't no one gonna help you now, Chapman. You're a dead man. Breathe in." And that was the last thing I heard.

CHAPTER 1

"**D**uane, Duane. Big Daddy, wake up. You're dreaming again." Beth gently shook me as she often does when I have a nightmare. It took me a second to realize I was safe.

Hell, it took me a second to realize that I was still alive.

I'd been having a lot of bad dreams lately. I get scared once in a while, especially when things are going good. I was enjoying the success of my first book, *You Can Run, but You Can't Hide,* which debuted number one on the *New York Times* bestseller list. The charges against me in Mexico for the capture of Andrew Luster were about to be dropped, and my show on A&E was enjoying great success. When things are going like that, I often wonder if I will wake up someday and realize it was all a dream.

There's some deep hidden fear inside me that all of my hard work and perseverance don't mean squat—that it could go away in the flash of a moment. When I let my thoughts go there, I try to snap myself out of it so I don't dwell on the negative, but rather focus on the positive—all the good things in my life that surround me. Ever since I went to prison in Mexico, I've frequently had terrible dreams of doing bad things like robbing a bank or, worse, killing someone. When I wake up after having one of those dreams, I have to remind myself, *You didn't commit that felony. It was only a dream. You're the Dog! You don't kill people, you help them. It'll be OK.*

Thankfully, I didn't kill Magic that day in Boulder, but I could have. What actually happened was that I did take a shot at him, but I purposely shot too low. I missed the front of his bike by an eighth of an inch. I saw my bullet ricochet off the pavement. I don't know why I pulled my gun at all, but I guess I just wanted to show off. Or maybe I wanted Magic to know he couldn't . . . or shouldn't mess with me.

I didn't want anyone to know I had chickened out and purposely missed, because that went against everything I was as a Disciple. The Lord was right. There is a fine line between success and failure. I walked it for years. I have been to the edge many times, but I'm no killer. Never was, never will be. Even so, ever since Mexico, I keep having those dreams and they scare the living hell out of me.

For those of you who might not know about the Andrew Luster situation, here's a quick overview of what happened. In the summer of 2003, Tim "Youngblood" Chapman, my son Leland, and I went to Mexico to track down Andrew Luster, the heir to the Max Factor family fortune. Luster was arrested in 2000 suspected of eighty-seven counts of rape and was standing trial in Ventura County, just north of Los Angeles.

Luster was considered a wealthy playboy who spent his days surfing off the beaches of Southern California and his nights partying at his beachfront home or college bars in Santa Barbara. He was a complete womanizer with $31 million in the bank to support his party-boy lifestyle.

Beth and I were flying from Honolulu to Los Angeles on January 5, 2003, when twenty minutes into the flight Beth woke me up to show me the headline from the *Los Angeles Times:*

HEIR TO MAX FACTOR FORTUNE MAY HAVE JUMPED MILLION-DOLLAR BAIL

By the time our plane landed in L.A., Luster was officially on the run. He failed to show up for his court date. He had removed his court-ordered ankle monitor two days prior and hadn't been heard from since. By the time we deplaned, he'd been declared a fugitive and a warrant had been issued for his arrest.

We knew finding Luster would be a challenge, which made hunting him all the more interesting. Beth took the reins to make sure we did everything by the book. She also was intent on seeing to it that we all really understood who we were chasing. We viewed Luster to be an arrogant, rude, opinionated, and egotistical punk. But we had to be careful because his family was rich and powerful, which meant they had friends in high places.

To find a fugitive, you have to think and act like him. You have to understand his needs, desires, strengths, and weaknesses. You have to know everything about the person you're looking for. Who is he? Who is his family? Who are his friends? Where does he hang out? More information means greater insight into the mind of the man you're chasing.

On January 15, 2003, Andrew Luster was charged with flight to avoid prosecution. That put him on the FBI's Most Wanted list. It also made him "Dog's Most Wanted." I went up to Ventura County Court to get a copy of the warrant. I told the court clerk who I was and said, "I'm the guy who is going to capture Andrew Luster." As charming as I thought I was, she told me to wait in the corridor while she went to talk to Judge Riley, the judge who was presiding over the case. When she came back, she handed me a copy of the warrant, Luster's mug shots, and a personal message from the judge.

"He said, 'Good luck,' Dog."

On February 18, 2003, a jury found Andrew Luster guilty of eighty-six of the eighty-seven criminal charges against him. The jury was deadlocked on one count of poisoning. These convictions were enough to get Luster 124 years in jail and he was sentenced in absentia.

By the time he was convicted, Luster had been on the run for more than a month. He might have changed his appearance and begun living under a new identity. He could have been thousands of miles away or right under my nose. I had no idea where he was, but I knew I would find him.

Months of research and investigation went by before all signs pointed me toward Mexico. I took a giant leap of faith, as did my son Leland and Tim "Youngblood" Chapman, and we headed for the border. On June 18, 2003, we finally got our guy in Puerto Vallarta.

I wrestled him to the ground, cuffed him, stood up, and said, "You are under arrest in the name of the United States government and Mexico!"

We took Luster into custody so that we could hand him over to the Mexican police. The station was only a couple blocks away from where we'd captured that son of a bitch. On the way, we were pulled over by the Mexican police and ordered to get out of our truck. I didn't want to move. I had the fugitive in my grips, and nothing was going to stop me from handing him over to the proper authorities—nothing, except a bunch of Mexican police officers pointing machine guns at me.

I tried to explain that I was Dog Chapman and the man in custody was Andrew Luster, who was wanted in America. When they asked Luster his name, he replied, "David Carrera." That was the name he'd been living under while he was on the run. Luster started speaking Spanish. He told the police officers we had kidnapped him, that he was the victim.

I knew this couldn't be good. As they began to uncuff him, I pleaded with the officers, telling them they were making a huge mistake. They took us all to the station to get confirmation of the story. Despite Luster's story being bogus, the authorities decided to throw Leland, Tim, and me in a cell until our story could be verified.

I had walked out of the Texas State Penitentiary almost a quarter century earlier. I promised God I would never go back to jail. From the moment I left Huntsville, having served eighteen months on a bunk murder-one rap, I had dedicated myself to living a good clean life. No more crimes. My number one purpose as a bounty hunter has been to serve truth and justice. I swore I would never hear the sound of the steel door slam shut and lock behind me again. Now here I was, sitting in a Mexican prison, with thin steel bars between me and freedom. My heart ached from the thought of being back in hell. And I was scared, too. The next day, we were told that the boys and I were being charged with kidnapping. I was nauseous at the thought that we could all go down for twenty years for capturing a rapist. Even though we'd done everything by the book, at the time it was Luster's word against ours.

Within a couple of days, Luster was sent back to America to serve his sentence, while the boys and I remained locked up for two weeks. Unable to make the kidnapping charges stick, the judge charged us with "deprivation of liberty," a paltry misdemeanor. We were released from jail but were told to stay in Mexico to appear in court for that charge.

While we were waiting for our court date, my Mexican lawyer told me there was a rumor around Puerto Vallarta that some guys connected to Andrew Luster were in town looking for me. My lawyer had heard they were flashing around a lot of money to influence certain people in the Mexican legal system to reinstate the kidnapping charges. He also told me he'd heard there was a hit man looking for me, too. His professional legal advice was to flee. I wasn't comfortable with the idea of running. Even though I was staying at the Westin and was out of jail, I was still under house arrest. If I ran, I'd be a Mexican fugitive for the rest of my life. I didn't want that hanging over my head, and besides, I've always said, "This blood don't run." I was the guy who chased fugitives. I wasn't about to become one. But the alternative was to stay in Mexico until my case went to trial. It could be six weeks, six months, or six years before that happened. No one knew for sure.

I thought long and hard about what my lawyer was saying. He told me I was as good as dead if I stayed. That's when I realized he was probably right. It was time to leave Mexico. I was assured that the misdemeanor charge was nonextraditable, so if I somehow made it over the border, there was no way I'd ever be sent back.

I called Beth to let her know we had concocted a plan, but I had to be cryptic in my explanation because I was certain that the feds were recording all of our calls. She understood what I was telling her, even though no one else who might have been listening could have. The boys and I packed up our stuff, loaded it into a rented van, and headed out as if we were going sightseeing for the day. I tried to act cool, but deep down I was scared to death. If we got caught, we'd be doing a lot more time than we were already facing. Thankfully, we were able to make it over the border without anyone catching on. I fell to my knees when I realized I was back in America. I looked up and saw the largest, most beautiful American flag waving above me. I was free, blessed, safe, loved, relieved, and very lucky. I kissed the ground beneath me. Thank God, I was home.

I had been counting on receiving at least $300,000 in compensation for capturing Luster. I'd funded the apprehension of this criminal with my own money under the assumption that I'd be entitled to recoup my cost plus a fee for his return to justice.

Unfortunately, the money never came through. When I went to collect my fees from the state, Judge Brodie, the judge who was now overseeing the reward case in Ventura County, California, said he wouldn't give it to me because I broke the law in Mexico. He was duped into believing the allegations against me because of a document he had been given that had been signed by twenty-five hundred California bail agents expressing their displeasure with me and my conduct. Although the judge believed the document was authentic, it was not. An administrative person at the California Bond Agents Association offered up the letter without the consent of the organization's members, making it look like the entire association was against me.

The judge persisted in his belief that I was a wanted man in Mexico and therefore wasn't entitled to a dime. He told me that he wouldn't "condone my vigilante tactics." I couldn't believe the judge saw me as a vigilante. It broke my heart that my good deed and pursuit of justice were being misconstrued. I was one of the good guys, and yet here I was being painted as a criminal for something I had done for my country, the state of California, and Ventura County. Let's be honest. No one—not one single person but this old dog—went out of their way to search for and capture Luster. Where was the crime in that?

I want to believe that Judge Brodie would have ruled differently if he had been given a brief from our attorney that would have clearly outlined how I'd captured Luster, why I expected to get paid, and the case law that supported my claim. We didn't face any objections from the district attorney, so the hearing should have been a walk in the park. We used a very high-profile lawyer who we expected would work his magic on this pretty straightforward case. Man, were we mistaken. When it came time to go in front of the judge, our superstar lawyer was ill-prepared, didn't know the facts of the case, hadn't read a single document before the hearing, and presented our story all wrong, even claiming Beth had posted the bond on Luster, which she hadn't. When the judge began asking our attorney questions, he got all flustered, fumbled around, and blew it for us. We were destroyed in court.

Somewhere in the middle of the judge's "holier than thou" speech that day, Beth and I stood up, grabbed each other's hand, and turned our backs on him as we walked out of the courtroom. I didn't understand his anger toward me. I had just spent my life savings helping the United States government capture one of their most wanted fugitives and all I got was a lecture on my conduct? It was absurd. No one wanted to pay me for the work I had done. *America's Most Wanted* didn't pay, Crime Stoppers didn't pay, and now Ventura County wouldn't pay us. The FBI didn't pay us either. All of the rewards that had been offered for Luster were jive. We had nothing and would get nothing.

What little money we had left was constantly going toward our legal expenses and to put food on the table for my family. We were flat broke, living hand-to-mouth, literally surviving by writing one bond at a time and living hand-to-mouth with each one. We'd write a bond and pay a bill. Write a bond, buy some groceries. Write a bond, pay our rent. We owed thousands of dollars on our cell phones because of roaming charges we'd racked up in Mexico. It was terrible. We were seriously behind in all of our expenses, and whatever money we did have was going to our lawyers.

During those months of scraping by, our financial stress was so bad that even the power to our house was shut off several times. The last time they shut us off, all of the fish in my aquarium died. I was devastated. Anyone who has ever had fish knows what it's like to come home to find them floating upside down. I stared at that tank for an hour before I could bring myself to scoop the poor guys out.

We had no money to speak of until December 24, 2003, when A&E came through with a deal for our television show. They gave us a small down payment of twenty-five thousand dollars to get us through the holidays. That was the only sliver of money we had seen since before my capture of Luster earlier that summer. Although the twenty-five grand was a lot of money, we were so far behind on everything that it didn't make much of a dent in our debt.

As we began filming the first season of *Dog the Bounty Hunter*, the excitement I had from finally having my own television series was offset by my constant fear that I could be sent back to Mexico at any moment. I was scared to death because I felt there was nothing I could do about my situation but wait it out and put my absolute trust and faith in the Lord, my lawyers, and the judicial system. At the time, the Lord was the only thing I knew, without any doubt, I could truly trust. The lawyers and the system were still very much in question.

CHAPTER 2

The impact of what happened in Mexico was hard on the entire family. It took all of us some time to adjust. But after nearly three years, we had gotten back to living life as usual.

Everything seemed fine until the morning of September 14, 2006. That was when a team of federal marshals stormed my home in Hawaii and arrested me for kidnapping Andrew Luster. As far as I knew, the kidnapping charges were never reinstated in Mexico. The idea of the United States government arresting me for a crime I didn't commit and wasn't even being charged with was absurd beyond my wildest dreams.

It was so crazy that for a moment, I thought I was being *Punk'd*.

But I wasn't.

They had what looked like a valid warrant for my arrest but no search warrant. They only had the essential paperwork to take me into custody. My first inclination was to run. Jump. Go out the back door, down the street, head toward the beach and disappear. I was innocent. Not everyone who bolts is guilty. Some are overwhelmed by the system, others are just plain scared. The warrant they had expired in twenty-six days. I actually believed that if I could run out the clock, then everything would be fine.

But then I began to worry about Leland and Tim. Had they already been taken into custody? I wasn't about to let my son and brother from another mother take the fall alone. No, I was the leader of this gang. I had to stand tall and hold my head up with dignity. So I got dressed and let the feds take me in.

The law is very specific about setting bail in these types of situations. The bottom line is that there is no bail for a fugitive wanted on kidnapping charges who fled another country. The only way I could get out of the federal prison they put me in was to prove special circumstances, which is a phenomenally tough thing to prove. Brook Hart, my lawyer in Honolulu, never wavered. He was able to convince the judge that Leland, Tim, and I were not flight risks. We had no place to go. Somehow, he got the judge to agree. A day and a half later, I was released on a $300,000 bond while the boys each had a $100,000 bond. When I asked why mine was so much more than theirs, Beth just laughed.

"Oh, right," I said. "I am the leader of this gang."

We were ordered to wear electronic monitoring ankle bracelets so that we weren't tempted to run. I hated wearing that thing around my ankle, but I detested bounty hunting with it on even more. It was hell booting in doors wearing a monitoring device that made me feel like the people I was chasing. If a fugitive caught a glimpse of it, he'd rib me for it. I took a lot of crap for having to wear that thing. And it was ironic that I was now wearing an ankle bracelet just like the one Luster broke out of when I began my hunt for him. A judge finally agreed all three of them could be removed in November so we could go back to work, doing things the way we used to. The week that bracelet came off my ankle, I caught my first jump in months. It felt good to bust out my rusty cuffs.

From the beginning in 2003, there was a lot of confusion in our case. We were referred to a lawyer named Bill Bollard, who came highly recommended to us through some friends who worked at *Dateline NBC*. He handled all of their Mexican-American cases. They sent me a videotape of Bollard in an interview so I could see what he was like before meeting and then making my decision about hiring him. I liked what I saw. He was a clean-cut man of Mormon faith. I thought he seemed secure, stable, and honest. I could get by with that type of guy handling my case. At least I thought I could. I hired Bollard and his Mexican co-counsel Enrique Gandara to handle the charges still pending in Mexico, while I had Brook Hart, the lawyer I knew from Hawaii, heading up the extradition case in the Hawaii federal court.

Brook Hart was set to argue our case to the federal judge in Hawaii, to prove that the only charge we faced in Mexico was "deprivation of liberty," which was just a misdemeanor. There was a lot of confusion and rumors as to whether the court documents had been translated incorrectly somewhere in the chain between Mexico and Hawaii and interpreted "deprivation of liberty" as "kidnapping," which is a felony and an extraditable crime. Several hearings took place from October 2006 through February 2007 and my legal team argued my case and why I should not be extradited to Mexico on the lesser charge. Despite their best efforts, in February 2007, the Mexican Federal Court cleared the way for me to be extradited by ruling there was no reason not to try me on the charge of deprivation of liberty, a minor charge in Mexico. Several politicians rallied behind me during this time because they truly believed that an injustice of massive proportion was taking place. Finally, on March 7, legislators in the International Affairs Committee of the Hawaii State House passed a resolution asking the Mexican government to drop the extradition proceedings.

Earlier that year, A&E had hired powerhouse San Francisco–based attorney James Quadra and another lawyer named Lee Levine, who specialized in First Amendment law, to represent the network and us in a lawsuit that had been filed by a small group of people from the Hawaiian Islands who didn't like the way their heritage was being represented on our show. Lawsuits that have no merit are a part of fame and stardom, so the nature of this particular suit didn't surprise anyone. Even so, the network hired two top-gun attorneys to handle the case and make it quietly go away.

I didn't know anything about either man before the network hired them. When I met Lee for the first time, I understood exactly why he was considered the very best. He is an honest and a straight-to-the-point type of guy. After that meeting, Lee sat down with me for a few minutes.

"I want to talk to you, Duane. In your world, you are considered the greatest. In mine, so am I," he said.

I told him I had heard that from several people we knew in common. He wanted to lend me his support in my pending case against the Mexican government and offer me some professional advice.

"You can win this case. You have to persevere and fight as hard as you can," Levine said.

The reality was that I had been seriously considering surrendering because the stress and lack of progress in my case was wearing me down. I had been contemplating going to the border and turning myself in. I didn't tell anyone what I had been thinking, because I knew they would try to talk me out of it. I also knew that if I did go back, I'd have to capture my surrender on tape so there would be no confusion about what I chose to do. I didn't want to give anyone the opportunity to say they caught *The Dog*. I privately shared my thoughts with one of the producers of my show and my most trusted cameraman, who both agreed to meet me on the border when and if it ever went down.

Lee's words were heaven-sent. It was divine intervention to have such a powerful man like him tell me not to surrender to Mexico. God knew I'd listen to a guy like Lee. I'm not sure a man of lesser stature would have had the ability to convince me. Of course, I wanted to hire Lee on the spot to be my own lawyer. I told him a little about my case and my growing concern about the legal advice I'd been receiving. He listened closely.

"You know that James Quadra speaks fluent Spanish, right?" I had no idea Quadra was bilingual. Lee told me how much we'd like James Quadra and that we ought to discuss our case with him to see if he could assist.

"He's the best I know. He'll like you a lot. And more importantly, Beth will like him." He was right. My Beth has to get along with whoever is in our life or they won't be in it for very long.

With Lee's endorsement, and since Quadra had done such a great job for us in quickly settling the lawsuit in San Francisco, we thought we'd meet and tell him about our case. I wanted to get his professional insight on what he thought we should do regarding our case in Mexico.

When we finally had our first conversation with Quadra, the chemistry was there from the start. He was one of us and immediately became my brother. He never tried to push his way into the Luster case. Never. We told him that we had been working with a lawyer named Bill Bollard and shared our concerns with the way things were going. He wanted us to tell him everything.

We explained that Bollard was calling the shots every

step of the way. I told Quadra that I was worried that the criminal case in Mexico was not proceeding in our favor.

Beth and I thought that something wasn't right. She has incredible instincts on many things, it's extraordinary really, and she shared with our manager her concerns that the pieces of the puzzle were not fitting together properly and she had a terrible feeling about our legal team. The defense costs were ongoing and Bollard had asked us and our manager to make some payments which made us feel uncomfortable. I was dumping every last penny I had into lawyer fees to keep my family and me safe from extradition.

I told Quadra how Beth and I were shouldering the brunt of the day-to-day stress of the case. We didn't want the boys to know what was going on. They put their faith in us and buried themselves in their lives while we got things figured out.

Once there was finally some money coming in, I still wasn't able to save any from the first three seasons of my show because of the extraordinary legal fees involved in my case. Beth wasn't even paid a salary for the first two seasons, so she couldn't help out either. I had one of the top-rated television shows on the air and the number one show on A&E, yet I was short on money. It was frustrating and maddening. I didn't deserve to be in this position after my successful capture of Luster and I felt all my hard work was eaten up in legal fees.

I sometimes sit back and think how different things would have been for Luster if he had been caught by me before he was convicted. Could I have saved him or made a difference? I would have told him I could help him. I would have encouraged him to take a deal, serve his time like a man, and put the situation behind him. I would have treated him like any fugitive I capture, by trying to help him get his life on the right track. I guess I'll never know, and at the time, I had to focus on my freedom.

A&E bought two specials from us, *The Fight for Freedom* and *The Family Speaks*, as their way of helping us out financially. Everyone who worked on those two shows donated their fees to our legal defense fund. We were overwhelmed by that demonstration of support from our A&E family. The encouragement we got from the staff was a tremendous help, and the love and adoration we'd received from our viewers and fans was beyond my wildest dreams. There is safety in numbers, and we were surrounded by millions of people who gave us strength when we needed it the most. And still, as fast as I was raising money for my defense, it went out the door quickly. Bollard was calling upon us to make more legal payments that would hopefully make our case progress easier, including payments to people on the ground in Mexico who would be able to gather information for us, as he was telling us there were still people associated with Luster attempting to thwart my case.

The situation in Mexico created so much fear and panic in me that I'd sometimes just shut down. If I shut down during production, the show came to a screeching halt. If we weren't shooting, we fell behind schedule, which costs money—a lot of money. It wasn't fair to anyone, especially the network.

I felt like Bollard was slowly pecking away at my flesh—taking every dime I had and then some. He'd ask for money and then warn me that if I didn't pay we'd suffer the consequences. So I sent him the money. He'd send e-mails with yet another reason he needed additional cash. His e-mails scared me to death so I'd send the money.

In one particular e-mail, Bollard explained that Enrique, his co-counsel in Mexico, had been warning the lawyers that while the magistrates in Mexico were beyond the reach or influence of Luster's powerful friends and family, the court support staff could be reachable and could cause considerable "mischief." He went on to remind Beth and me that we had already seen examples of this, especially in the case of the late-night announcement by the court typist which included misstatements attributed to our lawyers that caused considerable confusion.

Bollard said that Enrique was concerned about additional incidents of "mischief," including misplaced files or notifications which could delay the process or disrupt them altogether. Unfortunately, Bollard reminded us that this is a sad reality in the court system in Mexico. His suggestion to counter against this happening was to have Enrique use someone from his office to "babysit" the file and the court functionaries until such time as the hearing could take place and a ruling was made. Bollard knew that Enrique had been paying Enrique's staff to fly to Guadalajara and do this non-stop, but he was once again asking us for an additional payment of $35,000 to keep this vigilance going. He believed our "adversary's" efforts to interfere would soon be stepped up, as the matter had been formally assigned to one of the two appellate panels.

For us, this meant this was a case of the Luster family money against ours until this could all be sorted out. To be clear, the Luster family's pockets were much deeper than mine. Money was getting tight. That's when I started asking questions, which is how I gather information in everything I do from bounties to my fight for freedom. Still, I was worried if I didn't supply everything my attorney asked for, he'd throw his hands up, walk away, and abandon my case.

The lawyers kept telling me it could take years to go to trial. I was facing four years of hard time if I was found guilty. There's no "time served" credit whatsoever when you're waiting for a trial in Mexico, so even the ten days I'd already spent in jail there wouldn't count against a new sentence. If I was convicted, I'd start serving from day one. There was no doubt I was far better off in the comfort of my own country than I would have been surrendering.

The final blow came when Bollard asked me for that additional thirty-five thousand dollars to pay Enrique to hire clerks to watch over all of my court files so no one could steal them. This request made no sense. What were they going to watch over, my empty file folders?

When this call came in, I was deeply involved in a bounty hunt and couldn't face dealing with another threat or more drama. I couldn't deal with the request, so I called my accountant and told him to just pay the money. When I'm on a hunt, I've got the eye of the tiger. Bollard's requests were so distracting to me that I was really losing my edge. I couldn't let anything get in the way of capturing fugitives, but it was becoming nearly impossible for me to do my job like I used to.

The accountant was concerned I wasn't making clear choices, so he called Beth to tell her what was happening. Beth hit the roof when she heard I had okayed another payment to Bollard. Unbeknownst to me, she had already asked the accountant to slow down his payments so she could look into the validity of Bollard's requests. She and I got into one of the worst fights we'd had in years.

CHAPTER 3

Beth was positive something wasn't right. She instinctively thought things were not going well with my defense in Mexico. Whenever there was a press conference, Beth would stand by my side, acting the part of my supportive partner, but she no longer trusted anything happening with this case. Her female intuition was telling her something I suspected but didn't want to believe.

I made a decision to make a change of who should be representing me and my sons. But I realized I needed to be very careful about how to do this, as switching attorneys on any case can be detrimental. I realized it was time for me to get actively involved in the day-to-day proceedings of my case. Beth had been handling the brunt of it for so long, I owed it to her and the rest of my family to become present in the matter.

I discussed the situation with James Quadra and he told us that it was his recommendation to find highly qualified counsel in Mexico to evaluate the status of the case. We basically wanted a second opinion regarding the legal work that had been done. The network was reluctant for us to change the entire team as well. Everyone was nervous and not sure what to do. They asked if we could just shift our representation in Mexico to look at the case and evaluate the work that was being done. Quadra said he'd personally fly down to Mexico and check things out so he'd have a complete assessment together when we all met. This was huge because the network trusted James Quadra and agreed to let him investigate and see what was going on.

Quadra researched the best criminal defense lawyers in Mexico and then flew to Mexico City. One lawyer Quadra spoke to was a legal powerhouse named Alberto Zinser. He was very handsome, well connected, and quite debonair. When Alberto entered a room, you knew he was there. His co-counsel, Eduardo Amerena, was also at the meeting. Alberto relied heavily on Eduardo's expertise. He was the "get it done" guy, while Alberto was the presence and power. If you engaged Alberto's services, the message was clear: "We are not messing around." They weren't immediately aware of our case, however when Quadra mentioned "The Dog" they shook their heads in recognition of my story, which had become urban legend south of the border.

The three lawyers decided the best course of action would be to analyze our case so they could see firsthand what had gone down so far.

After several days of research, Quadra set up a teleconference with the lawyers and the executives at A&E to give them his assessment.

He explained that the only real hope we had left to win was to push the statute-of-limitations argument, which was our best legal shot at freedom. However, Quadra was clear that our case had to be presented in a very decisive manner or we could lose that argument, too. If that happened, we'd be screwed.

Quadra told A&E that we all ought to meet in San Francisco with Bollard to determine our next steps. Bollard agreed to meet us in San Francisco. The meeting was set for May 23. Quadra's plan was to show the network how deeply in trouble the stars of their top show really were.

We thought this would help the network feel more comfortable about our desire to switch lawyers. How we presented our story had to be carefully orchestrated and executed if we were going to succeed in convincing them that maybe it was in our best interest to make some drastic changes.

CHAPTER 4

It had been a crazy couple of years for Beth and me, but at least things with our case were finally beginning to look up. I was still mourning the death of my daughter, Barbara Katie, who was killed in 2006 in a terrible car accident in Alaska, where she had been living with her baby daughter. Barbara Katie died the day before my wedding to Beth, so celebrating our upcoming first anniversary on May 20, 2007, didn't feel that festive to me. I will always share that blessed day with the sadness that filled my heart after Barbara Katie died.

As a way to dodge my inevitable pain, Beth and I decided to take a romantic road trip up the coast of California, which would get us to San Francisco in time for our big meeting with Bollard, Quadra, and the team from A&E. A break from shooting the show and dealing with the case was definitely in order, so Beth planned our first vacation alone since we became husband and wife to celebrate our anniversary. It had been years since we could leave the island without getting permission, because the Andrew Luster case had still been hanging over our heads there. My every move was being tracked, especially when I traveled.

Beth and I rented a Hummer H2 to take the drive up the coast from Los Angeles to San Francisco. Two minutes into the trip I noticed the front bumper guard was loose so it made a jittery noise the whole time. To make matters worse, the wind was gusting at speeds of up to fifty mph along the coastline, so the noise got louder as we drove. Beth turned on the radio to try to drown out the constant clanking, but it didn't really help..

There are parts of Highway 1 that get very narrow, especially along the water, which made driving a Hummer on these roads treacherous.

"Duane, look at the seals!" Beth screamed with utter delight as she saw a family of seals playing on the rocks below the narrow cliff I was trying to navigate.

"I can't look right now, Beth." I didn't want her to know I was nervous. I have an awful fear of heights, and I was afraid to look down.

"Oh, Duane, honey. Look how pretty this is!" Beth was enamored of the majestic sight of the glistening blue Pacific crashing against the rocky shore. I could see cliffs for miles ahead of me. Admittedly, I wanted to look, but I simply couldn't without steering us right off the edge.

OK, I have to let you in on a little secret. My entire family thinks my driving is terrible. If you watch my show, you might notice I'm hardly ever behind the wheel. So now that you know this, it'll make sense that while Beth was oohing and ahhing over the scenery, I realized her knuckles were white from holding on for her life.

"Weeeee. This is so much fun, Big Daddy," Beth squealed with joy, all the while quietly hoping I didn't drive us to our death.

When we got to a safe place to stop, I decided to pull over. My nerves were shot and I needed a smoke.

We made our way to our first stop, Santa Barbara, where we spent the night at Bacara, a beautiful hotel that was set way back off the road. All of the porters and doormen were wearing top hats and white gloves. The only time I'd ever seen men wearing white gloves was during a crime scene investigation. Beth explained that the staff dressed that way because it was a fancy hotel and wearing gloves like that was considered very formal. I've never been the type of guy who needed glitz and glamour, but my wife loves staying in fine hotels, so I usually just go along for the ride. Since this was supposed to be a celebratory trip, I did my best to enjoy it.

It wasn't hard. Our accommodations were gorgeous. There was a grand piano and a fireplace in the living room and another big fireplace in the bedroom. The place was romantic and inviting in every way.

Outside, I could smell oil burning from the refineries off in the distance. I was standing on the patio taking in the scenery when I suddenly saw a deer eating in the woods about thirty feet away. There's something about being in the center of nature like this that I find especially calming. I have a special connection with animals and nature that's hard to describe. It's a trait that I share with my daughter Bonnie Jo, who loves the outdoors even more than I do.

Later that afternoon I met a man from the hotel who showed me how to feed the falcons that were all around the property. I even got one of the birds to fly up to our balcony and eat right out of my hand. Just before sunset, Beth and I took a walk along one of the nature paths around the perimeter of the resort. It was freezing and the wind was blowing hard. Long hair and wind don't mix. However, we were able to run back to our room and get warm . . . if you know what I mean.

Even though we'd been married a year, it still hadn't really sunk in that Beth was my wife and I was her husband. The Bible says that if you're going to live with a woman, God will give you a divine blessing if you commit to her forever and take her as your wife. Beth and I had been together for fifteen years when we decided to make it official. The time had come for us to make that commitment to each other. Our youngest children had begun to ask us why we weren't married. And Beth was being referred to as my "life partner" or "sidekick." Those descriptions weren't fair to her, either. In my heart, I always knew Beth would be my forever wife. It was time to make it official.

Our first year of marriage went by so fast. Nothing really changed between us. Life was pretty much the same as it had always been. We were knee-deep in raising our children, running our bail bonds business, shooting our show, and fighting the charges in Mexico and the United States. The stress of the case was taking a toll on us. The timing of this trip couldn't have been better, as we would be totally relaxed and ready for a much anticipated meeting at the end of our journey.

When we got to San Francisco, I wanted to go back to Golden Gate Park, where I got arrested when I was sixteen. Beth wasn't very interested in doing that, but she was really excited about seeing *The Phantom of the Opera* later that night. Even though I grumble whenever she drags me to those types of events, I usually end up enjoying the experience. That show brought tears to my eyes. I loved the music and every minute of the musical.

Our meeting was set in Quadra's office the following day. A&E's lawyer, Beth, and myself were all seated in the conference room. Bollard came by himself.

As planned, we let Bollard talk first. He tried to convince us that everything was going as expected. Quadra began asking Bollard several questions on a couple of matters that he had explored.

It had become obvious to Bollard that we had sought the advice and opinions of some other experts when suddenly the conference room doors swung open with the dramatic flair of Zorro arriving to avenge the death of his father, and we heard:

"Hello! I am Alberto Zinser! Am I in the right place?" Alberto spoke with the greatest accent. He sounded like a Spanish matador. He was accompanied by Eduardo Amerena, who was silent, yet equally powerful.

I could tell that Beth wanted to jump up and start clapping when Alberto made his very impressive entrance. Zorro had arrived to save the Dog! All I could think was *Olé!*

Bill Bollard almost swallowed his head when he set his eyes upon Zinser, a legal legend in Mexico.

Zinser introduced himself to Bollard and began to have a dialogue in Spanish. Now . . . I had heard Bollard make dozens of calls to Mexico over the couple of years he represented me. He spoke what I believed was fluent Spanish. He looked at Quadra several times while he was speaking, as if he understood everything he was saying. I only picked up a few words here and there because Alberto was talking so fast. I could tell he was saying something about prison, a release, and so on.

Bollard shook his head, nodding, pursing his lips and then he answered Zinser . . . in *English*. It was painfully clear to me that my lawyer didn't speak fluent Spanish and was having a difficult time keeping up.

Bollard began explaining the situation to Zinser. "I can't get the judge to make a decision, and the team of people I have down in Mexico aren't really working, and . . ." Blah, blah, blah was all I heard while Bollard kept talking.

Alberto Zinser stopped Bollard by slamming his hand on the conference room table and saying, "You see? This is pissing me off. You are telling lies about my country. You are making liars of my people and they are not. And *this* is pissing me off." I glanced over at Beth, who looked like she was courtside watching the finals at the U.S. Open, her head darting back and forth as this exchange was taking place. Her Cheshire cat grin was hard to ignore.

Next, Quadra suggested we get Bollard's Mexican co-counsel Gandara on the phone. He thought Gandara might be able to help us understand or figure out the next course of action since he was on the front line. We wanted Bollard to tell our "consultants" from Mexico what was going on, so we didn't miss any important details.

Quadra, Zinser, and Amerena started asking Gandara questions, one after another like a rapid-fire machine gun. Eduardo and Alberto were speaking in Spanish, so it was hard for us to follow the conversation, but they later told us they were asking simple procedural questions about the judge, the case, filings, deadlines, and other things Gandara should have absolutely been aware of if he was on top of the case. I don't know if he was startled by their call or had been sipping margaritas by the seaside, but my new team was not satisfied with Gandara's answers to most of their questions.

It appeared we had not been told the whole story and had been billed for hours of work that didn't move the case along.

In the Bible, there's a verse in Hebrews that says "God will give you the shaking that comes on your spirit when things are not right internally."

For the first time in years, I was able to catch my breath because I felt I no longer had to worry about my lawyers. I finally felt that I had three lawyers working for me, and that was a good feeling—really good.

The meeting was successful since about halfway through it, A&E's lawyer asked to see Beth and me in the hallway. "I want you to know that A&E is behind you if you want to replace your legal team."

We went back into the meeting. We were stone-faced so we wouldn't let on what we knew was about to go down. We asked Bollard if he wanted to break bread, have some lunch as a way to extend the olive branch. We were never the type of people to tear someone down to the point of no return. I try to embrace everyone. Bollard declined lunch but asked if he could have a few moments alone with Beth and me before we took a break.

After everyone left the room, he began his speech on what a big mistake it would be to replace him. He asked us to have faith in what he and his team were doing.

"We're almost at the finish line. You need to stay with us." He repeated his request several times until I finally said, "We'll take that under advisement."

A lot of water had flowed under this bridge.

After Bollard left, I decided that Beth and I would fly home to Hawaii and meet with Leland and Tim to make a final decision. Within a few weeks, we decided to dissolve our professional relationship with Bollard and Gandara and to retain Quadra, Zinser, and Amerena to take over our legal representation in our fight for freedom. From the moment that decision was made, a heaviness that I had carried for years was lifted off my chest. I could breathe again. I had been suffocating and didn't even know it.

CHAPTER 5

O nce we had new legal representation, things began happening. Alberto Zinser and his team filed a new *emparro*, which is a legal document that has to be submitted in the Mexican courts for an extradition case. There was a lot riding on this new document. If the *emparro* was rejected, I would be on my way back to Mexico. My new legal team told me they'd strengthened our argument by clarifying the exact charges against me. Despite the lack of evidence and a charge to the contrary, the authorities down there still believed I had kidnapped Luster. For the first time since I fled Mexico in 2003, I finally had a hope of beating the charges.

By the end of July 2007, the statute of limitations on all criminal counts pending in Mexico had run out. So, on July 27 the Mexican judge from the First Criminal Court in Puerto Vallarta had no choice but to dismiss all charges and nullify the outstanding arrest warrants against Leland, Tim, and me. The order effectively canceled all pending charges. The ruling, however, was subject to appeal by the prosecution. If an appeal was sought, it had to be filed by August 8.

When I found out about the charges being dropped, it was as if I had just undergone a heart transplant. I felt like a brand-new man.

"*Viva la Mexico!*" I shouted as loud and proud as I could when I heard the good news.

That was a memorable week for many reasons. First, Mexico, and then the publication of my best-selling book, *You Can Run, but You Can't Hide.* I had worked hard to tell my personal story and was excited about sharing my life's journey with my many fans. I wasn't sure what to expect or how the book was going to be received. When I went to a local bookstore at the Kahala Mall, near our home in Hawaii, to do my first book signing, I was stunned and rendered momentarily speechless by the masses of people who showed up in support of the Dog. Seeing the crowd that day reminded me of the time several years ago when I was in a helicopter with Tony Robbins on our way to one of his events. Tony looked down and asked why there was so much traffic. I told him there had to be an accident or something that shut down the streets. That's when his lead man on the ground radioed up to tell us the crowd was there to see him. I never forgot that moment because that was the first time I vowed to myself that someday a crowd like that would be there to see me. Well, that day had finally come.

I had to fight back my tears as I stepped out onto the podium to greet all the people who had come to buy my book. I gave them a big shaka and then soaked in their love as they cheered. I hadn't felt that good in years.

Even though we believed the news from Mexico was good, Brook Hart was quick to point out that nothing was final until he received the order and the translation to determine what the Mexican government was actually doing, whether they planned to take any further action, and what the U.S. Attorney's office might do in response. So I was cautiously optimistic until I knew I was completely out of the woods.

As expected, Mexican prosecutors appealed the ruling. Their reasoning was that all but three cities in Mexico had no statute of limitations on the charges that we'd been facing. Lucky for me, Jalisco, the city where I was arrested, was one of the three cities that did have that law on the books. My lawyers had to go in front of the judge one last time to show that the statute of limitations had run out. The judge agreed and dismissed the case once and for all.

In my heart, I knew that Mexico was not mad at me. I applaud the Mexican justice system even if it did take years for them to come around. Now my next order of business was making sure the American courts followed suit.

When Leland, Tim, and I were arrested in September 2006 by the U.S. Marshals, I was freed after posting $300,000 bail for myself and $100,000 for each of the guys. Judge Barry Kurren agreed to release the three of us on our own recognizance on September 15, while he awaited a written statement confirming that Mexico had dropped the charges so he could make his final decision.

In the meantime, as a way of prodding the United States government, Beth and I asked our fans to write various public officials urging them to drop the pending charges against us. I had the utmost respect for our former administration.

As a citizen of the United States, I feel it is my responsibility to support our commander in chief. Even so, I had some issues with how out of touch that administration seemed to be with the criminal justice world. It shocked and appalled me that Condoleezza Rice was the person who signed my arrest warrant, actually believing that I kidnapped Andrew Luster and took him across the border. In order for her to sign the arrest warrant, she had to believe that this false story was true. I have to believe that she was never given the facts of the case. That's the only rational explanation I can come up with for her signing such a document, because anyone who knew the facts never would have let me face being sent back there.

There had been some confusion in court when the bondsman who had written our bail bond asked the judge for a written statement saying we would not have to pay another 10 percent or $30,000 to renew the bond. He wanted to be certain we wouldn't be on the financial hook for more money to keep the bond active. Thankfully, that issue was quickly settled—in great part due to so many caring friends and fans who bombarded Judge Kurren with e-mails and phone calls. Our fans' actions touched my heart in a way I simply cannot put into words. To be clear, we never asked our fans to write the judge. They did so all on their own.

Judge Kurren, however, didn't share my warmth and appreciation for all the mail and messages he received. He came down pretty hard on Brook Hart, telling him to relay his message:

"Tell your clients not to contact the court or suggest that their fans contact the court." He was quite emphatic in his response. Of course, we had no way of controlling our fans' decision to write in or call.

After that issue was taken care of, the only thing left to resolve was getting America to dismiss the extradition complaints and arrest warrants for me and the boys. There was no reason to pursue those charges any further when there were no longer any outstanding charges against us in Mexico. American law requires Mexico to have a valid pending charge if they want to pursue extradition. No charges, no extradition. It was as simple as that.

Even so, we had to go through the system, and that took some time. It was pure torture waiting out that decision. I called Brook Hart every single day to ask if the government had dropped the charges or if he thought they were still planning to bring me in. His answer was always the same: "I don't know, we're not sure." I was totally freaking out.

Although I was off the hook in Mexico, my own country refused to back down. People often said we did the right thing by capturing Luster, a convicted felon. I knew God had forgiven me for any wrongdoing in the matter because I took one of the bad guys off the street when no one else dared to. If I had grabbed the wrong guy off the streets of Mexico, I'd be speaking Spanish and eating Mexican food from my cell instead of writing this book. But I didn't. I nabbed someone who had fled America to dodge his sentence for eighty-six counts of rape, drugging his victims and videotaping their encounters. The morality in Mexico supported what I did. They don't want our rapists fleeing to their country to run free, raping their women and children. They didn't want to put me in prison any more than I wanted to be there, and they proved it by dropping the case.

Days after Mexico dropped all of the charges against us, I was on the road promoting my first book. So while I wanted to celebrate the good news that came from Mexico, I had embarked on a thirty-day tour that took us across the United States. What a whirlwind experience that was. I toured for four straight weeks, shaking hands with my brothers and sisters—white, Asian, African-American, Latino, young, old, blue and white collar—signing their books, and hearing how my story had somehow inspired them to live better lives. I was absolutely blown away by the cross-section of America that had turned out to receive me with open arms and love. I feel the same way about each and every one of them. Everywhere I went, from Atlanta to Los Angeles, people wanted to meet me, say hello, and thank me for sharing my truth. I will never forget the faces of the tens of thousands of you who took the time to read my story and let me know you liked it.

The book tour was the craziest experience I'd had in years. I felt like the world's biggest rock star as I made my entrance to each and every venue. The fans roared and cheered when they got a glimpse of Beth and me. The feeling I got when I heard the crowd reminded me of my early boxing days. My dad once asked me why I was never really in the fight until I got hurt. At the time, I didn't care so much about the actual fight as I did the sound of the crowd cheering for me when the announcer called out my name. I told my dad how I felt. He said, "Son, why do you have to be in the ring to do that?" I didn't know what else I could do where I would receive that type of reaction—until now.

Most book signings are done in an hour or two. When that time runs out, regardless of whether or not people are still standing in line, the signing is over. "Sorry, can't sign your book, but thanks for buying it anyway" just wasn't how I moved through the world. I told Alan, my manager, to make sure the store knew that I would stay and sign every last copy. Outside of my family, my fans are the most important people in the world to me. I vowed I would do my best not to disappoint a single one.

The crowds were enormous and bookstores were running out of copies days before our arrival. Alan told me he'd never seen so many people at a book signing. He was as surprised as anyone when a thousand and often two thousand or more people lined up to buy my book. Forty-five hundred people showed up at a signing at a Walmart in St. Louis, and a few spent the night in the parking lot just so they could be at the front of the line. With Beth and my manager by my side, I stayed late into the night to make sure I met every single person who had waited so long to meet me. Then we were escorted to the freeway with three local police cars holding back the traffic so fans wouldn't chase us while we were driving back to our hotel.

There was another unforgettable appearance at a Wal-mart, in Arkansas, where people parked their campers in the store lot days in advance so they would be able to meet us and get their books signed. Someone told me those couple of days were the only vacation many of those people would take all year, and they chose to spend it with me. I was flattered and unbelievably appreciative.

It was sometime during my book tour that I realized I had finally fulfilled my lifelong dream of becoming a "celebrity." I had struggled, worked, and wanted to be famous my whole life. As the old saying goes, "Be careful what you wish for, you just might get it." I love all aspects of my public and private life, but my manager had to explain to me that a lot of responsibility comes with being famous. Alan told me a real celebrity is someone who other people look up to and love. It may seem like it's all glamorous and fancy—and to be honest, there are lots of perks—but there is also a certain amount of accountability too. Every action, word, or gesture belongs to the world to judge and critique. I listened closely when Alan shared those words and took his advice to heart.

Aside from the long, exhausting days, the book tour was loads of fun. It gave me a unique opportunity to go places in America that I had never been but always wanted to see. And while I didn't have many days off during the thirty-day tour, I made sure to make the most of that time when I did.

During a stop in Washington, D.C., Beth and I decided to take in the city and see the sights. I had never spent any time in the nation's capital. When I was growing up, we weren't the touring type of family. My father would stop along the way to see a landmark here and there, but we didn't take special trips or family vacations like that. We mostly spent our time away on fishing trips, something I still enjoy.

I've been invited to a lot of places since my show hit the air, including plenty of celebrity homes, but I was never more excited than I was to see the home of our country's first President. I've always loved American history, and what would this country have been without our founding fathers, especially my hero, George Washington? I have always loved George Washington and all that he stood for. He was a trailblazer who gave so much of himself to give all of us freedom and undeniable rights.

Mount Vernon is one of the most popular historic estates in America. It was the beloved home of George and Martha Washington from the time of their marriage in 1759 until his death in 1799. He worked tirelessly to expand his plantation from two thousand acres to eight thousand, and the mansion house from six rooms to twenty-one, during his life. Mount Vernon is located just sixteen miles south of Washington, D.C., so it wasn't far from the hotel where we were staying.

The homestead rests on the banks of the Potomac River. We were invited to tour the mansion as well as a dozen outbuildings, including the slave quarters, kitchen, stables, and greenhouse. George and Martha Washington's final resting place is also on the grounds. They're buried in a tomb where memorial ceremonies are held daily. The Slave Memorial and Burial Ground are also close to the tomb.

Seeing Mount Vernon was extremely emotional for me. I didn't expect to have the type of visceral reaction to it that I did. Washington's spirit and all that he stood for drew me to Mount Vernon, and being there deeply moved me.

When we got to the home, we were assigned a bright young tour guide to drive us around and show us the site. He pointed at an apple tree and said, "That tree has been here since the house was built." I asked if I could take an apple off the tree. I wanted to plant the seeds at my home in Hawaii. These were apple seeds from the same tree George Washington ate from. That was huge. I knew that this visit would be significant to me, but I had no way of knowing what a huge impact it would end up having on my life.

The guide began telling us stories about George and his best friend, who happened to be one of his slaves. Even though the man was George's closest confidant, he had to call him a slave so no one else could own him. I asked the guide how he knew these stories. He explained that George Washington kept meticulous notes on his life and left them behind so that we could all know his history.

That story reminded me of my good friend Whitaker, who was my cellmate back at Huntsville prison, where I had been sentenced to serve five years for first-degree murder, a crime I didn't commit, though I had some involvement.

I got to Huntsville in 1977, when it was still a segregated prison. The prison population was predominately black. The two-story cell block had white inmates on one side and the blacks on the other. They painted the white section a pale lime green. It was dreary and dull, the kind of color you found inside an old hospital.

It took me a while to get into a groove in prison. I was a cocky twenty-four-year-old biker who thought he had all the answers. Everything I did, I did the hard way. I had no idea what the easy way meant. Six months into my sentence I still hadn't learned how to pick my battles. What seemed like minor disagreements were of major importance in the joint, because that's all you have on the inside—right and wrong. A few days after a scuffle I had with the Muslims, they sent a guy named Whitaker after me. I felt confident going up against him because we were about the same size. We stared each other down. I always talked all kinds of bull before my fights to try and psych out my opponents. To my surprise, Whitaker was aware of my game. Before I could throw my first punch, he landed a few on me, but I never went down. I've taken a lot of punches, but I've never felt anything like Whitaker's. He was the strongest man to ever hit me. The few punches I landed on him had no effect on the guy. Whitaker kicked my ass that day. Because I never backed down, I earned the respect of the other inmates, and Whitaker and I emerged as friends. I was so impressed with his technique I asked him to teach me how to fight like him so I could become a better fighter.

Not long after Whitaker and I got into our fight, Huntsville was desegregated. It was the last Texas penitentiary to be integrated. Feds surrounded the prison with guns and said, "Integrate them today." The warden looked over to see the white prisoners standing to one side and the blacks on the other. Nobody was moving. I was the first to proudly walk across the yard to stand tall with my black brothers.

A giant and very dark-skinned inmate looked at me and said, "You're on our side of town now, Doggie."

"No matter what side of town I'm on, I'm still the Dog," I barked back.

Just then I noticed a guy I called Cadbury standing right beside me. He had walked across the line too.

"I'm his sidekick," Cadbury said.

Pretty soon twenty-five white guys had crossed over. The warden looked at one of the feds and said, "We'll integrate by morning."

Remember, this was 1970s America. The rest of the

country had already pretty much desegregated. As a half-breed, I never wanted anyone to judge me on the color of my skin. I was proud of my heritage and figured the brothers in prison were too. Sure, we used the "N" word in the joint, but it wasn't a derogatory term, at least not the way I heard it being used. It was just the way the black inmates talked to one another. In a way, from the moment I crossed the segregation line I believed I had become a brother too. The more I hung out with them, the more I started to use the same language they did because I wanted to fit in and be like them. The men I served time with never once told me I was out of line or about to get my ass kicked for using the "N" word or any other slang term I picked up along the way. I didn't realize the "N" word was bad or insulting. Never. Did that make me ignorant? I suppose it did, yet, in retrospect, perhaps in an innocent way. I just didn't know any different and no one ever told me otherwise.

On the night the prison integrated, one of the black inmates asked me why I came over to their side. I didn't know the answer. I just did what I thought was right. I wasn't raised to see men as black, white, red, or yellow. I didn't think of any one person as being lower or less important in society than another. To me, we were all the same, especially inside the joint.

Ironically, Whitaker, who had once been my foe, ended up becoming my cellmate and a good friend for the rest of my incarceration, which thankfully lasted only eighteen months of the full five years I was sentenced to serve. Whenever inmates saw Whitaker and me walking together, they'd shout, "There goes Salt and Pepper." We keep in touch to this day.

I spent most of my eighteen months in Huntsville hanging with the homies. After I crossed the color line, I became a counselor to a lot of those men. The white boys didn't require counseling—they got whatever they needed through the system. For some reason, I was the guy the black inmates came to with their problems—like when their woman wrote to break up with them or their momma died. I helped these men cope with their loss so they wouldn't do anything stupid like trying to escape, though some ended up trying to anyway.

My bounty hunting career was unofficially launched at Huntsville when I captured Bigfoot, a prisoner who was trying to make a run for it. Lieutenant Hillegeist, also known as Big Lou, drew his .38 and took aim at Bigfoot as he ran. We all knew Big Lou had the right to shoot the escaping convict.

"Don't, Big Lou!" I yelled, without considering what I was saying, then took off after Bigfoot. Once I started chasing Bigfoot, I swear that I heard the click of Big Lou's gun being cocked and felt the bullet pierce my body. But he never pulled the trigger. Fortunately, I was able to catch up to Bigfoot and tackle him to the ground.

"Stay down or you will die," I said.

Big Lou had made his way over to us by then.

He threw down his handcuffs and said, "Hook him up, Bounty Hunter."

Bounty Hunter . . . I liked the way that sounded.

I had to make the other inmates understand that Big Lou had a gun and he was aiming to kill. If I couldn't convince them, they'd think I was a rat—and rats don't last very long in prison.

Later that night, I pleaded my case to a group of Muslims who were very powerful and persuasive inside the joint. If I could convince them, I knew I'd be safe from retribution.

"They told Bigfoot that his momma was dead," I told them. "He went crazy and took off running for the creek. I didn't want to see Big Lou shoot him because his momma died."

The Muslims seemed satisfied by the explanation. It was a great relief because I knew they'd spread the word I wasn't a rat.

I became the great white hope of Huntsville after that. The prison guards often told me they'd never seen anything like how all of the inmates turned to me when they needed a helping hand or shoulder to cry on. I often think back on my days at Huntsville with nostalgia. Even though I was an inmate, I learned a lot of valuable life lessons. One of the most poignant was the friendship I formed with Whitaker and many of the other inmates. The men I met inside those cold stone prison walls were the strongest, most loyal men I have ever come across in my entire life. They were and still are my true brothers.

I got the education of a lifetime in Huntsville. It prepared me to confront any situation without having to go look up some answer in a textbook. It was a time in my life when every choice had a sudden and often horrible end result. Accepting the consequences of my actions taught me the true meaning of responsibility. The Texas Department of Corrections broke me down and built me back up again. They taught me what it truly means to be a man. I guess that's why I began thinking about Huntsville as Beth and I walked the hallowed grounds of Mount Vernon that day.

The tour guide took me down to see the grave site where George and Martha Washington were laid to rest. He told me about the three hundred slaves that lived on the property over the years. They had run the home, cooked, baked fresh bread, and worked the fields. He pointed to a hilly area of the property where all of the slaves were buried. When I asked why they were laid to rest there, the guide explained it was the resting place where each of the property's slave owners always buried their slaves. I was surprised to see there were no grave markers. Just a hill.

"You might find it interesting to know they were all buried with their feet pointed toward the Potomac River."

"Why is that?" I asked

"That's how they wanted to be buried, so their spirits would head up the Potomac when they left their bodies, which is the opposite direction from where they arrived."

I was choked up at the thought of all of those people who were buried under the ground that I stood on. While the others headed back to the car, I asked if I could stay a few more minutes. I wanted to pay homage to my brothers and sisters.

As I peered out over the rolling hill and toward the river, my mind wandered, conjuring up images of what this property had looked like in its day. I closed my eyes and could see all the families all together, children dancing around a large bonfire with their parents. I imagined George Washington having fun with his people and what it would have been like if I had lived back in that time.

The guide could see that I was visibly upset.

"Why are there no markers here for the dead?" I asked.

He stammered over his words, saying, "We don't really know who is buried where. We don't have their names or know the location of each body. They are scattered all over this hill."

His answer angered me. Did the great civil rights leaders of our time know about this? I wanted to shout over a loudspeaker, "Someone needs to get these graves marked!"

The Mount Vernon Ladies' Association had purchased Mount Vernon from the Washington family in 1858. They opened the property to the public in 1860. Since that time, nearly 80 million visitors have toured Washington's home, and no one has thought to mark the graves of the slaves who worked there? I was fuming. The guide explained to me that Mount Vernon runs independent of the government, and no tax dollars are expended to support the five-hundred-acre estate, its educational programs or activities. I offered to pay for a marker myself. I told the guide money was of no concern. He reluctantly said he'd pass my offer along, though I could tell he didn't hold out much hope.

I've fought for many things in my life, but never for anything more worthy than giving these slaves their due. Again, I told the guide that I really wanted to pay for a general grave marker. I needed to get in contact with the right people to make that happen. I felt an inexplicable connection to the hallowed grounds of Mount Vernon that day, so much so that I wish I could be buried right there too. It would be an honor for me to lie beside these unsung heroes of American history with no headstone.

I felt jubilant that day because I thought I'd be able to contribute something of significance to the heritage of our county, and that made me feel really good. I was happier than I had been in years. I can't really give you an explanation on why, but there's not a single day that goes by where I don't think about those graves and how to get them properly marked.

In my life, I've always had the drive to help people I've met along the way who I believed had potential and were worthy of a second chance. I've used that intuition for years as both a bondsman and a bounty hunter. Bail bonds is a user-funded service. My clients have to give me some type of collateral to secure the money I put up for their release, to guarantee that they will appear in court. If they don't, all of my assets, including my checking account, my income—everything—are on the line and can be subject to garnishment.

A bail bondsman is someone who acts as a surety and pledges money or property as bail for the appearance of a criminal defendant in court. Bond agents have an agreement with the local courts to post an irrevocable bond, which will pay the court if any bonded defendant does not appear. The bondsman usually has an arrangement with an insurance company to draw on such security if the defendant skips.

A bondsman usually charges a fee of 10 percent of the total amount of the bail required to post a bond. It is a nonrefundable fee, and this is how I get paid for my services. So, if a defendant is on a ten-thousand-dollar bond, someone has to come up with one thousand dollars in cash before I will go down to the jail and post the bond to get that person out. For larger bail amounts, I can obtain security for the full value of the bond against assets the defendant or someone who is willing to help the defendant puts up for collateral. For example, I can accept the deed to a mortgage, pink slip to a boat or car or any other large item that will cover the full sum of the bond. As a bounty hunter, if the defendant fails to show up for a court date, I am allowed by law to bring that defendant to the court in order to recover the money paid out under the bond.

Since bail bondsmen are financially responsible for these fugitives, we're the ones who go out to find the defendants so we can bring them back to court to face their charges—all of this at no cost to you, the taxpayer.

Bondsmen have traditionally been given a bad rap because of their image as rough-and-tumble characters, perceived to be almost as crooked as the guys they're bailing out of jail. But as the profession grew, it became more regulated, which made bondsmen more respected and reputable.

Several years ago, when I was writing bonds in Denver,

I wrote one for Calvin Pope, the president of the Rollin' 30 Crips. The Crips are one of the largest and most violent associations of street gangs in the United States, with an estimated 30,000 to 35,000 members. They are known to be involved in murders, robberies, and drug dealing, among many other criminal pursuits.

I had caught Calvin's daddy and another one of his relatives, so I knew his family pretty well. Calvin had sixteen warrants and needed sixteen separate bonds. His sister, Lil, had originally contacted Beth to put up the bonds for him, but she was too afraid to write that many. So we ended up splitting them between the two of us. Calvin was often called the "king of the road" because he didn't give a damn about the law. The first time I went down to the station to write a bond for Calvin, he said to me, "I thought you were black on the phone."

"I ain't black, but I am the Dog." Somehow I thought that would matter to him more than the color of my skin.

Calvin was worried that the judge was going to sock it to him. I told him he had nothing to be concerned about.

"You're young, Calvin. As long as you get a reputable job, I think you'll be all right."

The case was going in front of Judge Marcucci, who hated every bondsman in the business, except, perhaps Beth. I think he liked her low-cut blouses and Italian moxie. They used to run into each other at volleyball games where his daughter and Beth's niece, Jacqueline, played against each other for their respective teams. None of the other bondsmen in Denver had that kind of social connection with the judge. For the most part though, other than Beth, he never gave any of us enough time to properly plead a case for our clients.

"Why are you here today, Chapman?" Judge Marcucci asked.

"I'm here to support my client, Judge."

"You know he's got to show up fifteen more times this month, right?"

"Yes, Your Honor, I'm aware of that. Do you think you could put all of those warrants into one bond?"

"No." He didn't even have to think about his answer.

The judge knew it wouldn't be easy getting a guy like Calvin Pope into court fifteen more times, so it was a setup for disaster.

"Mr. Chapman, how do you propose you're going to get Mr. Pope here for his next appearances?"

"I'm going to call him, Your Honor."

"Oh, is that right?" he said with more than a touch of sarcasm.

"Your Honor, I am going to call him on his pager. Would you like the number?"

"Yes, I would. For the court, we most certainly would!" Remember, I was promising the judge the phone number for the president of the Crips.

Our little cat-and-mouse game went on for several minutes—longer than any other exchange I can ever remember having with Judge Marcucci.

When we got into the hallway after the hearing, Calvin let me have it.

"What the hell, Dog?"

"I had to, Calvin." I knew the judge would probably be giving him time. Calvin backed down because he realized that I'd done what I had to do.

A few weeks later, Calvin called me up at home to tell me to look outside my window. For a moment I worried that he was setting me up for a drive-by shooting. To my shock and surprise, out there was a royal blue 1986 Buick Regal that had been lowered to the ground, had a landau top, custom rims, fur seat covers, and a special paint job. It was a major pimped out ride.

"That's your car, Dog."

I loved it. I drove that ride all over Denver. My license plates said, "DOG LEE," so everybody in town understood that car belonged to me. The Crips and other gang-bangers knew the Dog was coming to get them when they saw that car in their neighborhood. And I purposely used it to hunt down those brothers too. When Calvin gave me that ride, all of the other bondsmen in Denver knew the black bail was mine and off-limits to them.

If I hadn't been standing beside Calvin that day in court, the judge would have hammered him. I had grown frustrated with the justice system's apparent double standard. If a white kid gets busted with less than an ounce of marijuana, he gets a slap on the wrist. But if a black kid gets caught with the same amount of weed, he goes to jail. I had watched this happen too many times over the years. That's why I always went to court with my black clients. I didn't want them to get jacked around.

I once got really upset after another judge sentenced a young black kid to thirty days for a minor charge—one for which she could have easily let him off with a warning, probation, and a small fine. This kid's momma was in the courtroom and had to witness her son being taken away in handcuffs for something a white kid would have surely been let off the hook for.

I was enraged with the judge's sentence. "Your Honor, I thought the scales of justice were supposed to be color-blind!"

The judge freaked out, pointed her finger at me, and screamed, "Get out of my courtroom!"

I suppose I was lucky she didn't find me in contempt and sentence me to a night in the clink too. Even so, I thought her decision was totally unfair, and yet that type of thing still goes on every day.

Calvin's first court date was fast approaching. I was stunned when he told me that Judge Marcucci actually paged him on the day he was set to appear in court.

When we showed up, Judge Marcucci said, "I noticed you answered my page by being here, Mr. Pope."

I think the judge respected Calvin's willingness to face the music for the crimes he had committed and take responsibility for his actions.

Unfortunately, Calvin had too many felonies, so the judge had no choice but to convict him and send him to prison. Even if a judge likes you, he still has a responsibility to uphold the law. While serving his time, Calvin was diagnosed with leukemia. While he was in the hospital, Judge Marcucci showed up for an unexpected visit.

Calvin was so inspired by the judge that he decided right there and then to fight for his health and not give up on life. I knew he'd beat his disease for sure.

I stayed friends with Calvin over the years. He eventually gave up the gang life, got married, and had a few kids. The last time I spoke with him was in October 2007. He told me he was applying to be a security guard at the Cherry Creek Mall outside of Denver. He called to ask me how he should answer the question on his application about being a convicted felon. He was nervous to lie but didn't think he'd get the job if he confessed to all of his various convictions.

I told him to write "will discuss" on the line and then explain the circumstances during his interview. Calvin hesitated to take my advice, fearing that they'd discard his application with that type of vague response.

"Dog, I'm going to get in trouble if I lie."

"With who?" I asked. "The paper cops? By the time

they run your record and come back to you, you'll have been on the job for at least six months."

"Six months! Hell, I only need the job for two weeks! I'm just looking to make a few extra dollars."

I had to laugh because Calvin was sweating bullets and agonizing over his answer. I offered to call over to the person in charge of hiring and give them my personal recommendation if he thought that might help.

"You'd do that for me, Dog?"

"Of course," I said. "I can't promise anything, but I'll give it a shot." When we hung up, I called the woman in human resources and told her who I was.

"Hi. This is Dog the Bounty Hunter. I am calling on behalf of one of my good friends, Calvin Pope." I hoped she knew it was really me and not a prank call.

"Oh, sure. I remember him. He really impressed me." I wasn't positive if she was being sincere or not, but I decided to play along anyway.

"I've known Calvin for many years. He is a great find for you and will definitely be an asset to your security team. He'll be terrific in catching shoplifters and keeping an eye on things. He's really good—you should definitely hire him." I hung up feeling hopeful my call would seal the deal.

A few days later, Calvin called to say he'd gotten the job.

"Dog, they gave me a uniform and a badge, man." I could tell he was proud of his new career. When I asked Calvin how he answered the felony question, he confessed that he had left it blank. In my heart, I was proud of him for not lying. He was a changed man who was being given a second chance in life. It felt good knowing that despite his past, he too had eventually ended up on the "right" side of the law.

CHAPTER 6

October 31, 2007

"**D**uane," Beth whispered.

"What time is it?" I asked her.

"It's four A.M."

We'd been out celebrating Beth's fortieth birthday the night before. I never gave her a surprise party because Beth is hard to pull one over on, but I'd wanted to do something special for her for her big four-o. We met several of our friends at Duc's Bistro, a well-known restaurant in Honolulu. I was in bed at our home just outside of Honolulu and still pretty out of it when I heard Beth say, "We've got trouble."

The only time Beth wakes me in the middle of the night is when I am having a bad dream or when there's some awful news. In the past couple of years she has woken me to tell me my daughter Barbara Katie died in a fatal car accident and then when federal marshals were outside our door to take me away. If Beth wakes me up, it's never good. She's never once woke me to say, "We just won a million dollars!"

"The *National Enquirer* has you saying the 'N' word on tape. This is bad, Duane. Really bad."

I thought, *What's so bad about that?* "Bad" is one of the children is hurt. "Bad" is you're going back to jail. "Bad" is someone we love just died. The *National Enquirer* story didn't fit into any of those categories, at least not for me.

"Where are all the kids? Are they all right?" I asked.

Beth said they were fine. The only one I worried about these days was my son Tucker. Tucker went to prison in 2002 for robbing a Japanese tourist with a BB gun. He received a twenty-year sentence for armed robbery and was later paroled after serving four years. When he got out, Tucker came to live and work for me in Hawaii.

It wasn't long before he was hanging with a bad crowd. Within weeks of his release, Tucker had a girlfriend who Beth and I thought was a terrible influence on him. I suspected Tucker was getting high again and it broke my heart. He was making one bad decision after another, but there wasn't a lot I could do except tell him how I felt.

So when Beth woke me up that night, I figured it had to be about Tucker, though I had no idea what he'd done. When she told me it was a tabloid news story, I said I was going back to sleep.

"Duane, I don't think you get it. You're in deep trouble."

"Beth, it's me. Nobody's going to be angry with the Dog for using the 'N' word. I use it all the time." And I did.

I rolled over and tried to go back to sleep. I kept thinking this wasn't bad. I know bad. I thought this would pass. I had no idea my dream was about to become my worst nightmare. Beth knew she had to rally the family, so she immediately called our daughter Baby Lyssa to the house to help soften the eventual blow that before the end of the day would unravel everything I held dear.

Beth told me that my son Tucker had recorded a phone conversation that he and I had had several months earlier. I had to think back to exactly when that call took place. And then it occurred to me, it must have been back in March 2007.

Beth had been suspicious that there was something going on with Tucker for some time. None of us liked his girlfriend, Monique, from the very start. She and her friends had been hanging around the back door of our office in Honolulu trying to hit on Leland and Duane Lee. Ironically, the girls were working at the Kirby vacuum store, the same vacuums I used to sell when I first got out of prison. Whenever the boys were out back on a break, these girls would hover around them. We called them "Lot Lizards" because they were like the lizards that crawl all over our back parking lot.

Beth kept telling everyone to stay away from those girls. She worried about them right from the start. Whenever one of the boys would make a comment like "They're really nice," Beth would quickly say, "Stop it! You're not going to start socializing with people you met in a parking lot. You don't know who they are or what they're capable of."

While everyone thought Beth was being a little paranoid, the bottom line is that she is usually right. One day Beth hit her threshold of tolerance and finally told one of the girls to get lost.

"You're not a client and you're not a tenant. I don't want you hanging around here anymore, got it? Now, go!" She literally shooed her off the property. The girl was pissed and ran as fast as she could to tell her friends, including Tucker's girlfriend, Monique, that Beth had been mean to her. That's when we believe they hatched their plan to catch us doing something really bad on tape.

Monique is an African-American woman. I am sure she heard from Tucker that from time to time I used the "N" word. After the Michael Richards and Don Imus catastrophes, that would have been a perfect way to set me up or, worse, bust me in the press. Tucker must have said it upset him whenever he heard me use that word so he could seem sensitive and heroic for defending his girlfriend's honor. Shortly after Beth chased off the girl in the parking lot, an anonymous note was left under my office door that had the word "N***er" written on it over and over again. Who would send me such a note? It was a message, but I had no idea what it meant. I gave it to Baby Lyssa, who handed it off to Beth.

"This goes into the shredder." Beth was certain she knew who was responsible for such a reprehensible thing.

Beth warned me. She said, "Duane, these girls are nothing but trouble. In fact, they're outside our door again. I'm sure they're up to something no good. Don't fall for any of their tricks."

Beth was right, but she didn't realize one other important thing: These girls were out to get *her* every bit as much as they were me. Tim "Youngblood" Chapman came to us to say he'd overheard the girls scheming, and their alleged plan was to call Beth a "f*cking wop," which they were certain would start an argument or some type of altercation. They would tape-record Beth's reaction, hoping that she'd say something damaging and trying to get her to throw the first punch. It was a good plan, because everyone knows if you start calling Beth names, you've grabbed the bitch by the horns and it's on like Donkey Kong. Beth fights back, but she generally fights fair. If you call her a name, she'll come back by calling you a name. If you talk about her family, she'll go after yours. If you throw down a racial slur, she'll respond with one about you. There was no doubt she'd let loose, and throwing the first ethnic slur was the trigger they hoped would get Beth to say something racial.

I was furious. I called Tucker to find out what was going on. When I told him Monique was in our parking lot trying to set up Beth, he denied it.

"No she's not. She would never do a thing like that."

Tucker firmly stood his ground while defending his girl-friend and her actions. Little did I know that he too had a recorder running, waiting to get what he wanted from me on tape.

It had become pretty clear to Beth and me that Mo-nique's intentions toward our family weren't sincere. She and her friends talked about taking us down and making some money in the process. We both totally believed that her goal was to sell us out. Beth never wanted her in our home, for fear of something leaking to the press that would surely be taken out of context.

Tucker was always fighting with Beth about her refusal to let Monique come to our home. There was constant bickering between the two of them. And then one day, it all came to a head. Tucker was working for us selling T-shirts at our family-run souvenir shop in downtown Honolulu. He quit for one reason or another almost every other day. He was perpetually angry for reasons no one else could re-ally understand. And then one day he came over with a nasty attitude saying he was done for good. I don't really know what exactly caused him to quit that day. It could have been anything from a fight with Beth to our shooing away his girlfriend.

Because Tucker was a felon, it was hard for him to find steady work anywhere else. He was on parole, so I felt it was better to keep him close. I have always ridden Tucker hard to keep him in line. When he first came to Hawaii after get-ting out of the joint, he was actually really well behaved. Everything was "Yes, sir," "No, sir" and "Yes, ma'am," "No, ma'am."

Looking back, I see that Tucker had us convinced that he was a totally changed man when he first got out. And, for a short time, he was really great. That is, until those girls started coming around. Once he began dating Monique, everything started spiraling out of control. We told him from the start that we didn't like her, that we both believed she was a bad person. I tell all of my children, "You are who you hang out with." And it's true. You become who you hang out with. And still, Tucker refused to break up with Monique.

Beth would get frustrated with his half-assed approach to doing things, and that sometimes caused an argument between the two of them. He'd do whatever we asked without a major fuss, but he'd always only do it halfway. If I asked him to sweep the floor, he'd forget to pick up the piles of dirt. If I asked him to water the plants, he'd leave the hose unraveled and on the ground instead of putting it away when he was finished.

Tucker was a good kid when he was a youngster. Up to the age of eleven or so, he got good grades, never missed a single day of class, and was never in any trouble. It was around this time that he started going back and forth between my place and his mother's house. He visited her regularly over the course of the next couple of years. He'd go for a week or two and come back a totally different kid than when he left. I was shocked when I saw him for the first time after coming home from an extended visit with his mom. He had left a clean-cut young boy and returned two weeks later a petty thief with his fingernails painted black.

Beth and I began to notice random items showing up around the house that we both knew Tucker could never afford to buy—like a fog machine! The only conclusion we could come to was that he was stealing the stuff. Although I tried to talk to him about his behavior, the more I spoke to him the worse his attitude became.

As they got older, Tucker, Baby Lyssa, and Barbara Katie had each figured out how to play mom against dad.

It's a pretty common trait among children of divorced parents. Add stepparents into the equation, and you've got a recipe for constant conflict and drama unless all of the adults find a way to work together and in the children's best interests—something I should have done with their mother, but didn't.

The atmosphere at my ex-wife's house was decidedly different from the one at mine. For one thing, the kids told me there were no rules at her house. They said their mother had become more of a friend than a parent, which made for a pretty inviting environment for three prepubescent teenagers. They could stay out as late as they wanted, didn't have to go to school on a regular basis, and were exposed to a party lifestyle that impacted all three in unimaginable ways. My children were not only exposed to hard drugs, they were invited to join in on the partying. They were too young and impressionable to understand that what they saw their mother doing was wrong. By the time Tucker was thirteen, he was old enough to understand what was really going on at his mom's house. He said he didn't want to visit her anymore because he hated what he saw happening to his mother and sisters. I think it was a constant internal battle for Tucker, who tried but failed to keep his sisters out of trouble. He wanted to be the heroic brother who protected his sisters from harm. Despite his efforts, he couldn't stop them from acting out in ways that would eventually hurt them both.

Of course, when the kids returned to our house, Beth and I were always the bad guys because we had rules they had to live by. We set pretty tight boundaries and had expectations that had to be met. The kids all had chores and responsibilities, which they didn't like very much. Whenever Beth and I told them to clean their room or take out the trash, their usual response was "I'm going back to

Mom's!" I felt so bad, I usually caved in and let them have their way when I ought to have practiced some tough love and been stricter and more secure in my parenting.

Over time, I became aware of what was happening at their mother's house and tried to talk to her about it, but I never stopped any of the kids from seeing her whenever they wanted. Looking back, I realize that I should have forbidden them to be in her presence until she stopped her partying ways. I should have gone to court and demanded sole custody. I should have told my kids that I'd cut them off and that they'd get nothing from me if they didn't stop using drugs. But I didn't. I passively allowed things to continue until it got so bad that I had to put a stop to it.

When Baby Lyssa was raped and became pregnant at the age of thirteen by her twenty-seven-year-old boyfriend, I hit my breaking point. It was time to intervene. Tucker was living with me while Barbara Katie and Baby Lyssa were living with their mother. My teenage daughter's only influence was that of a woman who was partying hard and endlessly dating. She didn't pay any attention to the kids, often working or staying out until two in the morning and sleeping all day. I needed to get the girls out from under her before one of them ended up dead. Beth and I stepped in and brought Baby Lyssa to live with us in Hawaii so we could get her off drugs and look after her new baby. She hasn't left since.

In the meantime, Tucker was getting into more and more trouble. His stealing got worse. He was always taking things like money, jewelry, and other valuable stuff he could easily get his hands on. He'd steal from anyone without a care or thought about what he was doing. He showed no conscience. He even stole all of his little brother's and sisters' Christmas gifts one year, leaving nothing but the discarded wrapping paper under the tree. He cleaned us out, taking everything, including a laptop Beth had bought, jewelry I'd given to her, and even a precious ring my mother had given to me before she passed away.

It was hard for me, but I told Beth to call the police even though I knew we were reporting my own son. This was the first time I had ever done anything like that against one of my children. It was a painful yet crucial decision because he was out of control and there was nothing I could do to stop him from stealing. I thought the cops might be able to rattle him into straightening out. I was enraged by the situation, but I also understood my son needed help, help that he wouldn't accept from me. I could hardly bear to listen as Beth made the call. When Tucker was sentenced, the judge told him "there will be a time when your dad cannot and will not be able to help you." Thankfully, because Tucker was only seventeen and a half, the judge took mercy on him and sentenced him to probation because he was a juvenile.

Even though the judge was easy on him, it wasn't enough to deter his behavior or keep Tucker out of trouble. By the time he was eighteen years old, his stealing had become even more out of control. One night, Beth and I were watching the evening news when we heard a story about a robbery in a local hotel room. Two men had broken into a hotel and stolen computers and other electronic equipment from a Japanese businessman. They duct taped the man's hands and feet together so he couldn't move and covered his mouth so he couldn't yell for help. Beth looked over at me and said, "That sounds like something Tucker would do." And she was right, because Tucker always had duct tape around. At first he used it to amuse Bonnie Jo, who was just a baby. She loved touching the sticky part of the tape. And then one day we came home to find Bonnie Jo's hand taped to the side of her head. Beth warned

Tucker not to do that ever again. But that didn't stop him. Another time, we found the baby's wrists bound by the tape.

"Someday that tape is going to be the end of you!" Beth warned Tucker.

Although Beth had her suspicions, I never once thought that my son would commit such a serious crime. I have a knack for ignoring the obvious when it comes to my children. When Tucker came by the house the next day, I asked him if he had anything to do with the robbery. He was emphatic in his answer. "No way, Dad. I would never do something like that." His denial felt sincere and that was all I needed to hear to put my mind at ease.

Somewhere along the way, Barbara Katie, Tucker, and Baby Lyssa made a pact with one another: They would never rat on each other, ever. But I could tell something was going on because Barbara Katie kept telling me she had something to say but never offered up the information. Beth and I sat Tucker down again and reminded him of the time we called the police on him after he stole the Christmas gifts.

Beth said, "Tucker, if you've got something to tell us, say it now before it's too—"

"OK, I did it!" he confessed.

Beth and I looked at each other.

"Did what?" I asked.

"I stole the computers. I robbed the Japanese guy, Dad. I'm sorry!"

His confession put me in the worst position I have ever been in as both dad and bounty hunter.

"Son, you have to leave my house right now," I said. "If my phone was to ring and it's the police asking about you, I'd have to take you in. You need to walk out that door right now. I can't harbor a known fugitive in my house,

Tucker. I could go to jail. You have to go." This time, there was absolutely nothing I could do to help my son. He was on his own. The anguish and guilt nearly killed me.

Shortly after he fled, I received a call from local authorities who asked me to help them find Tucker. They knew for sure he was one of the guys who pulled off the heist.

"Listen," I said. "You're talking about my son. How dare you call and ask me to help you find him. The mayor's son has been wanted on drug charges four or five times and I am positive you didn't ask him to find his kid. You wouldn't call a fellow cop if you were looking for one of his kids. Why would you call me? I won't do it. I won't help you arrest my son." I slammed down the phone.

Tucker was apprehended a couple of weeks later, but not before putting up a good fight. In fact, I heard he was stopped in Honolulu.

"Tucker!" It was a local police officer.

Tucker spun around, got right in the cop's face, and said, "What did you just say to me? Did you just call me a f**ker? Who the hell are you to call me a 'f**ker'?"

Apparently a crowd began to gather as Tucker and the cop had this exchange. My son got the police officer so flustered, he let him go. OK, I'll admit, Tucker should have turned himself in right then and there, but I had to laugh when I heard about this incident because in a strange way, he made me proud with his Chapman charm.

Tucker was sentenced to twenty years in jail, a stiff sentence for the crime he committed. He served four years in an Oklahoma state prison before being paroled. When he was released in 2006, he came to Hawaii to live with Beth and me.

Prison had changed Tucker, but as his dad, I always chose to see my little boy inside the angry young man who stood in front of me. Growing up, I wanted to give him every shot I could at making something of his life. Instead of teaching him how to box like the other boys, I put him in front of a computer. I tried to keep him away from violence because I thought that would deter him from using drugs. It didn't work out that way. I tried to overcompensate for his circumstances, and much like his mother, I became more of a friend than parent.

There's a great danger in being a friend to your children. For me, it ultimately cost me the most precious gift of all—one of my kids. Just before marrying Beth, I was faced with one of the hardest decisions I have ever made. As difficult as it was for me to accept, my daughter Barbara Katie, who was living in Alaska with her mother, had gotten in a lot of trouble with drugs. Every time she called home for a little money, I sent it. It was always the same excuse—that she had lost her glasses. After the third call in a month, it finally occurred to me that I was being incredibly naïve. At last I asked, "Are you on drugs?"

"Oh no, Daddy." And like a fool, I believed her. I kept sending a hundred dollars via Western Union every couple of weeks, under different names so Beth wouldn't find out. It probably didn't matter though, because Beth no doubt knew what I was doing anyway.

Beth could see how serious Barbara Katie's problems had gotten. She insisted that I send her to rehab, but Barbara Katie didn't want to go. She worried that she'd always be known as "that girl who had a drug problem." Beth pleaded with me to send her anyway, but I still couldn't bring myself to do it.

Beth even suggested we go up to Alaska and bring her to Hawaii. But I couldn't do that, either. I knew if I brought Barbara Katie back to Hawaii, she and Baby Lyssa would reconnect, which I feared would have horrible consequences. I had spent an enormous amount of time straightening out Baby Lyssa and getting her off drugs when she came to live with me a few years earlier. I was terrified that Barbara Katie would somehow influence Baby Lyssa to go back to using.

Barbara Katie had sent her young son Travis to live with us while she tried to get her life worked out. Our agreement was that I'd take Travis so she could go to rehab. I wanted her to go to Betty Ford or Promises, but she didn't want to leave home. She wanted to stay in Alaska. A week after she supposedly checked in to a local facility, I got a call from Barbara Katie saying that she was all better. But I knew she was lying and that she had never gotten the help she needed. Miracles happen, but no one gets clean in a week.

Each of my kids has a special place in my heart, but Barbara Katie was my oldest girl. She shared the same sensitivity I have, meaning she'd cry over anything! My mom was the only person I felt I could let my guard down in front of whenever I needed to decompress. We'd cry together for hours until I felt better. After Mom died, Barbara Katie became my crying pal. The night *Dog the Bounty Hunter* debuted on A&E, I was overcome with emotion. The first person I called was my daughter. As soon as she answered, we both lost it. Barbara Katie kept saying how proud she was and how much she hoped to someday be a part of the show. I promised her it would happen because she was family.

"Your dream came true, Daddy." She was so proud of me. Of all my memories from that first night on television, those are the words I will never forget. We were so close, and that's why it was extremely difficult to see her messed up on drugs.

Barbara Katie desperately wanted to come to my wedding. But I couldn't let her attend while she was so strung out. On the day she died, I heard that she'd asked her mother that morning if I had called yet to say she could come to Hawaii for the big day.

I loved her so much, but I believe *I loved her to death*. Every time I tell someone that, they tell me how sorry they are for my loss. The reality is they shouldn't feel sorry, because I have dealt with it in every way.

After Barbara Katie died, I received a call from a man who told me he was in a car that was driving behind the vehicle she was in when it flipped. He told me he saw the horrible accident as it happened. When he ran up to the overturned vehicle, he felt the pulse of the man behind the wheel. It was very weak. He told me he talked to the man and tried to tell him everything was going to be OK. Even so, the driver said he was going to die. That's when the man looked over and noticed another body too. It was my daughter. He explained to me that her head was hanging down to her chest. It was obvious she had broken her neck. The man on the phone told me that he watched the son of a bitch driver who killed my baby take his last breath. He said he called to tell me he was there when the guy died and wanted me to know it was a miserable death.

I thanked him for calling and hung up. I got up from the table, began walking in my backyard, circling the pool, and then I started to cry. Why didn't his phone call make me feel better? Why was I feeling mercy for the bastard that took my baby's life? I couldn't believe I wasn't finding any comfort knowing that man choked on his own blood.

"God, why? Why do I feel this way?"

And then God spoke.

"This is why you will go out there and share your message with people, Duane. You have a forgiving heart like me. That's why you're the Dog. This is what you're supposed to feel like."

Being angry with the driver wouldn't bring my baby back. It wouldn't heal my shattered heart any quicker, and it wouldn't allow me to set an example of the true meaning of mercy. Instead of cursing him, I forgave him. I haven't forgotten any of the pain from that experience, but I've let go of my anger. That act alone gave me the foundation to tell others that they have to do the same thing. Who pays the price when we carry around negative emotional baggage? We do. And where's the good in that? There is none.

So maybe Barbara Katie's death was a way for me to reach out and help others see what they choose not to in their own kids. Perhaps her death will remind you to take the blinders off, get your head out of the sand, and pay attention to *your* kid's addictions. Don't love your kids to death like I did. It's not too late to reach out and pull them from the abyss—but you've got to take action before something terrible happens or you will regret it for the rest of your life. It was too late for Barbara Katie, and now I saw the same thing happening to Tucker.

Tucker's attitude had become noticeably worse since meeting Monique. It was obvious that he was going downhill fast, and despite everything I knew in my heart, I did nothing to stop his spiral. He appeared desperate and without proper moral judgment. He didn't feel good about himself. He'd moan about his felony and the many tattoos he had all over his body that he now regretted. I don't think he felt desirable, so when Monique began paying attention to him, whether or not I approved of her was pretty irrelevant. She made him feel wanted, and who can blame him for that?

Tucker and Monique started spending a lot of time in clubs. It's a pretty well-known fact in our family that Chapmans and booze do not mix. It's a dangerous, deadly, poisonous combination. It basically turns us all into idiots, and Tucker was no exception. I never felt comfortable with Tucker and Monique's party lifestyle, and I now had a growing concern for my son's safety and well-being.

I didn't know if it was the alcohol or something worse, but his temper had become unpredictable and combustible. I suspected that he was on methamphetamines because I had seen him through another period of time when he was on that drug, and his behavior was exactly the same. I also began to notice that Tucker was losing a lot of weight and looked as if he wasn't getting enough sleep. He looked like hell. Then I heard that Monique had helped him buy a prosthetic penis so he could pass his urine tests in front of his parole officer by pretending to piss clean urine. He never would have been able to pass the test without it. That's when I knew for sure that he was back on hard drugs.

The day he came over to say he was quitting work once and for all, he actually threw a twenty-pound patio chair across the pool in a fit of anger. He was spiraling out of control. Drugs had to be a factor, because he was filled with so much rage.

When drugs get ahold of you, they take over all reason and rational behavior. There's nothing you can do to take back your life except to get off of them. My son didn't even admit that he had problem, which is always the first step to recovery. In truth, even though I could see what was happening to him, I still couldn't admit the extent of the trouble he was in, a mistake I will regret for the rest of my life. Beth knew what was going on from the very start. Somehow I put my head in the sand to pretend it wasn't happening . . . again.

The thought of Tucker being hooked on drugs upset me more than I can ever put into words. I should have stepped in to intervene, but I didn't. In the meantime,

Beth had even threatened to call Tucker's parole officer to tell him he was using drugs and using a prosthetic penis to pass his urine tests, because she knew he was in too deep to get off the drugs himself. I had been getting Tucker out of bad situations for years, but this time it felt like a betrayal to rat out my own kid. Since Tucker was on parole, an infraction like this would surely send him back to jail, something I didn't want to be responsible for, so I chose to do nothing. After losing Barbara Katie to drugs, I swore that I'd never allow another one of my children to make the same mistake. Everything inside me knew what I had to do so I wouldn't lose Tucker too, but still, for too long, I chose to do nothing.

When I finally decided to call Tucker to tell him how I felt, I really believed he would understand that what I was saying was for his own good. Like any hands-on parent, I wanted to help Tucker get away from the girlfriend I was convinced was adding to his problems.

That now infamous conversation lasted a solid twenty-five minutes, not the eight minutes or so that were leaked to the media. The call started off calm and cool, but the more I pleaded with him to leave the girl, the harder he pushed back, until I finally lost my temper. I became so pissed off that I couldn't get it through his thick head that I believed everything I was suggesting was for his own good. Tucker kept trying to convince me that since we never allowed his girlfriend into the house, we never spent the time to get to know her like he had. But we did know her, well enough to know we had to keep someone we were certain was out to hurt our family out of our home. No way, that would never happen. Not in my house! That's when I began saying things about Monique I now regret.

"I'm not taking the chance on some motherf**ker. I don't care if she's a Mexican, a whore, whatever . . . it's not because

she's black. It's because we use the word n***er sometimes here. I'm not going to take a chance ever in life for losing everything I've worked for thirty years because some f**king n***er heard us say n***er and turned us in to the Enquirer *magazine. Our career is over. I'm not taking that chance at all, never in life. Never. Never."*

Beth was standing in the courtyard outside our bedroom telling me to be quiet. She kept saying I needed to stop talking and hang up the phone, but I didn't. Nope. I kept right on talking. When I look at those words in print, it hurts my heart to think they ever came out of my mouth. It's obvious that I wasn't talking about the color of Monique's skin so much as the character, or lack thereof, that this young woman embodied, this young woman who had all but taken over my son's life. None of my sons had Anglo-Saxon wives or girlfriends, so my concern for Tucker had nothing to do with race.

I spent years studying and learning from Tony Robbins, who taught me that if a person doesn't understand what you're saying, you have to continue to change your approach until the person does. So I begged Tucker to leave Monique in every way I could, giving him all the reasons why I felt the way I did and why I thought she was bad news. I'd initially gotten on the phone to explain to Tucker why he couldn't bring her around my house, to tell him that she was trouble. But the more I tried to make my point, the less I thought I was getting through to him. Stupidly, I kept hoping I would somehow get through to his stubborn Chapman ass. Tucker didn't have much to say as I talked. One of the only things I remember him saying was "If Baby Lyssa was dating a black guy, you wouldn't be acting this way."

"If Lyssa was dating a n***er, we would all say f*ck you . . . and you know that. If Lyssa brought a black guy home ya da da

. . . it's not that they're black, it's none of that. It's that we use the word n***er. We don't mean you fucking scum n***er without a soul. We don't mean that shit. But America would think we mean that. And we're not taking a chance on losing everything we got over a racial slur because our son goes with a girl like that. I can't do that, Tucker. You can't expect Gary, Bonnie, Cecily, all them young kids to because 'I'm in love for seven months'—fuck that! So I'll help you get another job, but you cannot work here unless you break up with her and she's out of your life. I can't handle that shit. I got 'em in the parking lot trying to record us. I got that girl saying she's gonna wear a recorder . . ."

Looking back, I realize that, deep down, I instinctively knew this was going to end up in print somewhere. I was trying to protect everything I held near and dear—my family, my career, and most of all, my son. The son I'd delivered into this world with my bare hands. When his mother went into labor, she let out such a loud scream I thought she was dying. She passed out cold after her water broke. I picked her up, carried her into the bedroom, and did what I could to make sure she and the baby were safe. Thankfully, my mother didn't live far from our house. I called her to say I needed help getting my wife to the hospital. By the time Mom got to me, Lyssa was already giving birth. I could see the baby's head in between her legs. Even though I didn't know why I needed it, I told Mom to get me some hot water. I remembered watching episodes of *Gunsmoke* as a kid and hearing people yell for hot water and towels when a woman went into labor, so I did too. Mom came running into the bedroom with hot water and a towel.

I reached between Lyssa's legs and began to pull gently on the baby's head. She was screaming while I yelled, "Push, push!" I pulled until one little shoulder popped through and then the other. Within seconds I was holding Tucker in my arms. But something was wrong. He wasn't breathing. He wasn't crying, and now I noticed he was completely blue.

"He's dead," I said to Mom as tears streamed down my cheeks.

I put his little body to the side while I pulled on the umbilical cord. When the placenta came out, I thought it was another dead baby. I was absolutely beside myself with grief.

"Good job, Dad," a voice said from behind me. It was a paramedic who had arrived and then taken a large scissor and cut the cord.

Tucker began to cry. I never felt so proud in my life. I had brought this little baby into the world, and I felt a bond from the very moment I held him in my arms. I named him Tucker D. Chapman. His initials were the same as the Texas Department of Corrections. I looked into my son's eyes and thought, *This is the son that I'll be a good guy for.* I hadn't been a model citizen up until that point. But something about Tucker made me want to live an honest, honorable life.

I have a soft spot for all of my children, but the three I had with Big Lyssa have always had a special little piece of me because of my shame and guilt about the divorce. I spent years feeling responsible because they didn't have a mother who was around. There was nothing I wouldn't do for any of my kids, but those three in particular were impossible for me to say no to.

One Christmas, when he was just a little boy, Tucker begged me for a "My Buddy" doll. Unfortunately, I couldn't afford to buy it for him. Money was tight and the doll was really expensive. Even so, I didn't want to disappoint my son, so I spent all of Christmas Eve that year bounty hunting so I could earn enough money to buy the doll. I sat on the guy I was chasing for hours, just waiting for the right moment to get him. The cops wanted him as much as I did, but if they got him first, I wouldn't make a dime, which meant I wouldn't be able to bring home the doll for Tucker.

The cops drove by me from time to time over the course of the day and asked, "Are you going to get him?"

"I'll get him," I said. And then one of the cops said to me, "Why? Is he your buddy?"

I knew right then the Lord was going to let me catch this guy so I could get Tucker his My Buddy doll just in time to open it on Christmas Day. Sure enough, I caught my jump. I sang the jingle from the doll commercial all the way to the jail. The poor bastard probably thought I was nuts. By the time I handed him over, I barely had enough time to make it to the store before they closed for the holiday. When I got there, there was only one doll left. I took the box off the shelf as fast as I could so no one else would swoop in. I couldn't wait to give My Buddy to Tucker and see the look on his face knowing that his old man had come through.

I had a lot of great times with Tucker over the years. When he got out of prison, I knew he was feeling a little left out of the mix because he wasn't on our show. One of the last episodes we shot before going on break for the season was when Duane Lee, Leland, and I taught Tucker how to drive. We set up bright orange pylons in an empty parking lot so he could take serpentine turns through them. We put that boy through all sorts of torturous drills, but it was all in the name of family fun, brotherly bonding, and togetherness. When we finished, Duane Lee and Tucker were walking away, when I heard Duane Lee say, "Come on, I'll drive you home."

"How about I drive *you* home?" Tucker asked.

"No way! I'm not letting you drive my car."

We all laughed, but it was a really touching moment between my boys I'll never forget. It was probably the last good time we all had together.

I hung up the phone after going off on Tucker, somehow knowing that I would pay for losing my cool. I hoped and prayed he wasn't going to be my Judas, the one to sell me out, but deep down, I knew that he was capable of it. I wanted to believe it was because of what the drugs he was hooked on had done to him, and that he wasn't acting out of pure malice. That's an awful feeling for a father to have about his son.

Family is everything to me. I will defend my children to the bitter end against anyone or anything that I deem dangerous or harmful. I spent the rest of the day secretly fearing that I would now be in a position where I would have to defend myself against a member of my own family. I knew the bomb would eventually drop. I just didn't know when.

From that day forward, I became enemy numero uno to my son. Tucker had it in for me. He was angry about our conversation and harbored a lot of resentment toward me for demanding he dump his girlfriend. According to sources, he recorded the call in March 2007 but didn't make the deal with the *National Enquirer* until May, and didn't turn over the tapes until October.

By the time Tucker finally did turn over the tapes, his anger toward the entire family had grown out of control. It was like a time bomb waiting to explode. He'd spent years believing he was mistreated. He didn't get a lot of love from his mom, and as much as I wanted to be there for him, I was something of an absentee dad because I was always working. When he was growing up, I used to hug and kiss him all the time, but when he became a teenager, like a lot of kids that age, he didn't like me to do that anymore. I guess he thought it was embarrassing to have his dad smother him. I think Monique was the first woman in his life who loved him and showed him affection like that. I don't know if she became a mother figure to him, but she sure had a hold on him like his mother. Most people gravitate toward partners who are like their mom or dad because there's a comfort in that, especially when that type of love was absent while they were growing up. After four years in prison, Tucker was so starved for love and affection. I should have known exactly how he felt because I also felt that way when I got out.

It's not a secret there's no love lost between his mother and me. I blame her for the way she was with our three children, and she's angry with me for moving on with my life. In truth, I bear a great deal of responsibility for the way things turned out for Tucker because I played a role in many of the difficult events in his life. The strained relationship between his mother and me hurt all of our kids. If we had communicated better and learned to work with each other instead of against each other, perhaps Barbara Katie would be alive today, Baby Lyssa wouldn't have been raped, and Tucker wouldn't have gone to jail. I carry a tremendous amount of guilt for not having the courage to be a more strict dad and a more demanding ex-husband. The anger my ex-wife harbors toward me was funneled through to our children. She filled their heads with all sorts of stories that simply weren't true so she would be able to have a hold on them and turn each of those kids against me. Once I got Baby Lyssa back, she no longer wanted to hear her mother's rhetoric or propaganda. She could see how much better off her life was living with Beth and me. Barbara Katie played both sides until the day she died, so I never had the chance to turn things around for her before it was too late. Tucker was out of his mother's grip for four years while he was incarcerated, but it didn't take long after his release for her to sink her hooks back into him and begin to turn him against me. While I was doing everything I could to help Tucker adjust to life on the outside, his mother coddled him, preyed on his insecurities, and pushed our child to do something I am sure he now regrets.

Apparently, the *National Enquirer* sent the contracts for payment to Tucker's mother in Alaska so she could negotiate the deal on Tucker's behalf. He signed the documents but refused to turn over the tapes for several months. For whatever reason, he kept backing out of making that final destructive move that might sink my battleship for good.

Beth actually caught Tucker talking to the *National Enquirer* in June. She warned him that he better not be running his mouth off about the family or there would be hell to pay. My oldest son, Christopher, had already sold a story to the *Enquirer* that same month saying I beat him as a kid, which sent us all over the edge. Tucker could see that the tabloids were a real threat to us and an extremely sore subject with the network. He had found my Achilles' heel and planned to use it against me.

When I called Tucker that fateful day, I was still trying to reason with him. Of course, I know there's no reasoning with an addict. I wasn't giving him the kind of help he was so clearly crying out for, which I regret with all my heart.

Leland, Duane Lee, Beth, and I left for Texas a few weeks after my last conversation with Tucker. We were headed there to shoot our show for three weeks. Tucker was left behind with no positive influence in our absence. Since he was no longer working at the T-shirt shop, I heard he'd found work with a local construction company. He continued seeing Monique, falling further into a bad place. In addition to the drinking and drugs, Tucker slid even further sideways by listening to his mother and girlfriend say nasty things about me and Beth all summer long.

While we were gone, I heard a story about Tucker and Monique going to Lulu's, a club that on some nights allowed underage kids in to dance, but they couldn't drink. The underage kids have to wear wristbands so the bartenders know they aren't of the legal drinking age. Allegedly, Monique and Tucker had brought some underage friends to Lulu's with them one night and were giving them alcohol. One of the employees caught them in the act and they were asked to leave. While being escorted out, Monique began taunting the bouncer, saying, "It's because I'm black and he's white, right?"

There was a police cruiser sitting outside the club. When Monique saw the cops, she started yelling—throwing down the race card the second she saw them.

"It's because we're an interracial couple. You're just doing this because we're interracial!"

The officer overheard the ruckus, got out of his car, and asked if everything was all right.

"You kids need to move along now," the officer commanded. And then he realized he recognized Tucker, and he said, "Aren't you Dog's son?"

"Yeah. He's my dad."

"Well, I got a copy of his book in my car. Would you get him to sign it for me?"

Tucker rolled his eyes at him and said, "I don't really see him that much." Then he turned and walked away. The cop let them off with a warning but filed a report on the incident documenting the racial accusations. I could see a troubling pattern developing. Even so, I had no idea how bad things were about to get.

CHAPTER 7

When I was a young boy, my mother would often remind me of an old saying that goes, "Sticks and stones might break my bones, but words can never hurt me." I was trained from an early age that no matter what names someone calls you, you have to have a thick skin because they don't really mean what they're saying. From the time I was a little boy, I've been called a lot of bad things by people from all walks of life. When I was a boy, people called me Prairie N***er, Injun, Chief, Glue Head, Flatfoot, and all sorts of other names. As I got older, the names got worse, but they never cut me deep enough to hurt.

I grew up in a home with a father who never used a swear word. I remember being at work with him one day when I heard him curse for the first time. In a way, I was relieved to know he had it in him, but still I was shocked to hear Dad curse. My mother used to warn me to watch my language. She'd tell me if I wasn't careful, I'd end up like John the Baptist, eventually being handed my head on a platter if I wasn't thoughtful with my words. I tried to reason with her that curse words weren't literal, that it was no big deal to swear and call people names if you didn't mean it. Mom disagreed with me, trying to tell me I was wrong and that someday I'd understand what she meant when she warned me to watch my mouth.

My mother had warned me since I was twelve years old that my day of reckoning was coming, and it turned out that I should have listened to her.

I always tell people that the tongue is the most unruly part of the body and the hardest to control. To me, it is the most dangerous weapon we all possess. It can cut a person bare fists. Now, anyone who knows me also knows I wouldn't purposely hurt someone in such a manner. My intentions are genuinely pure. So when the *National Enquirer* story broke about me using the "N" word, I truly didn't understand what I had done wrong.

Even though I am white, up to that point I honestly believed that I was a "N***er" too. For as long as I can remember, at least since my days back in Huntsville, I always thought of myself as a brother. I thought the word meant "I've been enslaved, but now I'm free" and "don't mess with me." I believed that a "n***er" was someone who had gone through a lot of controversy, had endured a lot of troubles, and had survived. A "n***er" won by succeeding at something he wanted to do. For me, going from an ex-convict to becoming a successful bounty hunter and television star made me a "n***er."

People have called me their "n***er" for years. I never once thought that either of us was being disrespectful or derogatory. I viewed it as brotherly love. I thought I was cool enough to use that word too. There were always circumstances where I felt it was safe to use the word without fear of offending anyone, especially among friends in Hollywood. Because of my past experiences, I thought I had a pass to use the word without issue. When I did, it was always used as a slang term of endearment—never a racial cut-down.

I've been looked down on and discriminated against my whole life. Not just because I'm part Native American, but also because I'm an ex-convict, a seventh-grade dropout, an outlaw, and a biker too. From the bottom of my heart, I thought all of those things made me a "n***er."

The use of that word was never about color for me so much as it was about culture. It was more of a "been there done that" way of thinking. I know sophisticated people might not be able to understand how I felt. But they haven't walked in my shoes. I lived with thirty-six thousand black inmates in Huntsville. I chase and capture criminals for a living. The use of language that is offensive to so many people is simply a part of the culture I live and work in. I have a limited education. I was in a Texas state penitentiary until I was twenty-two years old. I spent my first year out of prison high on Valium while trying to figure out what I wanted to do with the rest of my life. Where would I have been taught that using the "N" word was wrong? Of course, as I got older, I realized that using that word in a public place is never acceptable.

How we talk is dependent on where we were brought up. For example, there's a perception that New Yorkers use the "F" word all the time. Rappers use the "N" word without having to worry about accusations of racism. In some communities, that language might be deemed acceptable, while it would be reprehensible in others. I was called a "half breed" most of my young life and never once thought it was wrong, because it describes who I am. If you're a white or Hispanic guy raised in South Central Los Angeles, you may sound more black than not. When Madonna moved to London, she began speaking the Queen's English even though she was born and raised in Michigan, and Eminem sounds more street even though he's a white guy from the suburbs. It's an effect more of culture than of the color of your skin. That's how I always viewed my use of the "N" word. It was never, ever about race.

Many of my most valuable civics lessons weren't learned growing up. They were picked up along the road of life. I didn't know it at the time, but this was going to turn out to be one of the greatest lessons.

About a year or so before that story hit the tabloids, I was at the MSNBC studio doing an interview with Dan Abrams. I used the "N" word off the cuff in between segments. My mic was still on, so everyone in the studio heard me say it. Dan Abrams asked me if I had heard about what happened to Don Imus. I knew who Imus was, but I never listened to his show. I asked Dan if Imus was the redneck guy who wore the big white cowboy hats. He said that was him.

"Well, I'm not surprised he would use that kind of language. I figured a guy like that might make a derogatory reference to black people from time to time. What was the big deal?" I asked. "You know, if I used the 'N' word to that guy right there," I said, pointing to one of the stage-hands who was black, "I don't think he'd care because I'm the Dog." Abrams looked shocked by my statement, but it was true. So much so that the stagehand agreed with me. "That's right, Dog," he said. He was treating me like we were equals, as if I was a brother and my using that word was not a problem for guys like him. It had never been an issue in the past.

I looked back at Dan Abrams, shrugged my shoulders, and opened my hands, as if to say, *You see? My point exactly.*

I never gave the use of that word a second thought because I believed everyone felt the same as that stagehand.

I kept thinking, *Why on earth would anyone care if I used that word?* Strangely, Abrams took issue with the word more than the stagehand that day. My best assessment was that the stagehand understood I wasn't being rude or disrespectful, so he was never made uncomfortable by the exchange. I don't think Abrams could possibly understand where I was coming from because he has never been in my shoes. He's a newsman, not a bondsman. He's not in the field chasing down punks. As far as I know, he's never done time. It didn't make either of us right or wrong. It made us individuals with very different backgrounds.

So when the story hit, I personally didn't think it was very newsworthy, at least not to me. But I knew it could be damaging. I assured Beth everything would be OK and that she didn't need to spend one minute worrying about the fallout. Of course, I was being naïve, because the story was growing by the second.

Now, telling Beth not to worry is like telling a food addict not to touch that platter of homemade cookies. It doesn't matter how many times you tell that person to back away from the plate, those cookies are goners.

I had already survived the screaming phony headlines of the tabloids for years: DOG SMOKES CRACK, DOG AND BETH TO DIVORCE, DOG BARES ALL! The tabloids' sole purpose in life is to devastate and destroy people. Not long after Barbara Katie died, a reporter from the *Enquirer* called to tell me they had photos of the crash. They were planning on running the graphic pictures along with a story about my dead daughter. I was furious. I threatened the man, saying I'd hunt him down and kill him with my bare hands if they printed those photos. Her lifeless body splattered all over the pages of a tabloid magazine was more than any parent should endure after losing a child. How far will these reporters go before it is too far? As humans, we can only take so much before we reach a breaking point. I have been tested so many times in my life, but this was one time I didn't feel like I had to turn the other cheek. Up until then, it was never the lies the papers printed that bothered me so much as the people who were telling them. But, then the "N" word story broke and I thought, *This time, they just might beat me,* because that was definitely my voice they had on tape. There was absolutely no doubt it was me.

As the day went on, the story grew into something much bigger than I could ever have imagined. I went from thinking it would all blow over to worrying that I was done. I couldn't believe that, of all people, I was about to go down for something like this. It seemed impossible. I thought I was invulnerable from the enemy, the devil, the guy who robs you of everything if you give in to the temptations of his world. I didn't think I had done anything wrong, but with each passing hour, the story blew up faster than a deer tick on a dog. By mid-morning in Hawaii, a six-hour time difference from New York, it was one of the lead stories on the news—around the world.

Larry King, Sean Hannity, Greta Van Susteren, foreign press, CNN, MSNBC—everyone called Beth wanting a comment from me. By the end of the day my manager called to say life as I'd known it was done—over. He said I was the plague.

Poof.

Gone.

It was all gone.

An irreversible cyclone began to spiral my life out of control. Even though I went back to bed that morning, I never actually fell back to sleep because Beth kept me up with her constant updates of what was happening. I was getting Google alerts on my iPhone about it every fifteen seconds or so. Within hours, Beth was on the phone doing what she does best, dealing with the media and handling the drama. She fielded calls from news organizations, producers, the network, our publicist, lawyers, my manager, friends, family, and everyone else who has a hand in my daily life. "We can help, we can help" was the general message. Everyone had thoughts on how to handle the fallout. My life had gone nuclear, and I never even heard the bomb drop.

Hollywood spin doctors warned Beth that I could never recover from this mess. Some of them wanted to help us turn things around but suggested that it might be futile at best. Their job is to help get celebrities out of trouble, but many thought this job was too big, would take too much manpower, and ultimately we'd never survive it anyway. The ones that did say they could help said it would cost me a minimum of *twenty thousand dollars* a month. And for that money, their advice was to deny everything. They suggested I make a statement claiming it was not my voice on the tape, which, of course, was absurd because it was so obviously me.

One particular publicist suggested I should make a public statement that I was drunk and didn't know what I was saying. Then I'd have to make a beeline for the Betty Ford clinic or some other rehab center for thirty days while the news died down, despite the fact that most everyone knows that I don't drink.

"Exactly!" she said. "That's why it's a perfect excuse for you. Since you don't drink, you can say the alcohol had an unexpectedly weird effect. Easy as pie, Dog. The public will believe you." But I didn't have it in me to deceive everyone about what had really happened, not even to save my reputation.

Have you ever wondered why so many celebrities go to rehab after some big news story breaks?

Isaiah Washington went to rehab after making a disparaging remark about one of his coworkers' sexual preference.

Mel Gibson made an anti-Semitic remark to a cop during a DUI bust—off to rehab.

David Duchovny and former ESPN host Steve Phillips—off to rehab for sex addiction.

Pat O'Brien left a voice mail for a stripper telling her how he wanted to do cocaine off her naked body all night: Go directly to rehab. Do not pass go. Do not collect two hundred dollars.

Now you know the truth!

Since this Doggie don't run, fake rehab wasn't going to be my out.

When yet another spinmeister suggested that I look into my family heritage because there had to be some African-American blood in the line since I was part Native American, the only thing I could say in response was a confused "Oh . . . is that right?" I was dumbfounded.

None of these "solutions" made a whole lot of sense to me. Going underground wasn't my style. Hiding out until the dust settled isn't who I am. There had to be a right answer, one that worked for me, one that was reflective of how I live and one where the learning experience I was going through could serve as a positive example to others as it played itself out. I prayed God would give me the right answer and show me the way, because I was coming up short.

Later that night, I had a dream that I was going to judgment in front of God. Three people were standing in front of me acting crazy. As they turned around, I realized that they were the three Hebrew children who wouldn't bow down in front of King Nebuchadnezzar. In Daniel 3 in the Bible, Nebuchadnezzar ordered that all those present bow down before the golden statue, but these three children refused to follow his direct command. They defied the king and remained standing. Angry and enraged, the king ordered they be thrown into the fiery furnace. Miraculously, they survived. When they emerged, the king's soldiers looked at each other in total disbelief. There were four people standing before them. They ran to tell the king they saw the three Hebrews and a fourth man standing there too, the son of God. Confused, the king ordered the three men be brought to him so he could see this miracle for himself. When he saw with his own eyes that they were alive, he publicly praised the God of Israel, saying, "He sent his angels to rescue his servants who trusted in him. They defied the king's command and were willing to die rather than worship any god except their own God" (Daniel 3:28, New Living Translation).

I couldn't believe I was standing behind the three Hebrew children.

Ugh!

Just my luck.

These three only did good deeds their entire life. After everything I'd been through, how would I look to God when I came walking in after their day of judgment? I knew God would see the raw, unedited truth about my life, what a whore I'd been in the past, the mistakes I made and the hurtful words I often said that I now regretted. I looked over and noticed a fourth man standing in front of me too. At first, I thought he looked like a pimp—with his big afro, velvet suit with a satin pinstripe down the leg, and platform shoes straight out of the 1970s disco era. I let out a loud sigh of relief because I figured he'd sinned more than I had. Surely God would show mercy on me after meeting with that macked-out pimp daddy dude. But then something strange happened. When the guy turned around, it was the Reverend Jesse Jackson! The realization that it was him freaked me out enough to wake me from my dream.

Even though I couldn't fully explain the dream at the

time, seeing the Reverend Jackson, a man I respect and admire, standing in front of me told me to be bold and confront my mistake. As far as I knew, no one had faced their public lashing for something like this head-on. The world was watching my every move. I had two choices. I could go underground until the dust settled, or I could own up to my wrongdoing, become a role model for others, and take whatever the Lord had planned for me like a man. The Bible says "the unsaved watch us all the time." They're judging everything we say, do, and whether or not we will live up to the standards they've set for us. I have tried to live by my convictions, my morals and values. If you are willing to sacrifice yourself for what you believe in, God will be there, and so I finally had my answer and knew what I had to do.

My survival instincts kicked in right there and then. I asked God if His plan was to brand me "N-Dog" for the rest of my life. Was this going to be my burden forever?

His answers to both questions came back "Yes."

How can you argue with the Lord and His almighty plan? That's simple. You can't. The only thing I could do was speak my peace, apologize, and hope America would take mercy on my ignorance.

And while it took me some time to buck up, Beth had already shifted into doing whatever damage control needed to be done. One of the first things she did outside of juggling the media was send Baby Lyssa up to the house where Tucker lived to get Travis out. Tucker would have to weather this storm on his own. When she got there, Tucker and Lyssa almost got into a physical fight as she delivered the news. He ended up calling the police on her and then contacted photographers from the *National Enquirer* so they could come over and capture the confrontation. Ka-ching!

More money for Tucker if they got the shot. It was clear he wasn't going to leave without a struggle.

Luckily, Baby Lyssa got away by the skin of her teeth and without harm. The cops showed up just as she was leaving, and the photographers were too late to capture the exchange.

Someone told me Tucker had gone to work that very same day saying, "Ain't gonna be no more *Dog the Bounty Hunter.*" He was gloating. My own son was basking in the hurt he had brought upon his own family.

Mutiny, by definition, is "a rebellion against legal authority, especially by soldiers or sailors refusing to obey an order and, often, attacking their officers." While my children have made lots of mistakes over the years, I never once believed any of them would knowingly and purposefully try to destroy me. Sell me out? Yeah. It had happened once before this incident with my son Christopher. But he was just chasing money, not catastrophic retribution. The tabloids make it so easy for someone to make a few bucks by selling information—whether that information is true or not. But this time they had gone too far. They waved more money in my son's face than he had ever dreamed of making. All he had to do was throw his old man to the wolves. He never looked back. What Tucker did was a mutiny of disastrous proportion, the depth and impact of which was painfully becoming more clear with every passing hour.

And if I had any hope about my son feeling remorse or guilt at the time over what he'd done, it was put to rest later that night after Tucker phoned Baby Lyssa. At first, she thought he might be calling to apologize for his behavior. Instead, he said to her, "Here's your future" and flushed the toilet. It hurts my heart even now, thinking that my son feels this way about me. But I wasn't the only one hurt by this.

I'm the Dog to you, but to my kids, I'm just Dad. They grew up in a house where I was pretty much always right, but this time Dad was wrong—*very* wrong. The family fallout was immediate. If Beth and I hadn't had our young children, the impact of this blow might have been a little easier to take. Unfortunately, it wasn't just me who took the hit. My entire family was attacked that day.

My nine-year-old daughter, Bonnie Jo, and my seven-year-old son, Gary Boy, came home from school on the day the story broke and said they heard the news from some of the kids in their class. Of course, we hadn't thought to tell them about it before they left that morning because I thought the whole thing would blow over.

"Dad, you can't use that word, you're not a rapper," Bonnie Jo said.

I just about died. I didn't want any of my babies ashamed of me, but especially the little ones. I couldn't stomach the thought of them hearing that their dad was a racist, or worse.

Duane Lee and Leland came over the morning this was all going down too. They sat in my living room and broke down. They were in tears over the news. Duane Lee told me about an exchange he'd had with Tucker two nights before the news broke. He confronted Tucker with his anger that Tucker was refusing to go to court with Beth to be a witness on a case she was involved in.

"You have to be in court to help the family, Tucker," Duane Lee told him, doing his best to compel Tucker to do the right thing.

"No way. I'm not going to court." Tucker's response was so angry. Of course, I now understand he had his fingers in his ears just waiting for the bomb to explode at any moment. But at the time, none of us could understand why he was being so short-tempered with everyone.

On a hunch, Duane Lee asked Tucker, "You haven't done anything to hurt Dad, have you?"

"Ugh! I can't believe you would ask me something like that. What kind of dick do you think I am?" Tucker was so defensive that Duane Lee backed right down. But now, two days later, as Duane Lee shared this story with us, Tucker's erratic behavior began to make sense.

Duane Lee and Leland insisted that I cut all ties with Tucker. His actions had a trickle-down effect on everyone associated with the show, including those boys, who felt as betrayed by Tucker as I did.

They pointed out that their own brother had failed to take his brothers and sisters into consideration. It was pretty obvious that he didn't care about them. He didn't care about Big Travis, the father of Barbara Katie's son, and someone who was his roommate and a close friend, nor did he consider the impact on little Travis, who looked up to Tucker like a big brother. He didn't consider the fallout this would have on our bail bonds business or the television show that had clothed and fed not only all of us, but many others who had depended upon our show for their livelihood over the past several years. Producers, cameramen, editors, and hundreds of others worked at the network, where a hit show helps pay the salaries—and all with families of their own. None of those people entered his mind when he sold the tape of our conversation. He couldn't even fathom what he had done. His only thought was to hurt Beth and me.

By mid-afternoon, prominent leaders in the black community were already calling for my television show to be pulled from the network. Roy Innis, who has served as the chairman of the Congress of Racial Equality, also known as CORE, a United States civil rights organization that played a pivotal role in the civil rights movement, was leading the charge, saying I shouldn't have my show and that I needed to answer for my behavior. He was asking A&E to take swift action in response to my statements. And he wasn't alone. Several civil rights leaders were pretty much saying the same thing.

Almost immediately, Alan Nevins, my manager, and Beth were fielding calls from various groups who had booked me to do special appearances and were now saying they were canceling. I was scheduled to be the grand marshal at Mardi Gras in New Orleans—canceled. Grand Marshal of the Fiesta Bowl parade—canceled. I had a deal in place to launch my own line of slot machines in Vegas— canceled. All of my licenses went away. Online sales of merchandise tanked. Stores yanked my products off their shelves. My first book, which had been enjoying a long ride on the *New York Times* bestseller list, was pulled from almost every store and returned to the publisher. It was devastating. I suddenly realized that all of my eggs were in the A&E basket, something that I had been grateful for but was now quite concerned about.

I didn't know what I would do. Bounty hunting was all I had. I could still do that, but the probability of doing it in front of the cameras ever again seemed to be quickly slipping away.

CHAPTER 8

Although we were already wrapped for the season, the network announced the same day the story broke that they were halting production on any remaining shows. They thought that by doing this they might appease civic leaders who were applying tremendous amounts of pressure on them to take the show off the air. We held our breath for two days hoping that the craziness would die down. No such luck. The debate was just getting started. Two days later, after two main advertisers pulled out from the show, A&E, under pressure from so many different sources, called us with the bad news. They were making the announcement that *Dog the Bounty Hunter* was off the network's schedule for the "foreseeable future." The wording of the announcement made it clear the show wasn't being canceled, merely shelved. Regardless, that news impacted the lives of eighty-six people who depended on my television show to support their families. When A&E shelved us, every single one of those people indefinitely lost their jobs too.

Beth was angry about the network's decision. She called Marty Singer, our entertainment lawyer, in Los Angeles to assess the situation and talk about our options. There was no way I would ever agree to bring legal action against my own son. Beth argued that Don Imus walked away with half the value of his contract when he was fired for racially insensitive comments and wondered if Marty could work out some financial arrangement too.

It's funny when I think back to those first few days because money was the last thing on my mind. I didn't care about contracts and felonies. Everyone was arguing that Tucker had recorded a personal conversation that we'd had in the privacy of our own home. I didn't go on a public racial tirade like so many others before me. I was having a heart-to-heart conversation with my son. Yeah, I heard a lot of "justification" over those first few days on how I was victimized and getting burned. The more I heard it, the more I wanted to scream *STOP!*

I knew in my heart that I wasn't the victim in all of this. Private conversations ought to still follow the path of right and wrong. And, in this situation, I was way wrong. No ifs, ands, or buts . . . I was out of line. Just because my words were used in private didn't lessen the impact, especially coming from me, a guy who was supposed to be a role model for my family, friends, and fans. My sole focus was on figuring out ways to fix the damage, to repent, and then to heal.

The network begged us to lay low for a while and let some time go by. They made it pretty clear they had to back off and wash their hands of the mess I had created. Civil rights leaders weren't satisfied with their decision to remove the show from the schedule. Several coalition groups sent letters to the network demanding our cancellation. The timing couldn't have been worse since Citadel Broadcasting Corporation had just announced Don Imus's return to radio the day after my story broke. This enraged many people because they felt that Imus had been fired and shown the front door while CBC was quietly rehiring him through the back. A&E's open-ended announcement gave these groups enough fuel to say the same would happen with me.

Even with all of the drama surrounding A&E's decision, Beth was determined to fight for the show. Frankly, I didn't have much of a fight left in me. The show seemed so unimportant compared to making amends. Even so, the overwhelming sadness of losing my show combined with losing my son was taking a tremendous toll.

People in the entertainment industry had warned me for years that I could lose all of my success with the snap of a finger. Lord knows I'd come close many times. Though I always heard the message, it had never made more sense to me than it did in that moment.

But I had to get those thoughts out of my mind. You become what you think. I had no plan to roll over and die. I'd lick my wounds for a while, but I planned on coming back and emerging from the flames stronger than ever. And time was of the essence to me, because I couldn't shake the feeling there might be people who would die thinking I was a racist before I could get out there and apologize. There were no books or manuals that could help me navigate these uncharted waters. I was on my own to do what I thought was right. Don't ever count out the underdog, especially when that underdog is *the* Dog.

There were thousands of media requests for me to give an interview on the matter. After careful consideration, we went to two of the biggest names in television news, Sean Hannity and Larry King. I wanted to be certain I would reach as many people as I could with the limited time I'd get on these shows. When I spoke with Sean Hannity, he warned me in advance that I'd better be sincere or he would take me down for good.

"If I don't believe in you," he said, "you're done."

Beth put Sean and his team through the wringer before

agreeing to do his show. She insisted that he read my first book before the interview, even going so far as telling Sean she was going to quiz him by asking questions about it before I went on the air.

A&E was advising me to simply respond to the press and media with a standard "No comment," but to me that was the same as saying, "I'm guilty and afraid to face the consequences." I didn't think this would ever die until I spoke. So, against the network's wishes, I set up the two interviews, with Sean Hannity on November 7 and with Larry King the following night.

Knowing the interviews were all set up, I had less than a week to figure out what I was going to say. I sought out the advice of many trusted and more experienced advisors on what I needed to do to right the wrong act I had committed. The first person I wanted to reach out to was my pastor, Tim Storey, who is himself an African-American.

The Bible tells us that God will send people into our lives who are there to help us, but you've got to test them first to make sure they are who they say they are. When you test them, you'll see the truth. Fortunately, I'm a born tester, especially when it comes to holy rollers. Some are fake while others are the real deal. Tim Storey is more than the real deal—which is why he's *my* pastor.

Several years ago, long before I had my own television show, a friend invited Beth and me to hear Tim Storey preach at her church. She told me how cool he was and how inspiring his sermons were. Now, I was never the type of guy who went to church to connect with God. I felt I had my own relationship with Him wherever I was. I didn't need a steeple to feel like I could pray. Even so, my friend was adamant that I go with her, so I gave in.

Beth and I got dressed and made our way to the church one beautiful Hawaiian Sunday morning. We sat down in the second row; I was on the aisle while Beth was inside to my left. Tim was slaying people in the spirit, praying for them and casting out evil spirits. I was mesmerized by his dramatic and engaging style. Suddenly, I got a feeling about the next man going up to the altar. I heard the Lord tell me, "Watch out for that guy." An evil feeling came over me like a cloak.

I sprung into action. I instinctively knew something bad was about to go down. Tim prayed for the guy, laid hands on him, and knocked him back in the name of the Lord. That's when I jumped on the altar and pinned the guy to the ground. Tim was trying not to pay attention to the ruckus I was causing, but it was hard to ignore a six-foot-tall, long-haired blond man sitting on top of another guy. I reached into his pocket and pulled out a four-inch knife. I yelled for security.

I asked the guy what he was doing.

"God told me to stab Tim Storey," he answered. He was there to kill the pastor.

"Security, get this guy out of here," I said. Tim Storey was still preaching while the guards carried his assailant away.

After the service, Tim asked the local pastor if he knew who I was, because he wanted to meet me.

The pastor said, "That's Dog the Bounty Hunter." I'm not sure if Tim had any idea who I was, but he was eager to say hello.

One of the security guards came over to me and said, "Preacher wants to see you after the meeting."

I walked up to Tim and shook his hand like I was greeting an old friend.

"How ya doing, brotha?" I asked Tim.

"I'm fine. Let me tell you what that guy was going to do."

I interrupted the pastor and said, "I know, I heard."

"That was the second time he tried to kill me," Tim said.

"And if I'm ever sitting in the congregation, my brotha, he ain't getting past the first row ever again."

Suddenly, the pastor jumped up from his chair and started pacing, rubbing his hands on his head and firing questions at me, one after another.

"What do you do for a living? What do you know about the Lord?"

And then, he stopped cold in his tracks.

"Oh no," he said.

I knew what was coming next. God was talking to the preacher. I'd know that look anywhere, because it's the look someone gets when he hears the voice of the Almighty.

"Something big is going to happen with you. You've got to remember to put every bit of your faith, every ounce of it, your reserve faith, your mother's faith, in God's hands. He will see you through. You're going to be one of the biggest in the world, friend, but you've got to trust in God."

Whoa. "Where do you want your offering?" was all I could think of saying. When an average Joe tells you something like that, you might believe him. But when a preacher says it, you can bet he's telling you the truth.

Two weeks later, *MidWeek*, a Hawaiian weekly newspaper, ran an article with a photo of me on the front cover. We found out about the story on a Sunday afternoon, three full days before the first copy was expected off the press. Anxious to see the piece, Beth and I decided to bounty hunt down a copy before it hit the newsstand on Wednesday. We went to the warehouse where they distributed the paper. Luckily, we caught the foreman just as he was lifting the last load onto a pallet. He recognized us right away.

"Hey, you're the guy on the cover this week!"

"Yeah, that's me. I was wondering if you could find your way to letting us take a look at an advance copy?"

The guy invited us in to see for ourselves. We stood inside this massive warehouse staring at thousands of copies with me on the cover. I looked at Beth and said, "That's a good preacher!"

The next time I spoke to Tim, I told him the story about the paper. He shook his head and said, "No, I don't think that was the big thing God was talking about, Duane." I had no way of knowing it at the time, but he was right.

It wasn't until I was standing in a jail cell in Mexico that I fully understood what Tim Storey told me about faith and placing my trust in God. The district attorney came into the cell to tell the boys and me that the judge was trying to decide between the deprivation of liberty charge and kidnapping. I walked to the corner of my cell and wept. That's when it occurred to me that Tim had warned me that I'd be in a situation that would take all of the faith I had. *This must be what he was talking about*, I thought.

Earlier that week, before the arrest, the boys and I had visited a place in Mexico where the sea turtles carry in their gullet one grain of sand from where they were born. They swim for years and then come back to the exact spot to lay their eggs. Scientists have theorized that it's that one grain of sand that brings them home. The Bible says if you have faith even the size of a mustard seed, you can move mountains. I fell to my knees and prayed. For the next ten minutes, I prayed like Billy Graham. Shortly after that, we got word the Mexican authorities were going to release us. That's when I knew Tim Storey would be my preacher forever.

Whenever an extreme emergency hits, I reach out to Tim for advice and counseling. I know for sure that what God gives him about me is real, and I need to listen to what he has to say. No big decision is made in my life without first consulting my preacher.

When the "N" word debacle broke, I am proud to say Tim firmly stood by me. I told him I was planning to appear with Sean Hannity and Larry King to talk about what had happened. Unsure of what I planned to say, I asked Tim for his opinion of what message he thought I should convey during those interviews.

Tim began speaking like he was reading from the Bible. "I sayeth unto thee, open thy mouth and I shall fill it."

I spent the next couple of days thinking about that advice, hoping and praying that the Lord knew what He wanted me to say on television, because I didn't have a clue!

After talking to Tim, I wanted to reach out to my old cellmate from Huntsville, Whitaker. I tried to reach him all day but couldn't track him down. So I did the next best thing and called his momma.

"Those sons of bitches," she said. "Don't they know you can use that word?"

I explained how I tried to tell everyone the same thing, but then she got quiet and said something so insightful. "Well, Dog. You're out there in television land now, honey." She wanted to support me as if I was her own son, but she knew I had messed up.

"I'm very sorry, Momma Whitaker." That's all I could say before I began to cry so hard that no more words came out of my mouth. I was so ashamed. Calling Momma Whitaker was worse than facing my own mother, because I knew deep down that I'd hurt her with my words.

Now seemed like as good a time as any to reach out and reconnect with Tony Robbins. I had spent years training with him, and I also sometimes spoke at his seminars. He has been one of the truly great teachers of my life. Since both our schedules had become so busy, Tony and I had lost contact over the past few years, though we try to touch base from time to time just to check in and see how the other is doing. Tony has got a lot of kudos coming to him because he helped change my entire way of thinking after I was released from prison.

I first met Tony in 1985 through my friend Keith Paul, an FBI special agent I befriended in Denver several years earlier. I liked Keith from the day we met. Despite his youthful appearance, Keith had a daunting presence. But I was never intimidated by him. We spoke the same language and we both liked to get things done.

One night, after a bust, we went to the White Spot diner, as we often did, to recap the evening's events. Keith began telling me about a guy who'd come to the Academy to train all the agents in his office. He said this guy was just like me, except he used bigger words. Keith was insistent I meet him. "His name is Tony Robbins," he gushed.

I had heard of Tony because of my exposure to motivational speakers while selling Kirby vacuums. I knew that guys like Tony changed people's lives, but I had no idea how meaningful his lessons and insights would become in my own.

A few weeks later I received a call from Tony. I was stunned to hear his deep and very recognizable voice on the phone. He called to ask me if I'd be interested in coming to one of his upcoming seminars in Texas as a guest speaker.

Texas? Did he say Texas? The day I walked out of Huntsville, I swore I'd never step foot in Texas ever again.

"No way, buddy." That was my firm and definitive answer.

Tony isn't the type of guy who takes "no" sitting down. He's a smooth cat, and before I even knew what had happened, I was on my way to the Lone Star State.

At first, I was worried that it might be some type of setup, that someone had made a horrible mistake by paroling me early. I thought the Department of Corrections had tricked me into coming back to Texas under the auspices of speaking for Tony Robbins. All they had to do was get me over the state line, where I figured they'd be waiting to take me back to prison.

But a few hours after landing in Austin, I found myself on stage speaking to a thousand strangers. I loved every second of it. I was so pumped up from the adrenaline, I felt like I was back in the ring boxing, like when I was in the Disciples. I've always loved the sound of a cheering crowd, especially when they're rooting for me. I walked down the long aisle, giving high fives and shaking hands with everyone within reach. I felt like a rock star and couldn't get enough of the adulation.

When I had first arrived at the venue, I spotted Tony off in a corner, in the front row just left of the stage. He was enormous in stature and presence. He towered over me like a giant. When we shook hands, his devoured mine. He is an engaging, warm, and powerful guy in every way. He stepped on stage and introduced me.

"This is Dog Chapman. His story is one of the greatest examples I have ever heard of a criminal gone wrong. Please put your hands together and give Dog a great big welcome!" Tony said as I walked onto the stage to speak to the crowd.

I never forgot those words because it was the first time someone identified me as "a criminal gone wrong." He later explained that I was the antithesis of what most criminals become after serving hard time. I chose to lead by example, by making something of myself. I found my strengths and created a life that took my inner criminal out of the equation, while still choosing to use all of my knowledge and understanding to aid me in my pursuit of justice and upholding the law. If I'd been a criminal gone right, I'd still be on the other side of the law.

That explanation is classic Tony Robbins thinking. He has a way of helping people see things differently. Thankfully and gratefully, Tony and I shared an instant bond that day. Our interaction on stage was compelling and garnered a standing ovation at the end. I had tears of joy being on that stage next to Tony. From that day on, I was filled with the great hope and inspiration that I had the power to help change people's lives.

I totally believe that it should be mandatory for anyone coming out of the prison system to hook up with Tony Robbins. It ought to be a parole requirement because recidivism for parolees ranges from 50 to 60 percent. Most inmates coming out of the joint have spent their time getting hit with clubs and being mentally browbeaten, while living in a cage they're let in and out of under someone else's watchful eye. Then, one day, that same officer comes up to you, opens the door, and says, "Forget about all the crap you just lived through, learned, and suffered. Now, go out there and make something of your life." Someone like Tony Robbins has the skill set, knowledge, and experience to help these guys and girls not only get on but stay on the right track. Had it not been for my newfound friendship and association with Tony, I'm not sure if I would have made it.

From the day we first met, Tony became one of my most trusted mentors. I began speaking at his seminars on a pretty regular basis. I loved the experience for many reasons. Mostly to hear two little words: "thank you." I was a bad guy for many years and never heard those words from anyone. I had listened to Tony talk at numerous seminars over the years about the struggles of life, something I often heard my mom talk about too. I spent years with Tony being both speaker and student. He taught me how to navigate any situation and emerge with the result I was seeking. He taught me how to talk to people in a way that makes them feel like they're the only person in the room. He showed me how to be a good listener, a skill that helped me get whatever I wanted from people without making them feel used or unimportant. He helped me realize and accept that I am the only person who can change my circumstances. Whenever I found myself blaming others for something, I thought back to the choices I had made that led me there, which always made me realize that the problem I faced was one of my own making. Tony showed me how to take responsibility for those decisions, accept them, and move on. And above all, Tony Robbins taught me the importance of living a life of dignity, truth, honesty, clarity, and purpose. His influence has been tremendous. I am forever grateful for all the wisdom he added to my life.

As we spent more time together, our families began to bond too. His stepson, Josh, used to come spend a couple of weeks every summer with my family in Denver. Josh became another sibling to Duane Lee and Leland, and my boys tortured him like the kid brother he had become. They'd spray shaving cream on him late at night after he fell asleep or place a little doll under his arm and take a picture. They teased each other all the time, but it was all in good adolescent fun.

Josh's background was the complete opposite of my boys'. He grew up in the lap of luxury, surrounded by mansions, maids, and fancy cars. Our home was rather modest, with lots of rules. We also required all of our kids to do their chores. When Josh first came to stay with us he had no idea he'd have responsibilities to attend to, but he didn't seem to mind pitching in.

Josh would believe any story you'd tell him, so I'd make up these incredible tales about flying and other stuff, fairy tales. He soaked in every word like I was preaching the gospel. There were lots of nights when the boys and I would camp out in the backyard. Sometimes we'd pitch a tent, while other times we'd hang out in an old trailer I got from one of my fugitives. What was considered normal for us was definitely "roughing it" for Josh. It didn't take long for him to adapt to his new surroundings though. In fact, I think he began to like how different our lifestyle was from his.

As a boy, Josh spent endless days and nights traveling with Tony and his mom. He was constantly on the move. And while I suppose he had opportunities to see places most kids his age can only read about, I got the distinct sense that he liked being stationary when he stayed with us.

He spent a lot of his time working in our office answering phones and filling out bond applications. Josh quickly became completely obsessed with going on an actual bounty hunt with me. He was fascinated by the adventure of tracking down a fugitive. To be honest, what thirteen-year-old boy wouldn't love the chance to capture a bad guy and play cops and robbers for real?

In order to be on my team, Josh was going to have to learn the basics of the trade. I explained that hunting a fugitive was no different from anything else in life you really want. When a woman hunts for the perfect wedding dress, she knows exactly what she's looking for. She knows what it looks like, where it is made, what style flatters her, and how it will ultimately come together when she walks down the aisle. I told Josh it's exactly the same when you track down a human being. You have to know their weaknesses, who made them the way they are, who they love, who their enemies are, and where they hang out. You want to become their friend as naturally as possible. But you can't get too close to the fire. That's why I have no friends who are or were ever fugitives. Convicts? For sure. Fugitives, never.

The big day finally came. When I told Josh he'd be riding with me, he nearly jumped out of his skin with excitement. He was with me every step of the way while we chased a fugitive named Merrill. When I finally captured the guy, I cuffed him and put him in the backseat of my car.

"Slide in next to him, Josh," I said. I could see he was a little confused about the direction I was giving him. That's when I turned to Merrill and said, "I know you can see this kid sitting next to you. Don't be fooled by his appearance. He ain't no baby. He's got a first-degree black belt in karate and he's studying the ancient martial art of Dim Mak, also known as the touch of death. Make one suspicious move and I'm going to have my partner here take you out once and for all, got it?"

Josh was shaking in his shoes. He didn't know karate or any other kung fu stuff and he definitely didn't know how to put a death touch on someone. Even so, I looked back at Josh in my rearview mirror so he would catch a glimpse of my eyes. He knew I wanted him to get it together and not make a liar out of me, so he did the only thing he could do; he sat straight up in his seat, leaned forward, turned toward the fugitive, and let out a little growl. At that move, Merrill was more scared than Josh. I looked back in the mirror one last time before we got to the county jail. I gave Josh a wink to let him know I was proud of him, real proud.

CHAPTER 8

My life has been filled with trying moments when my faith has been tested over and over again. Tony Robbins used to say that there was great power in positive thinking and positive confession. The words you speak are crucial to how you live. Your mind believes whatever you tell it. If you constantly tell yourself, "I'm so fat," or "I'm lazy," eventually that is how everyone will see you because that's how you'll act. If I move through the world like a leader, people will see me as one.

All those years studying with Tony Robbins helped me realize that every challenge is an opportunity to strengthen my faith, to make it stronger and to use that situation to learn and grow. Even knowing this, calling Tony after the *National Enquirer* broke the story was a lot harder than I'd expected it to be. I was certain he'd heard the news by the time I phoned. What I wasn't sure of was how he would react. Back in the days when I first started working with Tony, his wife Becky used to tell me that I needed to improve the language I used. She said I didn't speak with enough sophistication. She even gave me a dictionary to study so I could find ways of saying things that weren't so blunt or abrupt. I thought about that as I listened to the phone ring, waiting for Tony to answer on the other end. If I had taken Becky's advice back then, perhaps I wouldn't have found myself in the jam I was in. I guess it didn't matter much now.

"I don't know the answer, Duane, but you do." Those were the words Tony spoke when I asked him what he thought I should do. He said I could come to his home in Fiji and hide out for a while if I thought that was the best solution. He told me and Beth to fly on down for a couple of weeks. He was there doing a seminar, but he'd be able to spend some time talking it through if we wanted to. I gave his generous offer a lot of consideration. Two weeks halfway around the world on a private island sounded pretty appealing. I could hide from the world if I wanted to. But in the end, after a lot of deliberation, the answer was still no.

For the same reasons I didn't choose to go the "rehab" route, I didn't want anyone to judge me for seeking the advice of a guy so many view as a "guru" rather than as the good friend Tony Robbins has been to me. The more I thought about how Tony had answered, the more I realized that, once again, he was absolutely right. I didn't need two weeks in isolation to find out that the correct choices lived inside me. All I had to do was find the right words, let them flow from within, and hope I wouldn't make things worse.

It wasn't until I reached my fifties that I realized education wins out over stupidity every time. For years my manager warned me that educated men don't use the "N" word. Alan accompanied me to a speaking engagement in Canada a few months prior to the *Enquirer* story. We were driving to the event when I referred to a white girl as a "n***er."

Confused, Alan asked, "Why did you use that term on a white girl?"

"I've never used that word to describe the color of someone's skin. It's about who they are, how they operate.

It doesn't matter if she's white, red, yellow, or black. It's about who she is on the inside."

Although he understood what I was trying to say, he continued to strongly discourage me from using that word at all. I often tried to defend myself to Alan by rattling off a dozen names of educated Hollywood types who in fact use the word all the time—black and white men alike. Even so, Alan never bought into my rationalizations.

Growing frustrated and worried that my ignorance had now bit me in the butt, Alan said, "Please don't get mad at me for being the messenger, Duane, but this ridiculous, ignorant, stupid hillbilly dumb-ass act is going to be the end of your career. People will never understand you're not being prejudiced when you use words like that. You can't plead innocence and expect the educated person to believe you." Alan's words closely echoed the advice I'd heard from Becky, Tony's wife, years before that had so clearly fallen on deaf ears when she tried to impart her wisdom to me.

Alan Nevins is an elegant man who hangs around sophisticated people a lot more than I do. A guy like that always bets on the winning horse. He never takes a chance on the long shot. Alan was hired on the same day the federal marshals kicked in my door and arrested me for the Luster case. He had his work cut out for him from the very start. When we first met, Alan saw something inside me that made me a winner and someone he wanted to represent. Even with his undying support, I was beginning to wonder if I was too much of a loser to know when I had won. Was I really a dumb convict who just got lucky? Or was I like a moldable piece of clay that could be taught?

When I asked Alan what he thought I should say to Sean Hannity and Larry King, he deadpanned, "Anything but n***er." We both laughed for a moment and then Alan got serious. He told me that there wasn't much I could say that would make things worse than they already were, so I should just speak from my heart. He went on to explain that anyone who had met me and knew me already knew what was in my heart, and now the time had come to let the public see my true self and not hear only empty words when I spoke. Only then would they understand that I didn't say anything out of hatred for black people—it was just my naïveté. He gave me three or four pointers, reminded me that I am the Dog and that, for many people, that stood for something good. Other than those pearls of wisdom, though, for the most part, he left it to my own volition.

Within days after the incident, e-mails and letters of support began pouring in from fans. The officer who had encountered Monique and Tucker outside Lulu's earlier in the summer even publicly came out to share his experience with them that night to try and shed some light on what type of person Monique was. All of the support I received meant the world to me, but there was one letter in particular I received via e-mail that deeply touched my heart, so much so that I will never forget it. The e-mail was titled, "My Grandmother Is Crying. . . ."

It was written by a woman whose eighty-six-year-old grandmother religiously watched the show despite the fact that she didn't watch a lot of television. She said her grandmother disliked motorcycles, tattoos, long hair on men, bleach blondes, high heels, shorts, and overbearing men, but loved the Dog and never missed an episode of *Dog the Bounty Hunter.* Her grandmother said she admired me because I was not afraid to show the world I was human, believed in love and forgiveness, and would cry when my heart hurt. I had to stop reading the letter when I saw those words because I was overcome with emotion from the woman's kind words.

When her granddaughter told her about my show being pulled from A&E because of my remarks, she wouldn't stop crying because the one thing she looked forward to every week more than tending to her garden and cooking for her family was watching my show, and now it had been taken away from her. When the granddaughter discussed my situation with her, her grandmother imparted the following wisdom: "Christians come in all sizes, shapes, and from every walk of life. We don't all have to fit into one mold." She asked her granddaughter to write the letter to Beth and me to let us know she supported us no matter the outcome and to let A&E know she won't be watching their network again until they put me back on the air. She encouraged the network to give our advertisers the thousands of letters they had received like hers so they would be seen as heroes to stand by me instead of abandoning me.

What Tucker had done was tragic. He didn't understand that the hopes and dreams of so many, from little children to grandmothers, all over the country had been shattered. He had taken Dog off the air. But I was the one who had uttered the very words that brought me down. No one held a gun to my head. I said what I said without any thought it would hurt so many people.

I've read that e-mail several times since receiving it that day. I was hopeful the woman's words and sentiment would be representative of how most people felt, but I didn't count on it. Her understanding of my situation reminded me that there are lots of people in the world who get the meaning of compassion. Although I never met this woman or her grandmother, I feel like I will always be connected to them in spirit for the strength, kindness, and mercy they showed me in one of my darkest moments.

One of the most meaningful letters I received during this time came from my son Wesley, whom I hadn't spoken to in some time. I'd tried to reconnect with him over the years, but he always kept me at arm's length. I was surprised when Beth told me about the e-mail that came in shortly after the news of the "N" word incident. After years of limited correspondence, Wesley wrote to say he thought I could use a friend at my lowest moment. And boy, was he right. When I later asked why he chose to reach out to me at that time, he said, "So you could be absolutely certain I don't want anything from you." I was deeply moved by his love and support. His fortuitous e-mail opened the lines of communication between us in a way they had never been before. I would never have guessed it would take something like my public lambasting to bring my son back to me. I suppose the sad irony is I temporarily lost one son but permanently gained another from that experience.

For the most part, the letters I received were very kind. They assured me that I hadn't lost my fans so much as I had disappointed them. There was lots of love and support in the countless pages I read those first few days. Their kindness overwhelmed me, especially in the midst of the unbelievably untrue things that were being said about me by people who clearly didn't know me. However, I also received many letters that were angry that I was capable of saying something so cruel. Judgment calls were being made based on assumptions in the press and short clips from a twenty-five-minute conversation that were being used out of context. That was a tough pill to swallow, but I managed to let it go until my upcoming interviews with Sean and Larry, where I planned to explain everything the best I could.

The day before my scheduled appearance on *Hannity and Colmes*, I was finally given the good news that I no longer faced extradition to Mexico. Judge Barry Kurren had finally dismissed the extradition complaints and canceled the arrest warrants against Leland, Tim, and me, essentially making us free men. While the news was gratifying, I was very much focused on the events of the past week and my upcoming interviews. My troubles with Mexico seemed distant compared to the difficult and daunting task that was ahead of me.

Beth and I flew to Los Angeles to do the scheduled interviews with Sean and Larry. We had no idea what awaited us as we touched down on the mainland. I had been secluded and protected in my island sanctuary, so I wasn't sure what to expect. Our anxiety grew as we crossed the Pacific. We knew the press would be there, but we had no idea how many or how bad it would be. When we deplaned, Beth and I made the long walk down the corridor through the terminal at LAX. When we emerged from the long escalator leading down to baggage claim, I was relieved to see William, my longtime driver and friend, waiting for us. I was worried I had hurt William with my careless words, because he was a proud black man. I also knew he and I had a long history together and I considered him my brother in every way. We used to call each other the "N" word all the time. I can only recall one occasion where he whispered that word into my ear instead of saying it aloud. When I asked him why he'd whispered it that particular day, he said it was because he was worried there were a couple of people around us who would be offended by our banter. We looked at each other, with a knowing glance that he was probably right. Even so, it never stopped us from affectionately using that word—that is until that day he met me at the airport in Los Angeles.

William showed up with three of his coworkers, all black men, to protect us from the throngs of paparazzi that were there to greet us as well. William, Les, Isaiah, and

Ronnie looked like the front line of the Denver Broncos waiting to block anyone from our path. I was instantly relieved because I knew William's love for me transcended the story of what had happened. The guys quickly ushered us to a waiting bus while sending the paparazzi after two decoy SUVs they had brought to throw them off. We were so touched by their caring and warm welcome. It was ironic that the very people the media had said I despised and hated were the guys who met me, comforted me, and kept me safe throughout my time in Los Angeles. These guys had worked for me for years. They knew who I was inside my heart. They never once felt betrayed or dishonored by my use of the "N" word.

Not long after my appearances in Los Angeles, I was devastated by the news that William had been diagnosed with stage four cancer. He began chemotherapy treatments, but couldn't take what it was doing to his body. He called me from time to time to let me know how he was doing. I pleaded with William to continue with his treatments, but he couldn't do it. Every time we came to town, William did his best to see us until he got too sick and was no longer able to. I was so grateful for his friendship and loyalty over the years, I wanted to do whatever I could to make sure his last days on this earth were as comfortable as possible. I sent money to make sure he had groceries, could pay his rent, and was able to get whatever prescriptions he needed until he passed away. My friendship with William was as significant as my relationship with my old cellmate Whitaker. And, in a way, more so because he understood the ups and downs of living a fast-paced Hollywood life. He never gave up on me, nor I on him.

The interview with Sean Hannity was hard for two reasons. First, although I went in with a good idea of what he would be asking me about, I still didn't know what I planned to say. Second, I was incredibly emotional. I cry at the drop of a hat, and I knew this interview would rattle my cage a bit. Thankfully, whenever I broke down or started to sway into a bad place, Sean would stop me, rephrase the question, and essentially let me start over.

When I tried to tell Sean about my experience at Mount Vernon, it came out all wrong. Beth was off camera practically stomping her feet, begging me to just stop talking. I was so emotionally upset that I messed it up badly. Beth and Alan were in the back watching, and at the break they came rushing onto the stage. I thought they both were going to kill me. "You just told America you were going to be buried at Mount Vernon," Beth said.

"No, I didn't."

They both yelled at me, "Yes, you did!"

In my emotional state, I had told the world I had started the process to allow me to be buried with the slaves. What I'd meant to say was that I had contacted the foundation at Mount Vernon and hopefully started the process of buying them a marker for the slaves if they wanted to use such a marker. I also had wanted to tell Sean Hannity that I was so proud of my black brothers and sisters that I would be honored to be buried with slaves with no headstone. But, of course, what was in my mind and what came out of my mouth were not the same thing, causing a mini-scandal to erupt because I said I wanted to be buried at Mount Vernon. When we later called the foundation to offer money for a marker, they had been so bombarded with phone calls about what I said that they didn't even want to talk to us. I apologized to them for the misunderstanding. I felt so bad as they have preserved Washington's home with such impeccable detail so that we can learn and understand about the history of our country, slavery, and the man who gave so much for us. Even so, they still refuse to have anything to do with me—for now.

Unbeknownst to me, while Beth was freaking out, two African-American men approached her backstage. She didn't know who they were. For a moment she actually believed Sean Hannity had double-crossed us by bringing two black guests on to comment after my interview. That's when someone told Beth the man who was merely saying hello to her was the Reverend Jesse Peterson, who was there with his group BOND, which stands for Brotherhood Organization of a New Destiny. Beth was relieved when she met him, realizing he and his coworker were there to support me and not destroy me.

Reverend Peterson approached us after the taping was done. He looked a little like a gangster to me at first. I thought, *Here we go. My first public fight.* I couldn't have been more wrong about the guy. We began talking and sharing our thoughts on racism in America.

"There's no 'white bands, white TV networks.'" He was telling me that because of these types of stereotypes, he believes the black man is just as prejudiced as the white man. "I grew up on a plantation in the South. I've heard the 'N' word more times than you've taken a breath."

"Jesus, man. Shut up! I don't want to hear you talking like this!" I was stunned by his straight-to-the-heart style and manner, and nervous to be a part of any racially fired-up conversation. Peterson told me he knew a racist when he met one and he didn't believe that I was a racist. From that day on, he and I forged a friendship that began with what I thought was going to be a very sticky situation. Peterson and I don't necessarily see eye to eye when it comes to politics. In fact, I've never disagreed with a man more in my life than I do with Reverend Peterson, but I respect him and all he stands for. He's a radical nut and just the type of man I needed in my corner to help guide and counsel me through these times. We agreed to talk again over the next few weeks to see how we could work together.

I appeared on *Larry King Live* the next night. The interview was equally emotional. Tim Storey appeared with me for a segment, as did my oldest son, Christopher. Tim caught a lot of grief from other preachers in the community for standing by my side, but that didn't deter him from referring to me as his brother and supporting me through this situation. Even when others insisted I was a racist, Tim Storey refused to let them have their way, going so far as to make it evidently clear that he did not believe that to be true.

During the interview, my son Christopher told Larry King how the *National Enquirer* had approached him to talk about his dad, offering him quick cash for his story. They asked him a series of questions, which Christopher lied about in his answers so he could get the money. The *Enquirer* asked him questions about my alleged drug use over the years and about me being a racist. They encouraged him to say whatever he wanted by telling him "the more dirt, the better." When the paper gave Christopher a lie detector test, which they sometimes do as a precaution, the results were inconclusive. Even so, they went ahead and printed the story.

Since that incident, it appeared the *National Enquirer* had had an ongoing interest in stories about me. Christopher's interview was done months before Tucker sold the tapes. Christopher drove himself into the ground with guilt for what he had done. He went out of his way to reach me after the story broke, to apologize. He said he was after some fast money, which the paper made easily available for a few hours of the boy's time. Christopher, like Tucker, was vulnerable to their offer without realizing the consequences of his actions. I am a man who stands for second chances, and I was willing to forgive Christopher for his lack of judgment. Having a relationship with my son was more important to me than holding a grudge. That is why I asked him to be on the show with me that night.

After the Larry King interview, a poll revealed that 82 percent of Larry King's viewers said they didn't think my show should be taken off the air. That was a pretty big number of supporters, and it should have made me feel better about things, but it didn't. Even though it was a tremendous display of mercy, there were still 18 percent of his viewers who thought what I did made me a racist and I deserved to pay for it. I figured there was a small percentage of those people who had hated me to begin with. Yet for the 1, 2, or 3 percent of people who thought what I did was reprehensible, but whose minds I could still change, I needed to find a way to spread the word that Dog is a good man, a righteous man of principle, and someone who chooses to lead his life by example and not just words.

At the end of the interview, a young woman appeared via video clip urging me to never give up. She said, "Sometimes heroes make mistakes." And she was right. We are all just human beings who will, from time to time, stumble along the path of life. It is up to the hero that lives inside each and every one of us to turn our tests into testimony and our mess into messages. The message I was receiving was loud and clear: Don't give up.

After I taped *Larry King*, I bumped into Patti LaBelle in the lobby of the Four Seasons Hotel. We said hello and talked for a few minutes. She wrapped her arm around my elbow and said, "Let's walk into the bar together, Dog! I'd be proud to have people see you on my arm." Beth and I also ran into LL Cool J a couple of nights later and he was equally kind.

I've always been a controversial figure. The things that would destroy a weaker man make me stronger. Through years of challenges, I've learned to successfully turn my adversity into opportunity.

My barber's husband gave me some memorable advice a day or two after the story broke. He said, "Duane, the higher you go up the ladder in life, the more of your ass that shows. One mistake can ruin a thousand attaboys." This guy is a retired military man and married to a beautiful black woman. Throughout his military career, he was beaten down a thousand times only to be built back up stronger, smarter, and better than he was before. His brain was trained to get out there and throw his best at whatever life brought his way. I asked him for his advice on how to make things right. His answer was simple yet powerful.

"Get out there and get me another thousand attaboys." So far I'm at 398, but counting every single day.

When I was a young boy, I heard a quote by Jack Dempsey that I never forgot. I've since put my own twist on it and turned it into one of my new favorite Dogisms:

"Champions get knocked down, but they always get back up!"

Whenever I've asked God why something is happening in my life, His answer has always been the same: "I know you can do this, Dog." It is with that knowledge that I am able to take an absolute leap of faith, even if I don't know what lies ahead for me. I have the strength to move ahead and the belief that I can conquer anything, and that I always land on my feet.

So much of my training with Tony Robbins focused on how the mind perceives things. We only know life's ups and downs by how we represent them to ourselves. If we have a negative image of something, it can become larger than life and seem impossible to overcome. That negative thought can virtually paralyze us from moving past it.

On the other hand, if we take that same negative image and minimize it, then we are able to put everything in perspective as what it is and reveal what it is not. Doing this takes away its power and returns that power to you. Diminishing the impact of a setback, asking myself what the worst-case scenario is, and then realizing I can not only live through, but thrive from, those possibilities is my secret for turning adversity into opportunity.

Calvin Coolidge once said, "The slogan 'press on' has solved and always will solve the problems of the human race." When I'm on a bounty hunt, giving up and throwing in the towel are never options for me. My livelihood depends on a successful outcome. I took whatever fallout came my way when the "N" word story came out, because I realized that the Lord had a larger plan for me. He knew I could weather the storm, which in turn gave me the faith to endure through the months I spent making amends.

Instead of dwelling on my fears of losing everything, I chose to focus on moving forward. Tony Robbins taught me that wherever you place your focus becomes your reality. I was determined to place my focus on seeing the good that could come from this experience. I put myself in a positive state of mind and began acting on every opportunity that came my way to give back, until I no longer felt it was an obligation but rather a privilege.

We've all made mistakes and I owned up to mine like a man. I wish this event had never happened, but it did. I thought I had quit making bad mistakes, but I suppose as long as you're alive, blunders will happen. The only thing I could do from this point on was to forgive myself so others would do the same. To do that, I needed to make some very big changes in my life. I wasn't going to hide away or wish for some type of time machine to turn back the clock. I had to saddle up and ride the horse like I always did and face whatever lay ahead. I spent the next ten days or so reminding myself that I was an all-around good guy and a slayer of dragons. It was time to get out there and make that happen.

After taping the interviews with Sean Hannity and Larry King, Beth and I stayed in Los Angeles for a few days of rest and relaxation. We did a little shopping and then headed to Las Vegas to meet some friends for dinner. I was really looking forward to a fun night out. I handed my credit card to our server to pay for the bill. She came back to the table and politely asked if I had another form of payment since the card I gave her was coming up with a negative response.

I wanted to die on the spot from embarrassment. My card was declined . . . in front of several celebrity friends. I handed over another card, hoping that one would be approved. Thank God, it was.

When I left the restaurant, I called the bank that had issued the declined card to see what was wrong. It was our local bank in Hawaii, which we had done a lot of business with over the years. We had at least *thirteen* separate accounts with this bank, including our business, personal, and merchant accounts, which meant we put all of our eggs in that one financial basket.

There was a lot of street noise as I stood outside the restaurant making my call. The bank manager was having a hard time hearing me. On my third attempt to ask him what the problem was, I had to raise my voice so he could hear me.

"I've got a lot of money in your bank and I will take my

business elsewhere if you don't fix this problem right now!"

"Mr. Chapman," he said. "Please quit yelling at me." I wasn't yelling out of anger so much as pure frustration.

Unbeknownst to me, days before the "N" word story hit, the same bank had given Tucker a loan to buy a brand-new truck. At the time, he had no credit and no job. Tucker used my name, relationship, and the few thousand dollars he'd been paid for selling the tape to finagle the loan. Unaware of the storm that was brewing, Tucker talked them into extending him the credit he needed to buy his truck because we had such a strong and long-term financial relationship with the bank. When Beth and I got wind of this shortly after the story broke, we called the bank to let them know we weren't going to take any responsibility for the loan. Our relationship with the bank became strained after that conversation because they had been put in a bad situation by approving Tucker's loan. Apparently, after the credit manager saw the news story about the "N" word, the bank cut off all of our credit. I was confused by their decision because I'd never had any problems with them in the past. I didn't bounce checks, I was never overdrawn, I made all of my payments on time, and I kept a significant amount of money on deposit. When I asked why they cut my credit, their response was that since my show had been "canceled," I was obviously no longer employed and therefore I had become a bad credit risk. "Sorry." That's all they could say.

Beth wasn't about to take their decision sitting down. Our show hadn't been canceled. She wanted to make sure the bank understood what was really going on. She called the branch manager and said, "People lose their jobs every day, but we're still employed. Just because our show has been taken off the schedule, it doesn't mean we've been fired."

And, you know what? They reactivated the accounts. But a few days later they called and asked if we would kindly close out our accounts anyway. Instead of fighting over their decision, I kept my response simple and to the point.

"Sure. I'll change banks. No problem."

INTERMISSION ONE

PEOPLE OFTEN ASK ME ABOUT SOME OF MY
MOST EXCITING BOUNTY HUNTING STORIES,
ESPECIALLY ONES FROM MY EARLY DAYS.
I COULD FILL SEVERAL VOLUMES OF BOOKS
SHARING THEM ALL WITH YOU, AND MAYBE
I'LL DO THAT SOMEDAY. IN THE MEANTIME,
I'VE CHOSEN A COUPLE OF MY FAVORITES
THAT I THINK YOU'LL REALLY ENJOY. SO,
SIT BACK, BUCKLE UP, AND COME ALONG ON
THE HUNT!

When I started out as a bounty hunter in Denver I worked with every bondsman in the city. One day on my way back from court, I stopped into a bail office that had just been taken over by a new bondsman in town. I was taken by surprise when I met the new owner, a woman named Mary Ellen. I had never worked with a female bondsman, but I sure knew what the tattooed cross on the top of her hand meant.

"You used to be a black widow, huh?"

She never confirmed or denied that she was in the girl gang, so I automatically assumed she was once a member. I used to date a few girls from that gang, so I knew the symbol. I also knew these girls were tough. They're not the type of women you want to double cross. Later, she would confess she was never in the gang but she wanted me to think she was one tough cookie. She never let on to the truth when we first met.

"Are you Mexican?" I asked.

"Born and bred and proud of it," she said.

Mary Ellen was the only Mexican working bail in Denver, which made her a double minority—a Mexican woman in a white man's world. I knew right away she had the grit and moxie to make it big in the business. I was certain I'd be proud to work with her.

I was never averse to drumming up new business, and by the time I met Mary Ellen, I had already established a name for myself as the best bounty hunter in Denver. Even though I was usually busy, I was always happy for new leads.

"If you ever have a client who runs, let me know," I told her. There was something special about Mary Ellen. I liked her from the start. I walked her out to her car the day we met and noticed the rim around her back license plate that read, "We'll put your feet on the street." I thought that was a great slogan for a bondsman.

I began to spend lots of time with Mary Ellen and her husband, Fred. Whenever we walked into a bar or diner, everyone seemed to know her. The attention she got intrigued me. There was something else that made me stand up and take notice of Mary Ellen too: her kindness and compassion toward her clients combined with her wicked determination to make sure she didn't get ripped off.

Mary Ellen wasn't the type of woman who would just hand me her jumps. If I wanted her bounties, I had to be in her office first thing every morning to make sure I was there when the mail came. Mary Ellen never liked to open her mail. She'd tell the mailman to give it to me. He'd hand over all of her certified letters from the courts without ever looking up. I'd open each one and pull the coordinating file.

Mary Ellen had a work ethic that was the closest I've ever seen to my own. She is relentless, especially when her money is at risk. We could be out on a hunt all day, sometimes working until 11:30 P.M. If I told Mary Ellen I needed to call it a night because I had to get up and drive my kids to school the next morning, she'd say, "Well then, we've got seven more hours to find him, don't we! When we catch this SOB, we'll all go home together and happy. You'll be richer and I won't be out my money." Mary Ellen refused to quit until we got her man.

You have to have a mean streak to make it as a bail bondsman. We're not teaching Sunday school, we're dealing with criminals all day long. Mary Ellen's heart was bigger than mine, but it was also meaner. I'd often hear about people she wrote bonds for that didn't quite have all the money they needed to pay up front. She'd spot them the cash, but made it very, very clear she wasn't going to be so understanding if they ran. She wasn't going to let some thug lose his momma's house she'd used as collateral to save her son. As a precaution, she made sure her clients checked in with her on a weekly basis. If she didn't hear from them, there would be hell to pay.

Sometimes, when we brought a fugitive in to jail, I'd slip him a few bucks, only to have Mary Ellen yell at me for doing that.

"You didn't give that jerk any money, did you?" she'd ask, knowing full well I had.

"Of course not," I'd always say, only to find out the next day that she'd given him money too. Naturally, she usually denied it because she didn't want me to think she was soft, even though I already knew she had a gentle heart. She might have fooled most of the other bondsmen, but I could see the real Mary Ellen through that rough-and-tumble exterior.

Mary Ellen taught me to treat all of the jumps with respect. She reminded me over and over that they weren't running from us, they were running from the consequences of the decisions that got them to us in the first place. We had an obligation to the court to make sure they were brought to justice. We aren't the judge or jury. I have always respected that advice and have never forgotten those words.

I wanted to help Mary Ellen succeed, especially because so many of the Denver bondsmen were determined to watch her fail. Whenever I'd tell her I'd heard someone say it was only a matter of time before she was out of the business, Mary Ellen would respond with something like "Those sons of bitches are going to be waiting until hell freezes over before I give up!" I loved her determination, and I still admire it today.

It wasn't long before we began doing a lot of work together. Over the years she used me on hundreds of bail jumps and almost exclusively for her most dangerous criminals. She wrote every bond that rang in on the phone because she had me in her pocket. She'd write the bond and tell me, "This guy will jump so be ready to get him, Dog."

She warned her clients she'd send the Dog after them if they ran. "He'll beat you. You don't think he does whatever I say? You don't think Dog will kick your ass if I tell him to? If I send my Dog after you, he's going to rip your head off, I promise. I'm coming to your house and there won't be any white flag, pal, got it?" She loved using me as a threat so her clients wouldn't jump. I loved how cold-blooded Mary Ellen could be. Her cutthroat attitude helped build her business into one of the biggest and most profitable, eventually making her the Queen of Bail in Denver.

There aren't a lot of women who can push my Beth around and live to tell their tale. Mary Ellen once shoved Beth, and I thought Beth was going to kill her. Beth turned around to respond, but Mary Ellen was already in her face screaming, "You want a piece of me, little girl? Little bitch!" Beth backed down and did nothing. Oh, she and Mary Ellen still argue plenty, but there's a line that never gets crossed. There's a lot of love and respect between the two of them. In fact, a few years later, Beth worked with Mary Ellen, but that was after I'd left Denver for Hawaii. Good thing too, because I'm not sure I would have survived those two at each other's throats.

The more business we did together, the more money we made. I often teased Mary Ellen about her older model Toyota, until one day I told her it was time to get a new car. Bondsmen and bounty hunters drive their cars into the ground faster than most people because we put so many miles on the vehicle so quickly. I kept pushing Mary Ellen to come down to the dealership with me to check out a car, but she wasn't all that interested. About a week or two after I suggested she get a new car, she finally agreed to see what I was making all the fuss over. I had picked out a real beauty for her. It was a particularly slow day at her office, so we headed down to the dealership for a test drive. The manager and his salesman met us at the door.

"Hi," I said. "I'm Dog the Bounty Hunter. I'm the guy you saw in the newspaper last week." The owner recognized me right away. He rolled out the red carpet for us. He told Mary Ellen to figure out what she liked and he'd make it happen. Mary Ellen looked at every car in the showroom like she was inspecting racehorses before the Kentucky Derby. She kicked the tires, sat in the driver's seat, opened the trunk, and looked under the hood of every single car. She finally settled on the car I'd originally picked out for her, a maroon Coupe de Ville. She handed over cash for her down payment and drove off the lot in her brand-new car with a smile as big as the Colorado River across her face.

I called her the next day to see how she was enjoying her new ride. I was so excited for her, you would have thought I was the one with the new car.

"It's great! It's the nicest car I've ever owned. I got up and wrote six bonds this morning." I could tell she was ecstatic and that made me feel pretty good too. A couple of days later, Mary Ellen called to tell me the dealership was taking the car back, saying it had something to do with her financing. She told them to get screwed, pointing out she'd already signed the contract and the first payment had been paid. The financing was now their problem and not hers. I felt so bad thinking she was about to lose her car, I started giving her discounts on my fees so she would be able to make her car payments.

When I reminded her of this story recently, she burst out into uncontrollable laughter.

"Dog honey, that never happened. I was joking with you. For Christ's sake, what dealership would have let me keep the car if that were true? They call that grand theft auto, honey!" I had to laugh because I always thought that she'd held onto the car in spite of them wanting it back. Yes, Mary Ellen . . . you got me!

I was truly grateful for the work Mary Ellen threw my way. I paid her back by returning every single one of her fugitives. Well, almost.

Back in 1986, a guy named Michael Volosin and his wife got into an argument with their neighbor David Guenther on the doorstep of the Guenther home, about a party at Volosin's earlier that night that had gotten loud and out of control. The conversation escalated and began to get very heated. Guenther pulled out a gun and shot the Volosins, killing the wife with a bullet to the heart, wounding Michael in the thigh and wrist, and accidentally shooting a neighbor, who was injured from catching a round in the abdomen during the shooting.

Although Guenther claimed self-defense, saying he feared for his and his family's life, the cops arrested him. Mary Ellen posted the ten-thousand-dollar bond for Guenther. She had a bad feeling about him from the start, but she wrote the bond anyway.

Guenther's case was the first time the "Make My Day" defense would be tested. This was a landmark law in Colorado that protects people from any criminal charge or civil suit if they use force—including deadly force—against an invader of their home. The law is named for the famous line uttered by Clint Eastwood in the film *Sudden Impact*, "Go ahead, make my day." Guenther was acquitted on all charges stemming from that incident. Mary Ellen was just about to be released from the original bond when Guenther, who had a history of spousal abuse, shot his wife dead in front of their children. He fled the scene of that crime and was on the run. The district attorney called Mary Ellen to tell her Guenther was gone. Since she was still on the first bond, he was considered a fugitive. That's when Mary Ellen called me.

Now, most people know I don't carry a gun. First, I'm a convicted felon, so by law, I am not allowed to. Second, there are already too many unnecessary deaths from the use of firearms, especially by people who aren't trained to properly use their weapon. I am now and have always been adamantly against the bullet. However, several years ago I used to have a toy machine gun that was an exact replica of Bonnie and Clyde's Woody Woodpecker, a .45 Thompson fully automatic. No one knew it was a fake gun, because it was a perfect copy—not even Mary Ellen or Fred, who had both seen it numerous times. I used the gun on several bounties over the years in Denver, especially when I had to go into one of the city's rougher neighborhoods. I'd walk up and down the streets holding that gun up saying, "This ain't Avon calling!" I'd warn whoever I was chasing they'd better surrender or it would be rat-a-tat-tat time.

When Mary Ellen called about David Guenther, I told her and Fred it was time to bust out old Woody. I started developing leads on Guenther and was soon able to track him down to an old phone booth he'd used to make several calls. I took a black Magic Marker and left him a note right next to the coin slot that simply said, "David, this is Dog. I'm going to catch you."

People often ask me how I can tell when someone will respond to something like that. Here's how I know. Have you ever stood on line at a bank after coming right from the gym? You're wearing workout clothes, maybe a sweat-soaked shirt and a baseball hat, while everyone else in the bank is dressed up for the day. You feel grungy, but you stand there anyway so you can make your deposit or withdrawal.

Multiply that feeling times one hundred to walk into that same bank with a gun and say, "Everybody in this fricken place put your hands in the air!" That takes a lot of guts, bravado, stupidity, and a certain amount of smarts. Now, if someone moves to shoot, that's beyond guts. It's insane. That's the guy I look for when I'm out on a hunt. I ask myself, How far will this guy go?

I know the answer because I was once that guy, and still am that guy on the other side of the law. I know exactly how he thinks, and feels, and what his next move will be. He will go to the edge of death and I am willing to chase him to the gates of hell. When he has nothing to lose and I have everything to gain, the hunt is on. No one has ever outrun me and they never will. Sometimes I'll taunt those guys by saying, "You'll be famous if you can outrun me. You'll be the cat that got away from the Dog!" because I want him to run. If he does, I will catch him because he will, without a doubt, mess up.

Sure enough, when Guenther found the note, he called me.

"You're pretty good, bounty hunter."

"I'm the best."

"I'll kill myself before I let you get me, Dog. I'll drive my car off a cliff if I have to," Guenther said.

"I know you're somewhere between mile marker 144 and 148. There is a cliff at marker 146. Is that the one you're going to drive over?" I needed him to tell me exactly where he was so I could grab him before the cops did. At the same time, I needed Guenther to believe that I didn't care if he lived or died.

"Why do you need to know that?" Guenther asked.

"Because I get paid whether you're dead or alive. All I need is a print to prove you're the guy who ran on his bond. Hell, I want to be the first person to toe tag your body." I knew that would piss him off and I was right. He didn't like that answer one bit. If I rattled him enough, he'd make a move and most likely a costly mistake.

Tracking down leads for a case outside the Pagoda Hotel.

Briefing my crew before a hunt.

It can go easy or it can go hard . . . but either way, you are going.

This fugitive jumped out a third-story window to try to get away. She was later apprehended.

I try to give them something. In the backseat, it's just them, me, and God.

Kids always have the best information: Leland tracking a lead.

Back door guy and number one son, Duane Lee.

With Leland, Beth, Baby Lyssa, and Duane Lee in my office.

A stop on my first book tour in Atlanta, Georgia. Three thousand people showed up! I was grateful to have my fans come out and support me wherever I went.

An amazing portrait a fan made using the text from my first book, *You Can Run, But You Can't Hide.*

Beth and me at dinner with my manager, Alan Nevins.

This is the only grave marker these people had.
I am very upset that nobody had been named.

I always enjoy talking with local law enforcement wherever I go.
D.C. cops spotted me quick.

With Beth on Easter, 2008.

Duane Lee, Leland, and Tim at the legislature, being commended on their work in the war against ice.

My favorite thing to do is share my story.

Presenting a check to the Mooseheart Children's Home and School.

Beth at *Celebrity Family Feud,* where we played for the Mooseheart Children's Home and School.

Making my way through the media that had gathered, with Tucker by my side, after my release from federal prison.

At the press conference following my release.

Beth becoming suspicious.

Facing the media frenzy with my attorneys Bill Bollard and Brook Hart.

Meeting with our awesome legal team—James Quadra, Brook Hart, and Alberto Zinser.

James Quadra laying out our fate.

The team that saved our lives—Alberto Zinser, James Quadra, Tim, Leland, and Brook Hart. The only one missing is Eduardo Amerena.

Hanging out with my sons Duane Lee and Tucker.

The Chapmans.

Tough to say whose head is bigger.

Appearing on *Larry King Live*.

Doing the B.O.N.D. toy drive with founder
Reverend Jesse Lee Peterson.

Reverend Peterson stood beside me through all of my troubles.

With A&E's Vice President, Michael Feeney, in New York City.

Talking with Roy Innis and the CORE staff
at his office in New York City.

Giving thanks with Roy Innis at the CORE luncheon.

Christmas toy giveaway and charity event in
South Central Los Angeles.

Shopping for South Central toy drive with former heavyweight
champion of the world Ernie Shriver.

New York rookies sharing war stories.

At a charity event sponsored by Bodog.com with Snoop Dogg.
Bodog salutes the troops.

With designer Christian Audigier and Sylvester Stallone at an Ed Hardy fashion show in Los Angeles.

Beth and I present Winner's Camp Foundation with a check in Barbara Katie's memory at the A&E Recovery Project in Honolulu.

Winner's Camp Foundation provides cutting-edge leadership camps for teens, their families, and teachers.

Barbara Katie's final resting place.

At the A&E Recovery Project.

My preacher, Tim, is always there. Shown here at Baby Lyssa's wedding.

Baby Lyssa's final single steps. I gave my baby away.

Justin and me meeting Eric, a young fan from the Make-A-Wish Foundation.

Beth and me with our kids on a fishing trip.

This was the eagle I saw on our family fishing trip in Colorado.
It was a moment I will never forget.

"I'm going to catch you, boy," I growled.

"Not before I come get your mother." And then he hung up.

I told Mary Ellen that Guenther threatened my momma and was on his way to come and get me. He was a coldhearted killer who got lucky the first time he murdered someone because he got away with it without doing time. I figured he thought he was invincible, which made him capable of anything. However, once he brought my momma into the conversation, the rules of the game changed.

"That son of a bitch. Let him come." Mary pulled a tiny .38 from her desk drawer and called the district attorney to tell him she needed backup. She played like she was brand new in the business and this case was over her head. She told the DA that Guenther was on the highway coming to get us.

Later that night Fred, Mary, and I were driving around Guenther's neighborhood in Mary's Cadillac. Fred was driving, Mary was riding shotgun, and I was in the backseat, still holding Woody Woodpecker. When they spotted us, the cops waved us through the police line that had been set up outside Guenther's home.

"Look, it's Mary and her Dog." The cop shined his flashlight in the backseat, saw my gun, and said, "What are you hunting for, bear?"

"Naw," Mary said. "He's hunting Guenther."

"Yeah, I know. Good luck, Mary Ellen. Hope you get your man." They sent every available squad car and local highway patrolman they could get. They were watching for Guenther until they finally spotted his car on the highway and pulled him over. They snagged my capture but probably saved my life.

It was over. Although Mary Ellen was off the bond, I wouldn't get paid my thousand dollars because I didn't successfully make the capture. I knew he would have been gonzo, no one would have caught him if I hadn't left him the note in the phone booth. It was a bittersweet moment. I laid my gun across the table in Mary Ellen's office. She was happy, but I pretended to be really pissed. I turned Woody toward me and said, "Guess I'll end it all right now."

"Don't be stupid!"

"I'm going to do it, Mary Ellen."

"Whatever."

I began pulling on the trigger. Nothing. I pulled again. Nothing.

"Is that thing fake?" she asked.

I smiled and winked.

Then I said, "Look at this." On the gun it said, "Made by Mattel."

Every time Mary Ellen and I go out on a bounty it is a hell of a battle, and you never know exactly what's going to happen.

One time, I was headed up to Northglen, and I thought I was being sent to pick up just another punk who was dumb enough to jump his bond on Mary Ellen. On my way, I got a call from one of my kids saying their mother, Lyssa, was being beaten up by that very same bastard. And it wasn't until I got that call that I realized that the guy I was chasing was Michael Volosin, the same guy whose wife had been killed by David Guenther a few years before. Big Lyssa and Volosin had started dating shortly after she and I broke up. It was such a bizarre coincidence that even I had a hard time figuring out what was going on. But like everything else in my life, it must have happened for a reason.

By the time I got to the house, the cops had the whole place surrounded. I told them that my ex-wife was inside. The police recognized me right away and said Volosin had a rifle and was holding my ex-wife hostage.

"You tell that son of a bitch that if he doesn't come out of the house right now, not ten seconds from now, NOW, I am coming in after him, rifle or not." And I was serious too. Even though there was no love lost between Lyssa and me, that bastard was holding the mother of my children in there. At first the police were resistant to relay my message, but when they did, Volosin let Lyssa go and surrendered to the cops. I could see Lyssa wrapped in a blanket, but I couldn't bring myself to look at her battered body. I hopped in my car and drove away without another glance as they loaded her into the ambulance. The reason the Lord sent me up to the house that day was so I could stop Volosin from hurting the mother of my children. I knew she'd be fine, and I didn't want to get involved more than I already had. I drove back to Denver thinking about our kids and what they must have seen over the course of that abusive relationship. It broke my heart with every tick of the odometer home.

Despite the abusive nature of their relationship, Lyssa eventually got back together with Volosin. My only concern was for my children's well-being because I was well aware that their relationship was extremely violent. Twenty years had gone by without a single thought of that man. And then, sometime in 2008, I decided to reach out to him. My reason was an unusual one. As I've looked back on mistakes I've made in the past, my relationship with Lyssa is something that has haunted me. There's so much bad blood between us. I wanted to understand where all of her anger comes from. Was it just me or did she treat other men in her life that way? Volosin and Lyssa had parted ways years ago, and I thought talking with him might shed some light on the subject. When I phoned his home, Volosin's new wife answered. She was surprised to hear it was me on the other end.

"Dog, my husband made a terrible mistake twenty years ago and he is very sorry for what he's done. Can you find it in your heart to forgive him like you do other guys in the back of your car?"

"Of course I can." I didn't really have a beef with him. Our paths hadn't crossed much except for his relationship with my ex. Volosin and I spent about twenty minutes talking about life, Lyssa, and our kids. He told me about the son he'd had with my ex-wife, who she won't allow him to see. I felt his pain as he spoke because I had gone through the same thing with Duane Lee and Leland. I knew what it felt like to not be able to see your children. I tried to assure him to not give up the fight.

"Our children are worth fighting for."

No one should have the right to deprive a biological parent of the right to see their children. It's cruel and hurtful to all parties involved. I hung up from that call understanding for the first time ever that I wasn't the sole target of my ex-wife's anger. It was a bittersweet realization. I find no comfort in knowing this, only sadness in my heart for Volosin, his son, and the countless other families out there who deal with this type of loss and separation every single day.

Bounty hunting for Mary Ellen was never dull. Some of the greatest and most memorable hunts of my career in Denver were her jumps. Despite the fact that I always get my man, at the beginning Mary Ellen was always convinced they were gone and that we'd never get them. One day she called me about a big bond for a guy named Warren Halligan, who skipped. He was wanted on a $250,000 federal warrant. She was worried because losing him would have instantly put her out of business. I tried to reassure Mary Ellen that I'd find him, but my word alone wasn't giving her the comfort she needed.

Right in the middle of our conversation, Mary Ellen abruptly pulled her car over to the side of the road.

"What are you doing?" I asked.

"We're going to pray, Dog. God will help us find this guy. I don't deserve to lose everything I've worked for over this punk."

I was blown away by her commitment and determination, but even more so by her faith in the Lord. I can't say for sure when I began praying before bounty hunts, but I don't remember ever doing it before that day.

As Mary Ellen bowed her head and began to pray, I reassured her once again, "I promise you, I will find this guy."

Mary Ellen looked up with a crazed expression in her eyes. "Oh yeah? Let's see what you've got, Dog. Let me see you go. Prove to me you're the best."

That challenge was all I needed to hear. "Take me to his old house."

Mary Ellen stepped on the gas, spun her wheels in the gravel, and sped down the two-lane highway like a bat out of hell. When we got to the house, it was empty. The only things left inside were some random personal items, a couple of empty beer cans, and an old pizza box that was turned upside down. I flipped over the box and noticed a phone number written on the top. I recognized 941 as a Florida area code, so I whipped out my cell phone and dialed the number.

"Hello?" a voice answered after about a dozen rings. I could hear guys playing basketball in the background. I asked who I was talking to and where I was calling. He said he was in the yard of the county jail in Parrish, Florida.

"You're in jail?" I asked.

"Yeah. What's it to you, asshole?"

"Is there a Warren Halligan in there with you?"

"No. Never heard of him."

That's when I noticed a name written next to the phone number on the pizza box—Dan Fields. It was worth a try.

"What about a Dan Fields?" I asked.

"Yeah, he's in here."

"What does he look like?" I was starting to get a strange feeling that Dan Fields and Warren Halligan were the same man.

"He's got long brown hair, blue eyes . . ."

I interrupted him to ask, "Does he have any tattoos?" Warren had a distinctive tattoo on his chest.

"I have no idea, man."

"You've got to look and find out for me. It's worth a lot of money." I stopped myself from saying anything more, because

I didn't want to blow my cover if this Dan Fields in fact turned out to be Warren. "Look, he's come into a lot of money, but I need to make sure he's the guy I'm looking for. I'll call you the same time tomorrow. Can you help a brother out?"

"Who is this?" The guy was beginning to smell opportunity for himself.

"Never mind who this is. I'll make it worth your while if it turns out to be him. What's your name?"

"Chuck."

"Okay, Chuck. I won't forget this. I'll call you tomorrow," I told him and then hung up.

I didn't tell Mary Ellen about the new lead because I didn't want to get her hopes up just yet. Even if it was our guy, he was sitting in a cell in Florida, which meant I'd have to get him out before Mary Ellen could be released from the bond.

"Do you believe in God?" I asked Mary Ellen, knowing full well she did.

"C'mon, Dog. What kind of question is that?"

"Remember, G-O-D spelled backwards is D-O-G. Put your faith in me. I won't let you down." If things worked out, I'd be a hero. If this lead turned out to be a bust, I'd blame it on the big man upstairs.

I called Chuck the next day.

"It's him. He's got the tat," he said.

Blam. Got him.

When I told Mary Ellen the news, she was in shock. "It can't be," she said.

"Mary Ellen, I'm the Dog," I told her. "God's not going to let me fail. I'm one of His disciples, one of His messengers here on earth. God is always going to show me the way."

This was the first time I learned to follow my gut. We all have an inner voice that tells us the right thing to do. If that voice tells you to turn right, don't turn left! I had searched countless homes before, but this time my inner voice told me to flip over that pizza box. I instinctively knew a vital clue would be there. I knew for sure I had my guy. From that day on, I realized I had a special gift, something I call the "bounty hunter blessing." That's the ability to sense things others cannot feel.

For as long as I can remember, I've loved the story of Sitting Bull and his infamous Battle of the Little Bighorn. The battle was the most famous action of the Great Sioux War. Sitting Bull led the Lakota and Cheyenne tribes to victory over General George Armstrong Custer's Seventh Cavalry. This was the battle known as Custer's Last Stand because seven hundred troops fell to the leadership of Chief Sitting Bull, who had a premonition of his victory months before the battle took place. The chief saw bodies falling from the sky, which he interpreted as defeating Custer and his cavalry. Legend has it that Sitting Bull rode his horse in front of the cavalry sharp-shooters several times, but they missed with every shot. Not a single bullet hit its mark. "No white man's bullet can harm me," Sitting Bull is believed to have said that day.

Every time something happens in my life where I'm told I can't do something, I remember the words of Sitting Bull. I've never feared anything in my life because I know I will never be harmed. I told Mary Ellen the story of Sitting Bull and then promised her I would not let Warren Halligan get away.

"Bullshit." That was her response. "I know you think you're invincible, Dog, but you're not. Don't feed me your Injun crap."

I told Mary Ellen she was wrong and even decided to take it a step further. I guaranteed I'd pay her back every red cent of money it cost to send me down to Florida to capture Warren Halligan if I came back empty-handed. Of course, Mary Ellen knew that I was broker than broke and I didn't have thousands of dollars to give her if I didn't hold up my end of the deal. Even so, I had to put my money where my mouth was because I knew I was right. I offered to take her husband,

Fred, with me so she'd feel secure her investment was safe—
or at the very least, safer. And to be totally honest, I knew Fred
would pay all the bills since I didn't have two nickels to my
name to front the trip.

The plan was simple. We would go down to the county
jail and ask the warden to release Warren to us. I figured we
would show him our bail bonds badges and they'd hand him
over. Once I hit the road on a hunt, I'm all about the chase.
Game on. I've got my badge and the law on my side. There's
no more Duane. Here comes the Dog.

Fred and I flew to Florida and went directly to the jail. I
didn't think anyone would ask to see my credentials, but just
in case they did, I was ready. I called one of my FBI buddies
and told him the story and asked for backup if I needed it.

"You got it, Dog," he told me. "Let me know how it goes."

When we got to the jail, vivid memories of my time in
Huntsville flooded my head. When I stared up at the one giant
fan blowing hot air into the entire building, I thought, This had
to be built by Texans. It was so much like the prison I was in;
same color too. Before long, Fred and I were greeted by the
most redneck son of a bitch I had ever met. He was worse
than any officer or warden I lived with for my entire eighteen
months inside. Even so, I had to be cool because I needed the
officer to cooperate so I could get my man.

"Officer Chapman, I've heard an awful lot about you, son,"
he said.

I shook his hand and introduced him to Fred. "This is my
partner, Fred. Show him your badge, Fred." I could see a look
of panic come over Fred's face as I cajoled him along.

"That's not necessary, boys. What can I do you for?" This
good ol' Southern boy couldn't have been more accommodat-
ing as I began to tell him our story.

Just as I thought I'd closed the deal to hand over Halligan, my cell phone rang. It was my old buddy, Keith Paul.

He'd heard about what I was doing and thought he'd check in to see if I needed a hand. I played it cool, like Keith was my boss. I handed the prison officer my phone so he could talk to Keith, too.

"Keith Paul, FBI. The guy they're tracking is a sucker." Keith's unexpected call gave us the last bit of credibility we needed to get our man without hesitation from the officer. The only rub here was he now thought we were federal marshals, although we never said we were. Because of the call from Keith, the officer asked us to come back to the property room before he'd hand over the fugitive, so we could check something out they found when they arrested my guy. He opened up a jar full of clear liquid and asked me to smell it.

"What is it?" the officer asked.

"Jesus, you've got a half a million dollars' worth of speed in there," I answered. "It's liquid meth, bro."

The officer called the sheriff and told him what they had. The sheriff made a beeline back to the jail so he could see what was going on for himself.

"Let's go do a raid, boys," the officer said as soon as he hung up the phone. So the sheriff, Fred, and I, along with another eighteen officers, paid a surprise visit to every inmate's cell. I was pulling a wagon behind me because I was certain we'd need it for the evidence we were about to find.

"How you doing, fellas?" I asked the first two inmates we searched. "You know what this is? It's Christmas Day. Get out here while we search your cell." After turning the place upside down, I came out with several boxes of illegal contraband.

The sheriff was stunned by my discovery. "Jesus Christ!" he said.

Fred was nervous the entire time. He was worried they'd figure out we were just a couple of bounty hunters and not feds. I pulled him aside in the hallway and tried to calm his nerves.

"Let them assume whatever they want, Fred," I whispered to him. "I never told them we were the law. They came up with that all on their own. We've done nothing wrong here."

Unfortunately, everything I said failed to get through and calm Fred down. He became consumed with the idea that he and I were going to end up in jail for our charade. Fred's skin, which was normally of a dark complexion, had turned a light white. He was scared to death. Fred looked at me and said, "Do you remember cell number seven? I want that one because it was the cleanest we saw. We are all done, Dog. We are in the South. They'll never let us go. It's over. I know it is."

When we finally got to Halligan's cell, I immediately knew he was my guy. It was definitely him. When Halligan looked up and saw me standing there, all he could say was "Oh shit."

I took a step forward and looked him dead in the eyes through the bars of his cell. "Warren, my man," I said. "Who is the greatest bounty hunter in the world?"

"Damn, Dog. It's you," he answered.

"You ran on Mary Ellen, brotha," I told him. "That's a bad thing to do."

He was in total shock and disbelief he'd been found. Warren thought he'd do his ninety-day stint inside the joint and then be let out a free man. He already had a new name and identity. If he got through his sentence, he'd be long gone.

The sheriff informed Fred and me that we could take Warren the next day. He even offered to let us stay with him at his house, but Fred couldn't bring himself to take him up on it. He wanted to call Mary Ellen and tell her what was going on so she would know we were definitely going to jail. After all, we were still pulling the wool over the sheriff's eyes by continuing to let him think we were the law.

The following morning, Fred and I showed up at the jail as planned, to grab Halligan. All we had to do was get him in our car and we were out of there. But just as the officers were about to escort him out, the sheriff called us back inside. He told us to head over to the district attorney's office down the hall. When I asked why, the sheriff explained that the DA was the only person who could sign the extradition papers.

When Fred and I walked into the DA's office, there was another sheriff waiting for us.

"Who the hell do you think you are?" the DA asked. Man, was he pissed.

"I'm not sure what you are talking about, sir," I calmly answered. Under the circumstances, I thought being polite could only help things.

"You've been down here telling everybody you're FBI. Well, we just checked with the Bureau and they tell us you're a damned bounty hunter."

Technically, I had never told anyone anything, because no one ever asked. "Just because I had an agent on the phone doesn't mean I told anyone I was in the FBI," I pointed out to the district attorney. "If your guys jumped to that conclusion, that's their fault, not mine."

Fred was panicked by this exchange. He wouldn't even sit down in the DA's office. Throughout the entire discussion, he kept pulling me aside and saying, "We're going to jail, I told you, Duane. We're definitely going to jail." He sounded like Rain Man, repeating himself as he paced and said, "Oh my God" over and over. I kept telling Fred we weren't going anywhere but the airport. Jail wasn't in the cards.

I began laying into the DA for his dumb-ass sheriff not knowing about the dope he had in custody or that he had an inmate incarcerated under a false identity who was wanted on a $250,000 federal warrant or inmates who were hoarding all sorts of contraband.

"Listen, Mr. Smart Ass DA! I want my man," I insisted.

"The only thing I'm going to give you is a one-way ticket to jail unless you get your ass out of my town, and I mean right now!"

"I ain't leaving without my man," I repeated. Fred and I had come too far to go home empty-handed. Perhaps the sheriff knew I wasn't going to budge until I got what I wanted. He finally caved in, if for no other reason than to get rid of me, and said, "I'll give you a body receipt, but that's it. He's not going anywhere. He's our man now."

I was fine with that because a body receipt was enough to get Mary Ellen off the bond. I didn't care about Halligan or where he ended up as long as Mary Ellen and Fred were released of their obligations. The judge took them off the bond right away. This Dog always gets his man.

END OF
INERMISSION ONE

When I was a young boy, my grandpa used to tell me the story of Humpty Dumpty. Over the years, I adapted that famous children's rhyme to fit my personality a little better.

> *Humpty Dumpty sat on a wall*
> *Humpty Dumpty had a great fall*
> *All the king's horses and all the king's men*
> *Got together and put him back together again*

Whenever I'd repeat my version of the nursery rhyme, Grandpa was quick to point out I wasn't repeating it right. But I knew exactly what I was saying. I liked my version better because I've always been a fixer of men, not a destroyer. I never liked the thought of a man being so fragile that he breaks. I visualized the king's men busting out a giant tube of Elmer's glue and piecing Humpty Dumpty back together until he was as good as new.

In a way, that's how I see myself when I capture fugitives today. I am not out to destroy these people. My intent is to help them put their lives back together. I believe everyone deserves a second chance and an opportunity to right the wrongs they have done.

There's a human limit to how much pain someone can

take before they break. When I was in prison, I watched plenty of guys pay an inmate named Skinner to take his toilet brush and break their arms so they wouldn't have to work in the fields. When he hit their bare skin, their arm would break. You could actually hear the bone crack. The guys screamed in horrible agony for a few minutes and then, as quickly as the pain hit, it was gone. The mind takes over and protects the body by putting it into a state of shock so you stop feeling anything. I thought these guys were all nuts. There was nothing that would ever convince me to harm myself like that just to avoid hard labor.

Murder one didn't break me. Mexico didn't break me. Losing my daughter didn't break me. But there were times when I thought I just might shatter from the fallout of the "N" word debacle. I told Beth on several occasions I wasn't sure I would make it through. But she didn't buy into my self-pity. Beth has always been tough on me, but she is also my greatest supporter. When we took our vows to stand by each other through thick and thin, we both knew we'd be in for a heck of a ride. There's no one I'd rather have in my corner when the chips are down than my Beth.

After the *Enquirer* story broke, I met an eighty-five-year-old black man who put his arm around me and said, "Where I come from, Dog, that word means 'slave.'" He began to cry as he continued. "Growing up, all I heard from people was 'N***er, go get this and go get that.' It was not considered a bad word—it was just the way things were back then. I can promise you though, this will pass."

All I could manage to say to this man was "I'm sorry."

"Dog, I promise you, this is going to pass. You will be forgiven."

I didn't understand what he meant by "pass," because I'd spent the thirty years since I left prison paying for my felony. I didn't want to spend the next thirty paying for my ignorance.

The old man began to tell me a story about a guy who drove his car off a bridge with a woman other than his wife in the passenger seat. He got his seat belt off and was able to swim to safety, but he left the woman in the car. He fled the scene but didn't call the authorities until after her dead body was found the following morning. The next day he called the police to tell them his car was in the river and so was the woman. That's when he told me he was talking about Ted Kennedy.

"If America can forgive Kennedy for something like that, surely they will find mercy in their heart for you," the old man said. "What you uttered is nothing compared to that incident. You will be forgiven and yes, this will pass."

I have always been a huge fan of the Kennedy family and all they have done for our country. I think about the late Senator Ted Kennedy today and how the world loved him. His legacy will live on forever.

I understood the message the old man was trying to convey, and yet the words of the Old Testament kept coming back to me, "lest ye forget." I hoped and prayed the old man was right, but I feared he was just being kind and consoling. I had a long road ahead of me to turn around the thoughts of all the people I had hurt, but I believed it could be done, because I know most people have mercy and forgiveness in their hearts.

After my appearances on *Hannity and Colmes* and *Larry King Live*, the phones didn't stop ringing with requests to be on numerous other talk shows. Producers from *Dr. Phil* repeatedly called to see if I'd be willing to appear with two leaders in the African-American community, T. D. Jakes and Al Sharpton. I refused the invitation several times before they stopped calling. In my absence, Dr. Phil went on the air and called me a coward. No one does that to me without some type of fight, so I started referring to Dr. Phil as the "Great White Dope" in all of my interviews. Dr. Phil kept pushing my buttons by challenging me every chance he got, but I wasn't falling into his trap. He tried as hard as he could to get me to my breaking point, but he never put me over the edge.

Dr. Phil wanted the drama of a confrontation between honorable men and a supposed racist, all in the name of television ratings. I wasn't going to serve as his puppet. If I was going to be confronted by someone like Al Sharpton, I thought it would be much better and more effective to meet him head-on, so I called 411 and asked for his number. I hunt people who don't want to be found for a living. Finding someone who doesn't even know I'm looking for him is a cakewalk.

When the young woman operator gave me the number for Sharpton's organization, the National Action Network, I dialed it right away.

"Hello, is this Al Sharpton's place?" I asked.

"Yes it is. How can I help you?" The woman's voice on the other end of the phone sounded like she got a thousand phone calls like mine every single day.

"I need to speak to Reverend Sharpton. My name is Duane Chapman. I'm Dog the Bounty Hunter and I am in a heap of trouble."

There was a short pause and then I heard, "Yes, I believe you are, sir."

I was relieved the young woman on the other end of the line was so gracious when she heard it was me. I half expected her to slam down the receiver without another word, but she didn't. I explained I needed to get in touch with the reverend's secretary or assistant. I knew that would be my best shot to get my message directly through to him. I've learned over the years that assistants and sec-retaries hold the keys to the kingdom. That's pretty uni-versal in the world of business. If I could make a connection with one of Sharpton's main people, I'd have a shot with him too. Time was of the essence because Reverend Sharpton is notorious for setting up highly public displays when he is boycotting something. I was worried he was going to organize a march in front of the A&E headquar-ters to pressure them into firing me for being a racist. It was important to convince someone at his organization that I was a good man who'd made a terrible mistake. I was willing to beg for mercy if I had to.

"Look," I continued, "I know you've probably read the stories and heard the recording of the conversation I had with my son. I am so sorry about what I said, but I need Reverend Sharpton to know that I am not a racist." I was pleading with the receptionist to put me in touch with the right person.

"I think you've got an uphill climb, sir," she told me.

I swallowed hard. It was the end of the road. And then I heard something I'll never forget.

"I am Al Sharpton's daughter, Dog, and I haven't an-swered this phone in years," she said.

"Thank you, Lord!" I screamed.

"I heard the tape and I think it's all been taken out of context."

To hear Al Sharpton's daughter say she understood my situation meant so much to me. Now all I had to do was convince her to relay my message to her dad. Relief washed over me when she gave me a private number to call her back on the next day.

I phoned her as planned, but there was no answer. I called again. Still no answer. The third time I called she picked up.

"Hi, this is Dog."

"Hi."

"What's going on?" I asked.

"About what?" My heart was in my throat. I had hoped she was going to give me good news. On the contrary she started to explain that her father had decided to stay out of my situation.

I had no plan B. Everyone had told me how stupid it was to think I could pick up the phone and get Al Sharpton to back me. They said he'd hang me from the highest tree before joining forces. But I didn't see it that way. If I could somehow get his support, I believed everyone else would have to follow. I hesitated before I opened my mouth, but I thought this was my last shot at finding a way to her dad.

"I've got to resolve this," I told her. "Your father is one of the most courageous and fearless leaders in the black community. He's never backed down from controversy." I began rambling as fast as I could. She had me so nervous I was fumbling over my words and thinking I ought to go hang *myself* since that was what her father was about to do to me anyway. But then she interrupted me.

"I'm just teasing you, Dog. Dad said he is not going to say anything about the incident if you take care of a couple of things for him."

She said Reverend Sharpton wanted me to attend a rally against guns, which I was all too happy to be a part of. She also mentioned Dr. Phil was going to be there too.

"That Great White Dope? What a peckerwood!" I said. She started laughing on the other end of the line. "I'll go to the rally, but I'm not getting anywhere near that arrogant jerk."

To this day, Reverend Sharpton has kept his word. He never said a negative thing about me. And though there were several people I met along the way who offered me their support, it wasn't until a chance meeting in January 2008 that I thought I might actually be welcomed back into the African-American community.

Despite his efforts to get A&E to pull my show, I also reached out to Roy Innis and CORE to see if there was some way to make amends. Mr. Innis was resistant at first, but we were eventually able to set up a meeting to get to know each other. I knew I could turn him around if I spent some face time with him. His son also attended the meeting, and for whatever reason, he was wearing a name tag that read, "Niger Innis." After spotting it, I looked at Roy in total disbelief.

"Now, listen," I told him. "This is my life I'm trying to defend. You mean to tell me you named your son the 'N' word?"

They both broke out in uproarious laughter. "Duane, his name is Niger, as in the river," Roy said.

I was a little embarrassed to admit I didn't even know how to spell the word I'd uttered that brought us together that day. Roy was stunned by my innocence. He looked at his son and said, "He doesn't even know how to spell it, how could he be a racist?" Perhaps that moment helped him to understand how naïve I really was. Whatever the reasons, Roy got to know me that day.

"You don't fit any criteria for a racist, Dog," he told me.

Thank God I found an ally. I was looking for a leader to help me and found a friend. I began crying tears of joy and screaming "Hallelujah" at the top of my lungs. I wanted to shout from the highest mountaintop that I had been forgiven. I turned to Roy and Niger and said, "The Lord is on the mountain," quoting the great Martin Luther King. All they could say was "Amen!"

After hearing my side of the story, Roy realized that the controversy had unjustly spiraled out of control after the tapes were released out of context. He agreed to mentor me in my efforts to seek reconciliation and atonement for my careless language.

Before I left his office that day, I noticed that Roy's son was wearing a pin that had the letter "N" on it in a circle with a slash through it. I asked if I could have one.

Niger said, "Yeah, but I don't think you should pass them out!"

I wore that pin on every show and at every appearance I made after our meeting. Even today, I carry the pin Niger gave me in my pocket when I'm out on bounty hunts. Something about having it with me makes me feel protected.

One of the fights CORE was involved in that intrigued me was the belief that the "N" word is being abused by the entertainment industry. Niger, in particular, voiced his concerns about the industry's double standards, which allow comedians such as David Alan Grier or Dave Chappelle to be given a pass when doing skits using the "N" word, without public outcry. Rappers are also given a pass to use it with far more consistency and stereotyping. To some degree, my use of the word fell into the pass/no pass system being used in today's pop culture. David Alan Grier did a short monologue about my use of the word and used it over and over again to make his point. There were no headlines, no fallout for his show, *Chocolate News*, and no public outcry against his tirade. I wanted to do whatever I could to help CORE resolve this issue within the entertainment industry.

After our first meeting in New York, Roy Innis had a change of heart about old Doggie. Beth and I attended a luncheon hosted by Mr. Innis at the CORE headquarters in New York, where we posed for photos and got to know his predominately African-American staff, none of whom seemed reluctant to pose with us. It had become pretty clear to most everyone there that the papers had made me out to be something I wasn't. In fact, Roy Innis came out and publicly made a statement about the matter, saying, "Like many that heard the comments made by Duane 'the Dog' Chapman without the proper context, I was offended and outraged. After meeting with him and his wife Beth, and hearing his side of the story, we realized that the controversy had unjustly spiraled out of control without context."

His public statement vindicated me in the eyes of his organization, and I believe it started me down the path of recovery and reconnecting with the African-American community. After that luncheon, Roy invited me to attend a CORE dinner in late January 2008 honoring Martin Luther King. I was told I'd be attending with Senator John McCain and a host of other high-profile politicians and celebrities. I was deeply honored by the request and gladly accepted the offer to attend.

I have never forgotten a rebroadcast speech I heard Martin Luther King give on television when I was in Huntsville prison. He said, "The Bible says an eye for an eye, and a tooth for a tooth." At the time, I remember thinking, *Right on.* And then he said something like "America would be blind and toothless if we lived like that." I couldn't get his words out of my mind. I walked around the rest of the day thinking how great this man was. He made an unforgettable impression on me and gave me the gift of realizing that revenge has its price too.

CORE had asked me to speak at the Martin Luther King dinner. As I prepared for the evening, I wanted to find a connection to Dr. King that would make my presence relevant that night. And then it occurred to me that James Earl Ray had been wanted for breaking out of jail by hiding out in a bread truck, making him a flat-out fugitive when he shot and killed Martin Luther King. If I had been bounty hunting back then, he was just the type of guy I would have gone after. Knowing this fact gave me a purpose for being there and an inspiration to speak to the crowd. As I spoke, I thought I did a good job capturing the audience, but someone later told me that T. D. Jakes refused to listen to what I had to say and walked out before I was done.

After I spoke, an African-American woman approached me with her young daughter, a beautiful child wearing a pretty red dress. The little girl couldn't have been more than ten years old. The mother explained that her daughter was a huge fan of my show and wanted to meet me after she heard that I had said a very bad word. She said they saved up for three weeks to buy the young girl's dress so she'd have something pretty to wear when she met me. Later that night, someone told me they had actually saved up for months. I said hello to the little girl and told her how sorry I was for what I had said. She looked up at me, with a big ol' smile and simply said, "I love you and forgive you, Dog."

My heart melted on the spot and tears streamed down my cheeks. I was so worried I had disappointed this child— that she wouldn't understand why Uncle Dog used the bad word he did. I was ready to explain myself to her if need be, but she never asked for explanations. Her innocence, love, and acceptance showed me the great power in forgiveness— especially from a child. I will take her love and acceptance with me for the rest of my days.

After my positive experiences with Roy Innis and CORE, I spent the next several months going on what Beth and I dubbed my "Apology Tour." I knew I could change people's minds if I was given the chance. I was being horribly misrepresented in the press, and it didn't look like things were going to turn around unless I could convince people to give me a shot at redemption. If they could give me that, I was positive I would be in their hearts forever.

I attended several events, including holiday toy drives and drug awareness symposiums and town hall meetings, where I could give back to the community. I enjoyed getting out and talking with people at all of those events, but there was one local toy drive in Los Angeles I'll never forget. I met a father and son who touched my heart. The father, who was not more than just a kid himself, told me he'd never been able to save enough money to buy his son a toy for Christmas. Of course, I thought back to my struggle in buying Tucker his My Buddy doll and remembered how I felt. The young dad went on to tell me his son had no toys at home.

"I don't know why I'm here. I can't believe I'm doing this, Dog. I'm reaching out to you, of all people," he said.

All I could say was "Thank you."

I hugged the father and then knelt down and put my hands out for his son. He was the real reason I was there that day. I wanted to show how much love I have in my heart for all people, but especially for those who are less fortunate, because I have been there myself. I will never forget those hungry years and I am reminded so often, now more than ever, that we are all the same.

I made a big spectacle out of the three of us hanging out the rest of the day. I gave the young boy a toy truck I'd saved for one special kid. His face lit up with excitement as soon as he saw it. It was rewarding to be able to do something to brighten that young boy's day. There's nothing like the love you get from a child. It's pure, authentic, and real. If enduring the difficult experiences that got me to the toy drive that day was the price I had to pay in order to meet a family like that father and son, then it was all worth it. I'd sit through a grilling on national television every day for a month just to get one smile, one hug, and one "thank you" like I did that day.

My new association with CORE allowed me to affect change in some very unexpected areas. I even found myself in a roundtable discussion with members of CORE, the NAACP, and the ACLU, defending a Hassidic Jewish police officer's right to keep his beard because of his religious beliefs. I was stunned to hear that a police department was trying to force a good cop off the squad because of his facial hair, which is against department policy. After the ACLU applied enough pressure and threatened to go to court over the officer's civil rights, the police chief agreed to let him stay on the force if he only worked undercover duty. In the end, the officer called me to say thank you because he could keep on doing what he loved—being a cop.

It wasn't until I helped the ACLU and CORE to allow that cop to keep his job that I truly realized my mishap could allow me to help others who were suffering. Though I wouldn't have asked for the attention that was brought upon me after the *National Enquirer* tapes were released, I believe that much more good than harm has resulted from it. The controversy surrounding me was just another mountain I was forced to climb in my life.

In the beginning, my heart was bursting with tears of pain, but now I am filled with tears of joy for the opportunities I've had and the changes I've been able to make since the story broke. My new role gave me the responsibility of being a racial healer for our country. I was a changed man with a higher purpose.

The strangest part of the Apology Tour was that of all the people I shook hands with and met along the way, I found myself constantly surprised at how merciful the African-American community was, while the white community remained angry and unforgiving for what I had said. There was even a white supremacy group that was angry with me for apologizing for my careless slip.

In early 2008, I received a call from a well-known member of the KKK asking me to come to Texas to give a speech for their group at an upcoming meeting. I told the man who called me that I couldn't do it.

"You know me, bro. I'm not like that," I said.

He pleaded with me that I had an opportunity to use the situation to help lots of people who feel the way the Klan does.

"A lot of us are sick of it, Dog. We are sick of the crime, the assaults, all of it."

I was getting angry listening to him talk. I said, "You think white men don't commit the same crimes? I see it every day, brother."

Not long after that call I read an article on the Internet that said there was a $75,000 bounty on my head because I didn't promote white pride. I have spent my entire life knowing there is always going to be the presence of good and evil in this world. Evil can come in many forms, such as negativity, discontent, or plain stupidity. Believe me, those forces are almost as strong as the good. There were a lot of thoughts going through my mind when I read that article.

I said, "Come and get me!" after I finished reading the last word. I dared anyone to try to get my badge. I wasn't raised to give evil forces the power to win. I learned to go with the good because it always prevails. Some people will never understand that. They never gamble on doing the right thing. They see a crime going down and think, *If I get out to help that person, the bad guys will come after me, too.* Or *If I get involved in this robbery, they're going to shoot me.*

Me . . . I say, "Me and you, right now. Let's go." That's the old fighter in me.

So when I was confronted by a white supremacist from the Aryan Nations after a public appearance, about why I didn't stand up for what I'd said, the first thing I thought was *I could rip this guy in half.*

I remembered the Aryan guys I knew in the joint. I couldn't go around with them for two reasons: first, because of my friendship with Whitaker, and second, because I didn't support their way of thinking.

I looked the muscle-bound, tatted Aryan thug up and down while he was spewing his racist thoughts and knew I could take him for sure. Because I am in the public eye, physical confrontations are no longer my thing. But you can believe I got pretty vocal with that guy. He could tell he was going down the wrong path with me. I got right in his face and told him I didn't care what his homies thought, I was not a racist and I didn't think he should say the hateful things that were coming out of his mouth either. By the end of our twenty-minute dialogue, this poor fool was apologizing to me and asking for free *Dog the Bounty Hunter* T-shirts.

I started bawling after he walked away. I was stunned that I was able to turn his twisted thoughts around. I raised my hands in the air and said, "Thank you, Lord."

One down and, sadly, too many left to go.

Although I was slowly mending fences in the African-American community, I wasn't sure all of my efforts would be enough to convince A&E to give me back my show. I was hopeful that I'd be given the opportunity to prove I wasn't the bad guy the media had made me out to be, but I wasn't 100 percent sure the network would give me that chance. I'd seen plenty of guys bounce back from drugs or alcohol, but there aren't many who came back after racial tirades. If the network didn't believe in me, I would be done in Hollywood. I didn't care about the celebrity aspect so much as the platform, which allowed me to reach and help a great many people. Helping my brothers and sisters has always been the thrust behind my desire to be in the spotlight.

I worried about the network's decision day and night. Lots of people told me I had nothing to be concerned about, that after the dust settled everything would turn around. I still wasn't sure. And then one night I went to sleep and had a dream where I was standing over my own grave. I looked at the headstone and noticed the initials A&E in the bottom right corner. They had made sure I had a headstone. God was showing me everything was going to be all right, that I would get my show back and would soon be doing what I loved most. I woke up the next morning and told Beth about my premonition.

"We're getting the show back, Beth. I promise you, we will be on the air again soon."

Sure enough, through the efforts of many supporters and the mercy shown by the network, on February 20, 2008, A&E announced that our show was headed back to television. The executives told me their reason for bringing *Dog the Bounty Hunter* back was plain and simple: Since my show is predicated on second chances, they decided to give me one too. I was in Las Vegas working on a case when I got the good word. In an ironic twist, on the very same day the network gave me back my show, Jesse Jackson accidentally used the "N" word during an interview with Bill O'Reilly. I hadn't been able to figure out why he was in my dream a few months earlier until I heard that news. But when I did, it all made sense. Of course, there was virtually no fallout for Jesse Jackson's error. In fact, it was all but buried in the press. The upside was that from that day on, my name was no longer uttered every time someone made the same mistake.

The news of our return to television made worldwide headlines. I remember reading the scroll at the bottom of the CNN ticker with tears in my eyes. I was so happy and relieved that I broke down and cried. Everything I had worked for had hung in television purgatory for months. I knew I'd always be able to make a living, but without my show I couldn't reach the millions of viewers who tuned in every week, with my singular message to help them get a second chance at life. If just one viewer decides to get clean, give up crime, go back to school, or be a better parent because of something on my show, then I am satisfied. Now more than ever, I dedicated myself to reaching out to those folks in any way I could, so I could spread the word that I was there to help them take that first step.

I was looking forward to getting back to work and doing what I love most. Even though the network announced the return of *Dog the Bounty Hunter* in February, we didn't actually go back into production until April. We shot the new shows in Denver, where each capture we made became headlines in the local papers. Every news story written about me started out with a sentence that read something like this: *"Dog, who used the 'N' word, captured another fugitive . . ."* Once the show was back on the air, however, the tide began to turn toward the way things used to be before the *National Enquirer* story. For the first time in months I felt like people were once again judging me for the good things I was doing and were no longer just pointing the racist finger in my direction.

It felt great to be back in the saddle. I will always be grateful to A&E for their belief in me and the work I do. Everyone at the network assured me that they knew I wasn't a racist or the kind of person who stood for intolerance. Their kind words meant the world to me. Beth and I sent the president of the network flowers for thirty days in a row as a small token of our appreciation, but they could never convey just how grateful I was to have them in my corner. The card read, "Abbey: Have I thanked you today?"

When they told me they were putting the show back into production, the executives from the network said they had all the confidence in the world that our audience would be there for us when we hit the air—and boy were they right. Our premiere episode debuted with 30 percent more viewers than we had had when we were taken off the air. The Dog was back and bigger than ever.

By the time the show aired, I finally felt free. I was back on television, it felt like I had been forgiven for my ignorance, I was back to bounty hunting, and I was finally out of the federal government's hold. I no longer had to ask for permission to travel in the United States, as I had while my Mexican extradition case was still open. There were no more restrictions placed on what I could or couldn't do, and I felt totally and completely emancipated from the hell I'd been living since capturing Andrew Luster. It was as if the slate had been wiped clean—sort of. Despite my being able to travel in the United States, because of my felony conviction I still have to get permission to travel outside the country. I was recently contacted by people in London to go over and help Parliament create a plan to clean up the massive problem they have with violent gangs in and around the city. I was all set to make the trip when I was told England would not grant me a visa to enter the country because of my criminal history, even claiming that I had been convicted of the same crimes as Jack the Ripper! I was devastated because I was eager to get over there and help clean up their cities and streets.

With all of the good deeds I've done over the past thirty-three years, all of the fugitives I've brought to face their crimes, and the many hours of community service I've put in, I think there should be some type of absolution for my crime. I would rally for a pardon since I didn't commit the crime I was charged with, but if that wasn't in the cards for me, I'd like to have my rights restored so I can truly live as a free man. I want to vote in elections. I want to travel to foreign countries. I want to be able to wear body armor to protect myself if I have to. In some states, even if I'm working, I am not even allowed to wear a bulletproof vest. I may think I'm Superman, the man of steel, but out in the field, I have no right to any type of protection if I get shot. That doesn't seem fair to me. I should have the right to wear a bulletproof vest.

I am an upstanding, productive, respectable member of society and a citizen of the United States of America. I served my time and have given back to my community and country countless times in ways that no other man can match. What else will it take before my country sees me as a valuable asset? Even though we live in a free country, if you've been convicted of a felony, you will never really be free here. It's a harsh reality I have a tough time accepting. How do I win back the respect of my country so it will see me as worthy of these rights?

We all make mistakes in life. Lord knows I am a walking, living, breathing example of that, but I am here to tell you one thing I hope you never forget. As long as you're willing to take a risk, you will always get another opportunity to do things right. When I was leaving Huntsville, one of the wardens came over to me and said there was no second chance in the joint, only first chances.

"What do you mean by that?" I asked.

"Life is what it is, Chapman. If you screw up, you'll find yourself behind bars like you are now. When we let you go, that'll be your first chance to make whatever changes you need to live your life on the right side of the law. Mess that up, boy, and you'll find yourself singing the prison blues again. There won't be a second chance for a guy like you."

Even if I don't totally agree with what he said, I never forgot the warden's words that day. Unless they're back in the joint, I believe most everyone should be given as many chances as it takes until they get it right. So when I talk about second chances in life, I suppose I really mean your first shot at living a good clean life. It takes some people a little more time than others to get that right.

That first chance is the biggest risk of all because it

takes guts and courage to allow yourself or someone else to go there. And if you're lucky enough to get that chance, you better be damned sure you pay it forward. Even if you're the king of the world, friend, you will someday still meet the Almighty. If you have given your subjects mercy along the way, then the Almighty will surely give it to you. Where mercy is shown, mercy is given. That's why I never give up on anyone. Deep down, I know we can all turn our lives around if given the chance.

Many people showed me kindness and understanding through their forgiveness of the things I said to Tucker about his girlfriend. Since then, the biggest lesson I've learned from that incident is to watch what I say. I finally understood what my mother meant when she warned me about being handed my head on a platter. This was a tough lesson for me—really hard, because I think of myself as an interpreter for those who cannot articulate in a highly educated way. But now I understand I have to watch my language when I translate those messages. I've learned that names really do hurt some people, sometimes worse than the deepest cut of a knife or the sensation of a fist to the chin. There are lots of people in the world who can't get over that type of pain. I've been called so many names in my life that I've become calloused. That surely doesn't mean it's right. In fact, I now know it is terribly wrong.

I've also learned to be more humble and caring about people as a result of my reckless use of words. Before I open my mouth these days, I ask myself, *Who is this going to hurt?* I also know I have to make my point in a clear, precise, and educated manner because my old style of using slang isn't cool. It does hurt people's feelings—which was never my intent. As a result, I tend to keep my mouth closed and my ears open a lot more these days.

My mother and I used to talk a lot about the importance

of listening. Whenever I spend a few minutes with a fugitive after a capture, or a person who is lost on drugs, or someone whose love life is all screwed up, I'll take a few minutes to let them talk about whatever is on their mind. I'll sometimes sit for fifteen minutes without saying a word while they spill their heart and guts out onto the floor. Mom used to say that my patience and compassion with those people gave them the glue to put their lives back together. "By listening, you showed mercy, son," she'd say. Mom was the one who taught me that mercy and second chances go together.

Every single day I spent in Huntsville, the Lord showed me that someone there needed my help. I sucked up my eighteen months in the pen and served my sentence like a man because I made sure my time had purpose and meaning. At first it was only the inmates who came to me, asking for help rewriting their letters home, to their mom, girlfriend, and others, sobbing over the divorce papers that arrived during mail call, or getting the harsh news that someone close to them had passed away. But by the time I left, the guards were coming to me to talk about their lives too. Looking back, I became like the white Oprah of Huntsville.

On the day I walked out the front gate of that prison, the warden who talked to me about second chances approached me and said, "Can you stay out, Dog?"

"Damn right I can, Warden," I shot back.

"Do it for me, Dog. Make me proud." I knew he meant it too. I carried those words with me wherever I went from that day on because I knew there would be no second chance for me if I somehow found my way back.

A few months after *Dog the Bounty Hunter* went back into production, I received a call from Tim Storey. He asked me if I had any interest in giving a sermon at the Family Faith Church in Huntsville, Texas.

"Have you ever heard of Huntsville, Duane?" Tim asked. I had to laugh at first. I thought he was joking because I thought he knew my connection there.

"Have *I* ever heard of *Huntsville*? That's where I served my time, Pastor," I answered.

When Tim called, it had been almost thirty years to the day since the warden handed me two hundred dollars and wished me luck. The pastor told me the church was interested in having me come along and preach with him. I have dreamt of spreading the gospel since I was a little boy. My mother gave me a book by Nicky Cruz when I was thirteen years old, hoping I would read his message and embrace his relationship with the Lord. Despite her many attempts to get me to read it, I refused because as a teenager I never felt I needed a Bible to connect with God. I've always had my own special one-on-one relationship with the Lord. However, my first week in prison, I went to the library to see if they had a Bible I could study. Being inside the joint changed my mind about wanting to learn and follow the words of the Bible. Unfortunately, there were no Bibles to check out, so the librarian gave me a copy of the next best thing. The same book by Nicky Cruz that my mother had given me. It was a sign. I hadn't seen that book for a decade. Once I cracked it open, I was mesmerized by his testimony and style. I often wondered what it would be like to share the gospel in front of millions of people like Nicky Cruz. His book truly inspired me to follow my dream to someday preach. So when the pastor asked me to join him in Huntsville, I jumped at the opportunity for two reasons. First, I could share my life lessons through my own experiences with God, and second, I was going to have the chance to speak in Huntsville, a place I'd reluctantly called home for eighteen months.

After I hung up the phone, I immediately began preparing for the big day. I thought back to the first time I heard a preacher speak, at Bethel Temple, the church I attended with my mother when I was just a young boy. His name was Sidney Jones. When I heard him preach, I thought he was the greatest speaker I ever heard. When he ended his sermon that Sunday morning he said he was scheduled to be in Lyman, Colorado, the following week. I turned to my mom and said, "I've got to go hear him again. Will you take me?" Mom agreed.

When I went to watch Pastor Jones for the second time, I was extremely disappointed when he gave the exact same sermon he'd spoken at Bethel Temple the week before. Not one word was changed, even though the congregation was decidedly different. When I asked my mom why he repeated himself two weeks in a row, her best explanation was that it was because the material was so moving and powerful. Even so, I didn't like the way his repetitiveness made me feel. While I was deeply touched by his message the first week, it lost all of its impact the second time around. Somehow, it felt lazy not to change up the sermon. I figured if I could turn my life over to the Lord, the least this guy could do was tell me a different story week after week. I never forgot how his sermon made me feel and vowed I'd never make that mistake if I ever someday found myself speaking in front of a crowd.

Today when I give speeches, I don't write them out in advance and I rarely prepare more than an outline. I know there are people out there who may attend my events three nights in a row, so I want to make sure they get their money's worth every single time. That's why I usually say what's in my heart—I know the Lord will always fill my mouth with the right words to say. I'll alter my speech based on the reactions I'm getting from the crowd. You have to know who you're talking to if you want to have the biggest impact. I pay close attention to the looks on the faces staring back at me from the audience. If they're laughing at the right moments, I know they get my humor. If they're crying, I know I've touched their souls. When I see a mother swing her arm around her son's shoulders because she knows he's in trouble and loves him anyway, I've done what I set out to do—and that is to help people find the courage to take a second chance. Sometimes, not always, but occasionally I believe the Lord directs me at an event in ways I could never have seen prior to it, and my upcoming speech at Huntsville would be the biggest surprise on how impactful His influence can be.

The day we got to the Family Faith Church, I was stunned when I was told that twenty-five hundred people were waiting to hear the preacher and me. They were lined up as far as I could see. Someone from the church explained that the people waiting were not part of the actual congregation. They were what he referred to as "overflows." I had had no idea how huge this event would be. The crush of people called out my name:

"Dog, Dog, Dog."

Now, over the years I've gotten used to large crowds, but this time I was really nervous. I had studied the story of Jonah and the Whale for two weeks so I'd have the basis for my sermon. I was ready to get up on the pulpit and lead the congregation with my own unique take on the classic tale of how Jonah was swallowed up by the whale. I was all set—at least I thought I was until moments before I was called up to the podium.

That's when I heard a voice say, "You're not preaching Jonah today." I had to laugh because for once, I had actually planned out and memorized what I was going to say word for word. I figured it had to be the devil whispering in my ear because God would want me to tell His story even if it was in my own special way.

"You know it's me, Duane," the voice said. "You can't use Jonah today. There are some people here who need more than scripture from you. Use what you know, son." I was frozen with fear because I didn't know what I was supposed to say or do.

It sounds absurd, but I couldn't bring myself to veer off the path I had planned, for two reasons: first, Beth would freak out, since she and I worked on this speech together for weeks; and second, it was hugely important to me to get a positive reaction from the audience. I was worried they wouldn't respond to my usual "from the hip" style, which was what I had become most comfortable doing.

My nerves got even worse as I peeked through the curtain from backstage and took a look at the huge crowd as they filled the church auditorium. I closed the curtain, turned around, and began pacing back and forth trying to figure out what I was supposed to do—stick with my planned sermon or obey the Lord's request to speak from my heart.

Beth kept saying to me, "Do you have your notes? Are you prepared? You can't get up there and say whatever you want this time!" Her constant nagging wasn't helping matters. The more I thought about it, though, the more I realized she was right. So when I hit the stage, I asked the congregation to open their Bibles to Jonah, the sixteenth chapter.

I began to read out loud. "I was in the belly of the whale. The weeds came around my neck and choked me to death. My spirit cried unto the Lord. . . ."

And then I stopped.

I took a deep breath, closed my eyes for a single beat, and then said, "How many of you have been to a place where your spirit is so broken that you have broken down and cried?"

The whole church raised their hands. I turned my eyes upward, like I was looking toward God. *OK, big man. This must be what you wanted me to do,* I thought.

And then I said, "Well, welcome to the 'I barely made it' club!" The congregation broke out in thunderous applause. I began to tell the story of John the Baptist and how he was beheaded for the words he used. I did something I had never done before: I gave my testimony with various quotes from scripture along the way. This time I really let my words and emotions flow. I spoke of Jesus in a way I didn't always allow myself to, mostly because up until this moment, I had been told to keep my speeches fairly nonreligious. In the past, I was told not to include Jesus as much as I wanted to. This time, things were different because I was in a church. I allowed my true love of the Lord to fill my mouth and, therefore, the room. It was the most incredible experience. As I spoke from my heart for twenty minutes, the response nearly knocked me off my feet. I felt such love and powerful energy coming from the audience. When the preacher asked anyone with a problem to come forward for an altar call, I literally had to take my seat because I was being crushed by the intense energy and power coming my way. The Lord was showing me how strong the people's love was.

The whole time I was thinking, *Come get a piece of me. I'll be here for you if you need anything. I'll take the time out, whether ten seconds or ten minutes, to hear what you have to say.* And then I thought I should be saying what I was thinking in my head out loud.

I announced to the crowd, "Come up here if you need

something. Come forward." And they all came. I have never experienced anything like that outpouring of emotion. For just a few minutes, Dog and Jesus were as thick as thieves. It was the ultimate power trip and I loved every minute.

I was proud to be God's Dog that day, just as I have been proud to be Beth's Dog, Mary Ellen's Dog, and so many others over the years. In my mind, I have a direct connection to the Lord. If someone asks me to pray for them, I will. I don't always get an answer, but God always hears my prayers.

A few months after that appearance, I received a call from the people at the Make-A-Wish Foundation asking me to meet a fifteen-year-old boy who was dying. I try to fulfill these requests whenever I can because they are so meaningful to the terminally ill child and to me. When we met, the boy looked really frail and weak, and it was pretty obvious he didn't have long to live. Most of the time, parents of the sick children I meet will tell me that they haven't told their kid how ill they are and they don't know they're dying. The parents will ask me not to talk about it with their children, especially if the kids don't know they're terminal.

When I met this young man, he immediately told me he was scared. When I asked what he was afraid of, the young boy said, "Dying." I began to tell him the story of a dream I once had when I was about his age. I was walking along a path when a flower stopped me cold.

"Good morning, Dog," the flower said.

"Hello, flower," I answered. I wasn't sure why the flower was talking to me.

"Where are we?" I asked.

"This is heaven. Everything that was once alive is here now."

I looked around and began to see many familiar things.

There was Max, the horny toad I had when I was a boy. Behind him was my old dog, Cookie, and behind him was King, the dog my grandpa made me shoot because he got too old. There were three ducks and a bird, too.

"What did Max look like?" the boy asked.

"He still had the same fat yellow belly."

"And the ducks? Why were they there?"

The truth is, I wasn't sure why the ducks were there, so I shrugged my shoulders and said, "I drowned those bastards," which made the boy laugh.

I pulled a feather from my coat pocket and showed it to him. I told him some Apache Indian friends had given me this feather for long life, freedom, joy, and a peaceful soul. When I handed it to him I said, "Anytime you need strength, you take this feather in your hand and hold it close to your chest."

The boy reached out for the feather and wrapped his frail fingers around the stem. He looked up at me and asked, "What's going to happen, Dog?"

Whenever I find I don't have the right words to say, I always fall back on scripture because God always has the right thing to say.

"The Bible says, 'Yea though I walk through the valley of the shadow of death, I shall fear no evil for Thou art with me.'" I paused for a moment to make sure the boy was looking into my eyes. "When you die, son, there will be a light," I told him. "Get ready because you're going to walk through this valley called the shadow of death. It'll be spooky, but fear not, little brother, because He's there. He's like your bow and arrow, your tomahawk. As you walk through the valley, you may see demons flying over your head or to the side of you, but don't be scared. Just keep on walking through the tunnel of light. The Lord will be with you. When you get to the end, He will be there waiting."

"Do you think I'll see my pet parrot that died last year?" the boy asked.

"He'll be right there, waiting with God."

"This has been a good talk, Dog. Thank you."

I fought back my tears when we said our good-byes, because I knew my little friend wasn't going to make it. A few weeks later, I received a call from his mother saying he had passed away. She told me he started to cough a bit when he asked his father for my feather. His mother went on to tell me he laid it on his chest and smiled the biggest smile she had seen since he got sick. His parents heard him take his last breath, and then he was gone.

"Dog, do you mind if I ask you what you and my son talked about the day you met?"

I told her everything.

"You know, I believe he saw his bird there, Dog," she told me. In my mind, I had no doubt that he had.

I was sorry for her loss but felt lucky to have met this young man before he died. I'm the guy that has always said "All aboard!" because I know life is truly a journey and a path we all walk along. In the criminal world, I'm sometimes the last guy a fugitive sees a free man. As a lover of God, sometimes I am the last man a young boy sees before he closes his eyes for good. Whatever hat I'm wearing, I wear it proud.

CHAPTER 14

People rarely like to admit they've made a mistake, especially people in positions of power who can change people's lives with the snap of a finger. In 1997, I reluctantly surrendered my bond license in Hawaii for two years after reaching a settlement with Amwest, my former insurance company. They quickly revoked my appointment and essentially put me out of the bond business and on the street overnight.

This was the result of a terrible and frustrating series of events that began when Richard Heath, an insurance agent from Amwest, came to audit my books because his company suspected there were some unlawful dealings happening in my Honolulu office. After a couple of days of poring over my books, Heath was convinced that I wasn't the one responsible for any unreported bonds to the insurance company. It was clear they were being written by two former employees who were using my powers and then pocketing excess fees. Once Heath was certain it wasn't me, he sat me down as if he was the Godfather and made me an offer I had no choice but to accept. I knew he had the ability to rescind my powers by canceling my appointment. If he did that, I'd be out of the business. A few days later, Heath called me to a meeting. Despite overwhelming evidence to the contrary, he said my two former employees were willing to testify against me, saying I was the one stealing the insurance money. He knew they were lying because I had already proven my innocence. Still, it didn't matter because I was a convicted felon—an essential point Heath kept reminding me of over and over. If my case went to court, Heath told me, a jury would probably take me down forever. At the very least, I was looking at doing more time in jail.

As I listened to Heath talk, I began to wonder who would bail me out. None of the local bondsmen, that was for sure. They all hated me because I had swooped into town and changed the way everyone had to do business. I also began worrying about my children and what would happen to them. I couldn't bear the thought of any of my kids ending up in foster care. Heath said he wouldn't press charges if I agreed to get out of the bond business for a minimum of two years. After I reluctantly took the deal, life as I knew it was over. Suddenly, I had no job, no income, and no savings. With no phones ringing, it all stopped.

Rumors began spreading like a California wildfire. I heard people saying I had embezzled millions of dollars and even tried to kill a man, both of which were utterly absurd. There were whispers wherever I went.

One of the conditions of my deal with Heath was that I surrender my bond license during our two-year noncompete agreement. Since I had no license, several complaints were filed with the Hawaii Department of Insurance. There were lots of people who needed my service and who had already paid me in advance to oversee their bail and bond. When I was forced out of business, many of those people lost a lot of their collateral in bail forfeiture. What this boiled down to was that the cosigners were losing everything because the people they were backing had skipped out on their bail and I couldn't go after any of them. This was a rare opportunity where they could run with no threat of the Dog tracking them down. Nonetheless, my company still had to pay the insurer for the full value of the bond. During that two-year period, that meant liquidating my collateral to make good on the money owed. I hated doing it, but I was left with no choice.

Most of the complaints were settled outside the system. As for the other complaints, my problems started when the Department of Insurance began sending me notification letters at the wrong address. The notices went to an address I hadn't operated out of for five years. The strange part was that prior to my deal with Heath, I always received letters from the department at my current address with no problem at all. It was my legal address on every document filed with the state. It made no sense that they didn't try to reach me through my correct address.

I was patiently waiting for the two-year noncompete Heath made me sign, as part of our deal, to run out so I could get back to work in Hawaii and start all over again. That would have been the perfect plan had it not been for those complaints I never received. The problem wasn't the complaints, but my failure to answer. That was an automatic suspension of my license. If I didn't adhere to all of the rules and regulations, I was in danger of losing my rights as a bondsman.

I called the Hawaii Department of Insurance to make sure they had a correct mailing address so I could deal with any outstanding issues. The next letter I received arrived on December 27, 1997, informing me that my license was in jeopardy for failure to respond to the complaints. The hearing was set for October 29—two whole months prior to receiving the notification. In my absence, the commissioner had revoked my license for five years. The penalty for not answering a complaint is generally a thirty-day suspension and a five-hundred-dollar fine. The revocation of my license for five years was extreme and unfair.

Nobody in the bond business gets sanctioned as harshly as I did. I was also deprived of my due process under the law because I am entitled to get notice of a hearing before it takes place, not after they've already made a decision. It was very difficult to get people to listen to me. I knocked on every door imaginable, until finally one lawyer, Howard Glickstein, agreed that I had been robbed of my basic rights. He told me that it would be an incredible long shot, but I knew we had to go for it anyway. There was nothing left to lose.

It took eleven years of perseverance and fighting, but Beth and I fought my case all the way to the Hawaii Supreme Court, until we were finally able to show a panel of judges all of the clerical errors that were made leading up to my revocation. Finally, in late 2008, our lawyer was victorious. The judge ruled in our favor, saying the corporate division of insurance was wrong. He said the state was required to reinstate my license exactly as it was when they revoked it. The only problem with that ruling was that when they revoked it, I had already surrendered my license in my deal with Heath and moved to Colorado to wait out the two-year noncompete period. So, in essence, the state revoked a license that had already been surrendered.

The reason it took so long to win the case was because it was extremely technical. The laws in Hawaii had changed since I first lost my license back in 1997. Initially, the best compromise the state would agree to was allowing me to take the license exam again. That wasn't good enough for me. The Supreme Court had ordered my license to be reinstated because the state should never have suspended it in the first place. I could have sued for eight years of lost wages because I wasn't able to work, but I didn't. My hands were tied because I also couldn't go to another state to apply for a license since the first question they would ask would be if I'd ever had a license suspended or revoked in another state. I would be forced to tell the truth. This was exactly the same kind of situation I had found myself in numerous times since I was released from Huntsville, when asked if I had ever been convicted of a felony. My answer was always "Will discuss." I was conflicted for years by that question. In fact, it wasn't until most states started regulating bounty hunters all over the country that this common question became something of a problem for me. I had to fight hard to get states to make exclusions in their laws about bounty hunting so that I was not inadvertently put out of the business with the proposed laws.

In 2008, I finally got my official license reinstated, which gave me permission to write bail anywhere and everywhere across the country. For the first time in eleven years, I was legitimately licensed by the state of Hawaii. I already had credibility as a bounty hunter, but receiving my license back gave me the respect from my peers, the state, and the legislative system that had finally righted the legal wrong that had been committed against me.

I know the United States government will never admit that they made a mistake in my extradition case with Mexico, because they never do. I've reconciled that fact in my mind because even though I've lost many a battle along the way, in the long run, I won the war. I wasn't extradited—I was allowed to stay in America, my home, my country that I love with all of my heart and soul, plus Luster is still in jail.

Having worked in and around the judicial system for most of my career, I'm used to the government being less than perfect. It's just a fact of life. I don't expect much from the lower courts because over the years I've learned that real decisions aren't made until you get to the higher courts. I've learned to expect the bureaucratic flimflam. I believe judges in the lower courts are prejudiced. They use their decisions to work their way up the judicial ladder. Judges in the higher courts have already been there, done that. They don't need to lie or impress people like Andrew Luster's mother or her high-priced lawyers. Like it or not, justice is political. The system doesn't like guys like me who are out there fighting for both truth *and* justice.

There's always been a little rift between local police and bounty hunters, especially this bounty hunter. Even though bounty hunting has been around for centuries, it has never really been considered a job. I can't stomach picking up a newspaper or hearing a story on the news about inexperienced vigilante wannabes breaking into someone's home and accidentally shooting or, worse, killing them. These unqualified amateurs are the guys that give bounty hunters a bad name. It takes years of experience to learn the business—not guns or guerrilla tactics. We are officers of the court, but that in no way makes us police officers. It's hard for many bounty hunters who are just starting out to grasp the difference.

Bounty hunters generally have more authority to arrest than local police, because defendants waive all of their constitutional rights when they sign their bail bond contract. They essentially agree to be arrested by the bail bond agent if they break the terms of that agreement. A bounty hunter can nab a fugitive in any state except Wisconsin, Illinois, Kentucky, and Oregon, because bounty hunting is illegal there. Me? I don't care about the state law in those four states. As far as I'm concerned, if I know one of my jumps is hiding out in any of those states, I'm going to get him.

When I was a young boy, there was a local police officer my family knew and who I really looked up to. He was the officer who came to our school to give speeches about safety and awareness. For whatever reason, he used my name a couple times during one of his speeches, which made me feel special in front of my classmates. At the time, I worked the safety patrol, helping the crossing guard do his duties before and after school. One day I decided to take my services to a busy intersection in the middle of town. I stood in the street and began to direct traffic. It wasn't long before the cops came to pick me up. They called my dad and told him he had to come take me home. I had a great time that day stopping traffic and giving directions to all the drivers. From that day on, I wanted to become a policeman.

Shortly after that incident, I heard the officer had been indicted for burglary. I was devastated when I heard the news because this was a man I admired. When I went to school, kids began teasing me that my "cop friend" was a no-good crook. After he pleaded guilty to his crimes, I began to see all cops as phonies and criminals. I felt that way until I got to prison.

Once I started interacting with the wardens and prison guards, I once again began to respect cops and authoritative guys in the system. I'll never forget one of the prison guards telling me that he lived in Huntsville prison too.

"No, you don't," I said. "You get to go home at night, hug your wife and kids, and I don't."

"Sometimes, but mostly I am here more than I'm home. Sometimes I get a home-cooked meal, but mostly I'm in the joint doing time with you."

I gave it some thought and realized he was right.

For the most part, the guys on the force love me and appreciate what I do. They even send me their service patches from the departments where they work, and I proudly display them behind the desk in my office. I have patches, badges, and pins from policemen and others who work criminal justice all over the world. I'm always so appreciative of their support. However, there are other cops who will never see me as anything more than a felon—and to them, I will always be on the other side of the law. They're threatened by what I do because my experience and skills help me bring in the fugitives that they simply cannot bring in themselves. Many officers think my success rate makes them look bad. I'm not out to upstage the police. My only goal is to get my man. But some of these cops still see me as the bad guy, while they're the good guys.

When I started bounty hunting, I was always trying to prove to the police that I was one of the good guys too. I wanted to be a cop or a United States marshal more than a bounty hunter, but the choices I'd made in the past made that impossible. I love cops and want to work with them because I know we are stronger unified than we are apart. I want their respect for what I do and bring to the table as a fellow member of law enforcement.

Whenever a cop shows up at a scene we're working, we fear what type of cop he is. Will he embrace us and work with us? Or will he make it difficult for me to do my job? Every time we make an arrest, we always risk a cop siding with the fugitive and not us.

This is especially disconcerting because most police officers don't know the laws that protect bounty hunters. Unlike the police, I can enter private property unannounced and without a warrant. I don't even have to read a fugitive their Miranda rights before making the arrest. Some states require bounty hunters to be licensed, while others only ask for bounty hunters to register with them. They refer to bounty hunters as peace officers, officers of the court, and people who aid government officials. Whatever it's called, bounty hunting is an essential element to effectively fighting crime.

But every time I'm out on a bust, I never know if the cops I come into contact with in the field are friend or foe. Not long ago, we were out making a bust when the police showed up at the house where we'd arrested our fugitive. One of the officers began questioning the homeowner, who told him we broke into her house. When the cop asked me if that was true, I told him, no.

The cop said, "I certainly hope that's true, Dog, because if it's not, you're all going to jail. Now, get out of here!"

"I will not. I've got proof we got permission and I'll use it if I have to." Of course, I was referring to my camera crew, who'd captured the entire bust on tape. It's generally not a great idea to offer up my footage as evidence, unless I really have to, because the police will confiscate all of it. Usually if I find myself in a position where that's my only option, I'll take the arrest and defend myself later. The fact is, I ultimately have to be responsible to uphold the law when I am out on a hunt because not only could I lose my job with A&E, I could also go to jail.

It really hurts my feelings that some cops see me as the enemy. I've got thirty-plus years in the field chasing down criminals. I've had experiences most cops will never have throughout their entire career. I'd love to share my techniques and information on chasing fugitives with the proper authorities so they can share in the knowledge I've acquired over the years. I respect the police and the service they provide. Whenever I see cops in a restaurant, I make it a point to pick up their check as a small gesture to let them know how I feel. I always tell the waitress not to tell them who picked up the tab, because I don't want the recognition. I just want to say thanks for all they do. Unless the police and bounty hunters learn to work together, fugitives can use the system to keep themselves from being caught. Cops and bounty hunters are on the same side of the law—they ought to join forces to serve and protect citizens from dangerous criminals on the run.

There have been all sorts of laws proposed to govern the field of bounty hunting, ranging from not allowing the use of real firearms to restricting our right to enter a private citizen's home. To be clear, bounty hunters are *not* vigilantes, executioners, or police officers. It isn't our responsibility to execute the sentence, but merely to pick up the fugitive and deliver them to the court. Because the laws vary from state to state, I think bounty hunting has become a business that now needs some kind of regulation to govern what we can and cannot do.

I'm disappointed that the National Association of Bounty Hunters has never asked me to speak at a function and has never asked me to become a member of their organization. I think I would bring a lot of clout to the table to help establish our profession as a viable and respectable field. The only time they tried to associate, or should I say disassociate, with me was after I was arrested in Mexico, when they were quick to point out that they would have never apprehended Luster like I did. Well, I guess we all know how that story ends. Even so, I would be honored to be a part of the association one day because I know our collective voice would bring the right type of attention to our chosen profession. Since I have become the very best in the field, I would be an ideal advocate to help mediate between the association and the government, to come up with laws that would effectively regulate the business while taking the needs of both parties into consideration. Although I am the poster boy for the profession, many bounty hunters think I am the very person ruining it. For all of those doubters, I have one thing to say: You're sadly mistaken.

The higher up the rank of an officer, the better we generally get along. The rookies trying to make a name for themselves loathe bounty hunters. Let's face it: I'm the guy out there *catching* criminals while some of these guys are still *chasing* them. This constant tension with my profession combined with a personal feud I wasn't aware of led to a surprise meeting set up with a Honolulu police major and Beth and me. Let's just say he wasn't a huge fan of mine. One thing is for sure. He is not sitting at home on Wednesday nights watching my show.

Beth and I have never been known for our promptness, so of course, we were twenty minutes late on the day of our big meeting. James Lindblad, my good friend and the number one bondsman in Hawaii, was also at the meeting, but of course he arrived on time. When we walked in, Lindblad was just coming out of the meeting room. He said the meeting was over before it began.

I figured I could smooth talk the major into hearing what we had to say, so we walked into his office anyway. He barely looked up from his desk when he said, "You're late. Meeting's over. Leave."

When I was selling Kirby vacuums back in the day, I never took no for an answer. If a farmer's wife told me she couldn't afford the machine, I talked to her until she realized she couldn't afford *not* to own one. So when the major informed me that our meeting was over before it began, I fell back on my vacuum salesman days.

"Listen, Major," I said. "I am really sorry we are late. The traffic here in Honolulu has gotten so bad. I mean, you know, you live here too." I looked him straight in the eyes so he could tell I was being sincere. I thought he was going to eat right through one of his pencils as we tried to apologize for our tardiness, and then I did the only thing I could think to do: I introduced him to Beth, saying, "This is my wife." He didn't have the courtesy to acknowledge her. He couldn't have cared less that we were there to talk. It was pretty obvious the major wasn't going to budge. He didn't want to hear a word we had to say.

I was there to discuss an administrative procedure that states that as a bounty hunter, if a prisoner is hurt, I am supposed to take him to the hospital first, obtain a release when he is deemed okay by the attending physician, and then bring him to the local jail. I had a problem with the details of this procedure. If the prisoner is wanted, I'm not a doctor, so if he were injured, I wouldn't know how serious it was, but I don't want to walk him down to the hospital, where he could run or, worse, harm other civilians, and I don't carry a gun, so I wouldn't be able to deter him with a firearm if he got out of hand.

Beth and I tried to explain all of this to the major, but he was too angry to listen. Our words were falling on very deaf ears. Beth began to get a little heated at his lack of response. She pointed out that the police carry guns and are able to protect themselves against the unpredictable behavior of a prisoner. We don't and aren't. We simply find them and bring them in to the station where they become the police's responsibility.

Sure, I have been known to leave a prisoner cuffed to a post outside the hospital or police station so he's someone else's problem. But I walk away knowing where my fugitive is and where he will be. I get paid either way.

Now, these tactics don't make the cops all that happy, but to be fair, I don't practice them often enough for it to be a problem. But I have done this sort of thing a couple of times where it stirred a rumor or two that I do this for the sake of television. Not true. Everything on my television show actually happens just as you see it at home. It's not staged, scripted, or planned in advance. My show is true *reality* television. What you see is what you get.

When Beth's tone changed from sharp to sultry in our meeting, the major began to get even madder. My wife knows how to turn on the charm and use her femininity to the max. Guys like the major hate that in a woman. There are some men who don't like strong women, and he was one of them. Of course, Beth was well aware of this, so she used her strengths to prey on his weaknesses.

She pointed to the major and said, "Look at this guy. He's been giving me the stink eye for this whole meeting. Do you think he likes us when we bring prisoners in they can't find? We have the right to arrest a fugitive just like you do. This guy gives us nothing but problems for doing the job he can't."

If looks could kill, then Beth would have been a goner.

The major shot back a quick retort. "Yeah, you use your badges like you're cops, but you're not. What about that guy you nabbed at the airport a couple of weeks ago? You had no right to arrest him."

"Like hell I didn't," I shot back. "The guy was wanted on twelve charges of sexual assault. He was bonded for one crime or another for the past three years and was planning to leave before he got permission from the court. I couldn't take that risk, so I grabbed him before he fled. Would you prefer him safely locked up or out on the streets where he could commit more crimes?"

"How did you know he was about to run?" the major asked. "C'mon, it was a setup for your show, right?"

"No!" I told him. "A friend called to say he'd bought a plane ticket to Florida and was leaving on a flight the very next day."

I got to the airport just as the guy was standing in line

to go through security. When he saw me, all he could say was, "Sorry, Dog." He called his wife on the way to jail and said, "The Dog got me." I booked that son of a bitch with his plane ticket and boarding pass in his pocket.

The major was still dissatisfied with how things were going. Just as Beth and I were about to leave, he called me over. He started questioning me about all the places I traveled to around the world for my job. I thought this was my one chance to show the major I was a good guy. I wanted to break the ice and make him like me. Boy, did I have him all wrong.

"You know, Duane," the major started out, sounding a little like Barney Fife as he slowly began to make his point, "there are a lot of murders, rapes, and other types of crimes that happen all over the globe. Probably in places you might go or have already been to."

I still wasn't clear on where he was heading with what he was insinuating.

And then he said, "Are you aware of the law here in Hawaii that all felons have to have their DNA checked? I think we ought to be able to do it right now in the station while I've got you here instead of one of my guys having to pull you over and make a scene in public. You wouldn't want another scandal to make the evening news, would you?"

I was flabbergasted. "I've got nothing to hide. Bring it on. Go get your swab."

The major sent one of his sergeants to get the DNA kit. He must have run as fast as Carl Lewis because he was back in the room within sixty seconds or so.

I walked back toward Beth, who still wasn't sure what was going on. She was upset, but we both knew I had to let them swab me because it is state law. The major could run every possible DNA match there was, but he wasn't going to find anything, because I had nothing to hide. I suppose in a far-fetched world, it was possible that I was a "secret serial killer," because people surely have died in all of the places I have been. Anything is possible. Even so, the major didn't have to conduct himself like that. It was the height of disrespect and unprofessional behavior and everything I stand against when dealing with fugitives. I would never have acted that way—not even on my worst day in the field.

Not long after that meeting, I bumped into that same major again. I was delivering a prisoner to the local police station in Honolulu after a bust, when he came over and told me to move my car.

"You're parked in police parking," he said.

I tried to explain that I had a prisoner in custody and was entitled to use the spot.

"No, you're not. You're lay public, now move your vehicle before I have you towed!"

I was quick to point out that under *Taylor versus Taintor*, bounty hunters are acting in the capacity of the sheriff at the time of making an arrest. Despite everything I said and the case I cited, he still wasn't buying my explanation. The major went back into the building to look up the law and check the accuracy of what I was saying. In the meantime, I walked my prisoner to the door of the station and handed him over like I always do. When I came back outside, the major was standing in front of my car with a smug look on his face and his arms folded.

"Bounty Hunter!"

"Yes, sir?" I said.

"Move your car, civilian. You're in *my* spot now."

At first I thought he was just being a punk, but then he gave me the Hawaiian shaka sign, waving his thumb and pinky finger in the air to let me know everything was all right. It was a small victory knowing I had won the major over. Perhaps he wasn't expecting me to be cooperative when he called me into his office that day, or maybe he actually believed he would bust me for something after he swabbed me. Whatever his motivation was, he seemed to have a change of heart that day in the parking lot. It always makes me feel good when cops embrace the service we provide, but this time it was especially satisfying because this guy had been on my back for so long trying to trip me up. Thankfully, that day he was only yanking my chain. I looked over and said, "Thank you, sir. See you again, not too soon!" I smiled, got into my car, and drove away.

15

Jail is a wake-up call for most people. But once they're awake, what do you do with them? Having been in the streets for the better part of my life, I understand the inner workings of the criminal mind. I often think that the justice system should consult with reformed criminals to help make better laws to protect the citizens the system is supposed to save from harm.

The federal justice system is broken. It hemorrhages money, when in fact it could be generating billions of dollars in revenue. Right now, the only people making money off of crime are the criminals and the lawyers who represent them. The justice system that fights against the criminal loses money.

When a criminal runs, I know I am going to make some money, but I have to work damn hard and will earn it. As a bondsman, my money is in jeopardy if a client decides to run and I'm not able to catch him and bring him in. I've always claimed that my motivation to make sure every single person I bond shows up in court is to prevent the loss of my own money, something I don't like very much. I have to capture that person if they run, and do it within thirty days or I won't be able to put food on the table for my kids. That drives me to make sure I'm on top of the people I bond out.

And though it's tue that I don't like to lose money, between you and me, the real reason I'm in the game is for the chase. When someone runs, it's the best part of my job to know that I will chase them to the gates of hell if I have to.

Police don't have the same motivation as a bondsman. They don't have the deadlines or financial risk we have. They have every resource imaginable available to them, yet criminals run free. Our police agencies are terribly underpaid for the service they provide. Their departments are understaffed and slammed with more cases than they can handle. Because of that, the private sector has to be brought in to subsidize the workload.

If you have a skunk in your house or a stray dog gets loose, you can call your local humane society, which is supposed to come to your home and take care of these problems for you, courtesy of the taxpayers. Most people don't take advantage of this service because they usually end up calling an exterminator and paying for the removal out of their own pocket.

A bondsman works much in the same way as an exterminator. He is the person in the private sector who does a better and more efficient job than the state-run public sector agency. The criminal justice system ought to be designed to work the same way a bondsman does—to make a profit off of criminals. They're the house and the criminals are the players. The house should always win, but in the case of crime, the house continues to lose, and lose big.

Most bail bonds businesses are family-run operations that have been around for two, three, and even four generations. That connection makes it hard to walk away from the business, but there are also two years' worth of liabilities that have to be squared away before you can shut your doors. It makes good fiscal sense to keep the business in the family so that the next generation can take over. The good news is that most bondsmen get to learn the system from the ground up because they have been in the business from an early age, which means they understand how the system works inside and out.

I'm a criminal justice expert. If I could, I'd like to be appointed the czar of criminal justice by the Obama administration, so I could help create new laws and implement a better, more efficient system. Because of my years of experience in chasing criminals, I know what deters crime, which punishments work and which ones don't. If I had the opportunity, I would love to work with a dream team of the experts I've met and worked with over the years, including friends from the FBI, local law enforcement, and people I respect and admire in other government agencies. Together, we could really make some positive changes in the system where the current programs simply don't work.

Most states in our country have implemented a policy for certain offenders called "pretrial release." The program is designed as an alternative to incarceration for all defendants who are initially unable to post bail. Although the program is meant for defendants accused of minor crimes, who pose no immediate threat of flight or danger to the community, many jurisdictions offer the program to criminals who don't fit those criteria. It's a state-run program funded by the federal government. It's designed to relieve overcrowding and alleviate court burden for judges who have severely overbooked dockets.

The pretrial service interviews defendants so they can decide if that person is either worthy of a free bond or what is often referred to as a PR, a personal recognizance bond. In some states these are also called OR bonds, or own recognizance bonds. Any way you slice it, these are free bonds provided to defendants by the government, which in my opinion are nothing more than "get out of jail free" cards.

The program works by having a pretrial officer prepare a report based on the officer's limited interview with the defendant, which ostensibly helps the court make an informed decision about whether that person should be released or detained. If that person is released, the pretrial officer becomes responsible for supervising them, assisting in complying with the conditions of their release, monitoring that compliance, providing necessary support services, and informing the court of any and all violations of those conditions.

Unlike bondsmen, pretrial officers don't need a license to do what they do. They don't have to take a state-mandated exam like the one that bondsmen are required to pass. They get very little instruction beyond some administrative training and can't really assess whether a defendant is a true threat to society or if they'll ever show for their court appearance. The state doesn't employ bounty hunters and there aren't any who work for pretrial services. That job ends up falling on people who are called cops, which means that they'll issue another warrant if the defendant bolts, but only after that guy's file has sat on someone's desk for three to six weeks before it gets entered into the system.

The percentage of defendants who run from the pretrial system exceeds 70 percent, a staggering figure when you consider that many of these are hardened criminals who have been put back out on the street because the program believed they weren't risks. To put that into perspective for you, the percentage of my defendants who run hovers around 17 percent. Of those who are foolish enough to try to get away, I have brought 98 percent back to face their crimes. I'm still looking for the other 2 percent, and you and I both know who you are!

Unfortunately, none of our criminal justice departments can allocate the funds to send out a task force to reclaim all of these fugitives from the pretrial program, so they do the best they can, and don't end up achieving much. Forty to 60 percent of all defendants will be released under the pretrial release program, which means that the state is letting these criminals back onto the street as fast as the cops are picking them up. The defendant doesn't care if he shows up in court or not, because there is nothing to lose if he fails to appear. No one has the deed to his momma's house or the pink slip to his daddy's car, and he certainly isn't afraid that the Dog will come looking for him. There are no repercussions for anyone—not the defendant or the pretrial officer, who doesn't worry she'll lose her car or home if her client runs, because she has no personal stake in it. It's basically a system of "it's not my problem," because there is no deterrent. This inefficiency makes the pretrial service one of the most ridiculous drains on today's judicial system.

Regardless of the state's opinion, a bail bondsman offers a tremendous system of checks and balances. Because we secure bonds with a family member, a car, a house, or something of equal or greater value to the bond, we are also providing a "get out of jail card," but not for free. We will only get you out if you make a promise that you can financially back yourself up. If you can't pay for the crime, then you will do the time. Period. I personally see to that.

And if you can't pay the bail and act in a responsible way, I will take your momma's house and see to it that you can't get out of jail to commit more crimes. Repeat offenders should never be offered pretrial services—ever. The only people I believe qualify for this type of program and to be released on a personal release bond are first-time offenders who have never been in trouble before, have no criminal history, have committed a nonviolent crime, and have no reason to be looked at further than the jailhouse interview.

Illinois, Kentucky, Wisconsin, and Oregon are the only states in the union that do not allow bail bonds—they've actually outlawed them. They are the 10-percent-to-the-state states, meaning a defendant puts up 10 percent of their bail to the state instead of a bondsman. They only use the pretrial release program, which in my opinion has been absolutely disastrous for them. Thousands of victims will never get closure on their cases because their assailants have disappeared. In Chicago alone there are thousands of open cases on the books because the defendants cannot be found and they don't convict in absentia. It has to be terribly frustrating for anyone trying to bring a fugitive to justice in those states, because the pretrial release program works against them.

Bounty hunting has been outlawed in Oregon since 1974, but recently the state has seen the error of its ways and is now trying to bring bail bonds and bounty hunting back. The bill has already cleared the House and is set to head to the full Senate for consideration. Senator Jason Atkinson actually said, "In the faint hope of meeting Dog the Bounty Hunter, I will vote yes."

The state government in Oregon has recognized how much money it has wasted because it can't bring fugitives to justice. If it allows bounty hunting, I can find these guys so that their cases can go forward and the victims can be vindicated. Case closed. The state gets the revenue from the fines and crime goes down. I would volunteer my time to help any one of these states get its system in order so it could start making money on crime instead of losing it.

It used to be that the prison system was about incarceration *and* rehabilitation. Unfortunately, there's only incarceration these days. There are no Tony Robbins courses in jail to help the inmates become rehabilitated, functioning members of society when they get out. We aren't educating the inmates, teaching them how to read and write, or making sure they have a skill set when they're released, so we aren't preparing them to reenter a world where they have to make decisions all on their own. Their lack of decision-making skills is what landed most of these guys in the clink in the first place, so why on earth would we not offer them some type of program to help teach these inmates the skills they'll need to not only survive but thrive on the outside?

We break them down but never build them back up. There are some people who think we shouldn't offer prisoners anything—that they made their bed and now they have to lie in it. But to the prisoners I say, "Who cares what *they* think? You committed a crime, but you don't get to lie around doing nothing." That's nothing more than free, lazy living. When I was in Huntsville, I spent my days picking cotton in one-hundred-degree heat and humidity. I'm certain that kind of hard-labor punishment works, because I never want to go back there again. If prison weren't so easy, people wouldn't be content with going there. For too many, prison is a free ride on easy street. Those guys get an all-expense-paid vacation, and guess who's footing the bill? Me and you! In the meantime, your taxes go through the roof, your insurance rates are sky-high, and your identity is put at risk while the guy who stole your car stereo or used your Social Security number lies around in a cell for six months trying to figure out who he's going to harm next.

Jail should be reserved for repeat offenders, those people who can't get it through their heads that they cannot continue to commit crime. For first-time offenders, I've found that money is a great deterrent. Anytime a criminal has to go into his pocket and come up with cash, it's a big "ouch." Money hurts those guys the worst. In this economy and in today's society, we need to start looking for other means of punishment without it actually costing taxpayers money or becoming a burden to society.

Take someone like Leona Helmsley or Martha Stewart—two obviously brilliant women who had no prior criminal history. Their attitude and demeanor were why they ended up in jail. Like them or not, that's not supposed to come into play when a judge is making his or her decision on sentencing. Both women were made to pay back the money they owed, suffered tremendous public humiliation, and were still sentenced to jail, where taxpayers had to pay for their incarceration. I don't agree with that outcome. I think they should have been placed in welfare situations, sent to inner-city public recreation centers and schools, where they could have influenced the lives of those who were less fortunate. They could have had to spend their time showing people how to enter the workforce, helping them get back on their feet, and teaching them how to cook and sew. Surely their skills could have been taught to the underprivileged, easing the stress on our state budgets in the process. That would have allowed them to do something good for society without costing the state any additional money. And if the state still felt compelled to incarcerate these women, they should have been required to pay for their stay. They had the means and ability to subsidize the cost of their imprisonment. This type of alternative sentencing would have had a far greater impact on these women, because it would have knocked the chip off their shoulders. Instead, Martha came out of prison thinner, healthier than she had been in years, and with a television deal to do *The Apprentice*, while Leona Helmsley remained the Queen of Mean for the rest of her days, never showing remorse for what she had done to cheat the system.

There should be a government task force that gathers information from all of the white-collar criminals in the system, so we can learn from them how to better prevent these crimes in the future. Someone like Bernard Madoff will never be able to make up for the horrible crimes he committed against thousands of innocent people, but we certainly could tap into his brilliance to find flaws in the system so that no one will ever be able to get away with what he did again. He could work with a team of experts, the SEC, or the Federal Reserve to show them where the system is flawed and how he was able to get away with his crimes for so long. The government should make Bernard Madoff work with the IRS or financial institutions that are in the red, day in and day out, for the rest of his life. A guy like that knows the financial system inside and out. Force him to share his knowledge and expertise so that the government might have a shot at balancing the budget or shifting the economic downturn. All of this at no cost to the government because the criminals would have to provide it for free as part of their sentence. No vacations, no days off—Madoff would have to do nothing but hard work with a purpose for the rest of his life.

If we can somehow accept these criminals for what they've done and use them where they fit in to help improve our way of life, we could avoid letting them lie around in prison, where they do nothing and become an absolute drain on our economy. We're paying them to be there. We pay for their cell, their air-conditioning, their meals, the staffing of the prison, the sheriff, and round-the-clock babysitting by every guard on duty twenty-four hours a day, seven days a week. And if you are going to put these people in jail, bill them! Make them pay the two hundred dollars or more a day it costs to keep them incarcerated.

People often ask me if our judicial system can be improved. The answer is *absolutely*. The system can be fixed by involving more citizens and installing a harsher range of fines. For example, if a guy steals a car, we as taxpaying citizens will pay somewhere in the neighborhood of two hundred dollars or more a day to keep him in jail. In general, that thief will get probation for a first offense, putting him right back on the streets, where the likelihood is he will steal another car—or do something even worse. If he gets caught, he's going back to jail for three to five years. If it costs two hundred dollars a day to keep that criminal in the system, it will cost you, as a taxpayer, *$365,000* to keep that *one* offender in prison for five years. That's a lot of money!

Here's my idea on how we can fix the system for this type of crime. Hit them in the pocketbook. You fine the guy for every offense. The first time he is caught, it'll cost him five grand or he will get five years. I'm pretty sure that someone will come up with that money to make sure their son, brother, boyfriend, or husband isn't put away for five years. The next offense will cost double—ten thousand dollars or six years in prison. Again, someone has to come up with that money or he's going away for a long time. Every offense he commits will cost him more and more money, until the financial benefit of crime just doesn't make sense. If he boosts a car that he knows he can only get a few thousand dollars for, he's going to think twice if it is going to cost him triple that if he gets caught. Add up the cost of the lawyer, court fees, and fines and you're talking about a substantial amount of money.

The more serious the crime, the steeper the fine. Armed robbery would cost the perpetrator a lot more than petty theft. If you hurt someone while committing your crime, there's no option of a fine, just mandatory jail time.

If you're a drug dealer, that eight-hundred-dollar bag of heroin will cost you eight thousand dollars in fines.

I've made a lot of money on the criminal justice system over the years. Every time someone jumps, I laugh because I'm going after the reward, which I always get. If you fine people for their crimes, sooner or later they will give up their ways because they won't be able to keep coming up with the cash to get out of their situation. If they keep committing crime, they're going away for a very long time. Believe me, they'll get into a different line of work before they'll choose to do hard time.

Ever since my television show hit the air, jumps from my bail bond business have gone down because no one wants to be chased by me and a camera crew. The courts have seen a significant rise in attendance and I have seen a significant decrease in "failures to appear." Getting busted on television is humiliating for both the perpetrator and his family, but it sure is a great way to remedy crime. Beth calls this method "shame therapy."

Most everyone has seen *Dateline NBC*, the television news program where Chris Hansen traps online predators coming to the home of underage girls. When the suspects meet Chris Hansen and realize they're going to be on television for their crime, they are humiliated, embarrassed, and uncomfortable for their decision to be there. This type of bust is effective and really works as a deterrent.

If you want to catch a criminal, set up cameras on the streets. Start taping the comings and goings of suspected drug dealers' homes. They'll either move their entire operation in twenty-four hours—something most won't do because they don't know how—or blam, they're out of business. The cost of video surveillance is minuscule compared to the man hours it would take to set up a stakeout.

Another way to lower crime is to get officers out of their patrol cars and onto the streets. Policemen ride around in their patrol cars, protecting themselves from the very people they're out looking for. If officers began walking their beat, they'd have a much better sense of what's really happening in those neighborhoods. They need to knock on doors and talk to the people who live in these cities and streets that they protect and serve, to hear firsthand accounts of who, what, and where they need to be searching. They need to meet the citizens who pay their salaries and hear their concerns. Then, and only then, can they be more effective and successful in reducing crime in those areas.

I believe so strongly in my ideas to cut crime that I'd be willing to stake my badge on the results. If these ideas were implemented, I would expect to see a 50 percent or more drop in crime over a period of ninety days. I hope to someday have the opportunity to bring these ideas to fruition, to test my theories and to help finally bring more peace to our communities.

INTERMISSION TWO

CHAPTER 16

Your momma sure does have some sexy panties," I said into the phone. One of my favorite tactics to bring in a fugitive is to slam him with a bunch of phone calls in a row, so he knows I'm on his trail and to get him to reveal some valuable information. Most times they fall right into my trap.

"What did you say about my momma?" The voice on the other end of the line was that of a fugitive I'd been hunting for days. I was taunting him with all sorts of comments about his momma's lingerie.

"I went through her panty drawer and touched her bras too. Man, you have a fine momma," I told him.

And then I hung up. Click. For whatever reason, the guy kept calling me back. And when he did, I kept taunting him, hoping I would anger him enough so he'd call me back again, mess up, and reveal where he was hiding. I'd hit his mom's house earlier in the day, but he wasn't there. Even though we didn't grab him, I was positive he'd hear we were out looking for him. Every time he called me back, he blocked the number he was calling from so I wouldn't be able to see it on my caller ID. Whenever I saw private number flash on the screen of my phone, I'd pick it up and say something vulgar just to get his attention.

"Your sister is almost as hot as your momma. I'd love to see her naked."

Click.

And the next time he called I said, "Is this smell Febreze or at ease?"

Click.

My phone rang again, private number.

"Hello?"

"What did you say about my momma's panties?" the guy yelled on the other end of the line. He was getting angrier with each call. "If you ever go to my mom's house again, I'm going to kill you!"

"Oh yeah? Well, I'm on my way back there right now," I said. "Your momma's pink panties were really nice. And they smell good too. I am going back to see them again. Maybe she'll be wearing them this time . . ."

Click.

Eventually, I knew he'd trip up, forget to block his number, and blam, he'd be mine. Sure enough, the very next call, his number popped up on my screen. He was raging mad. He'd also found out I had been to several homes of friends and family looking for him. When I answered this time, I pulled a little reverse psychology.

"Listen, you can yell all you want, I don't have time to talk to you right now. I'll call you back." Beth was in the background yelling, "We got the number! Hang up! Hang up!"

So I hung up on him. Click!

I could practically see the confused look on his face when I hung up the phone. The next time he called, his number was blocked again. I wasn't sure he ever realized he'd already given us the break we'd been waiting for. Once I had the telephone number from the hard line he was calling from, I could pinpoint his location.

It wasn't unusual for me to taunt skips like this. Whenever I talked about their moms or sisters, I knew I'd get their blood boiling and it would be just a matter of time before they made a fatal mistake allowing me to make my capture. I've gotten really good at tripping the psychological triggers of fugitives over the years. The more personal I get, the easier they are to find. And whenever I can't get to them, I know I've got the person in my posse who can—my Beth.

I started bringing Beth on bounty hunts a couple of years after I met her in 1988, mostly because I would come home and tell her stories that she wouldn't believe. I said she ought to start coming with me to see what happens with her own two eyes. She was a real natural our first time out. Over the years, she has become an integral part of what I do, although her presence has forced me to change the way I work. I used to be able to use my charm and good looks to get information out of people, especially women. My sweet talk was my secret weapon. These days, whenever I try to go there, Beth is right up in my business making sure I don't. That's when I call in one of the boys and tell them to go talk to the woman for a while. I'll call him over, give him a wink, and send him into the lion's den until we get what we need. Duane Lee will go right over, no hesitation. If we send Leland in, Beth will tell him to let down his ponytail because there aren't a lot of women out there who don't think that boy doesn't look good with his long loose hair. And let's be clear, what's good for the goose is also good for the gander. If Beth tries to point her "double-barreled" so-called shotguns in someone's face, I tell her to cover those things up!

People sometimes think of Beth and me as the Bicker-sons, but there's nothing more meaningful to me than being in a relationship with a strong woman who believes in me, has a mind of her own, and totally understands everything about my life. Even if it doesn't always look like it, we're usually working toward the same goal.

It's true that I debate with her a lot and let her win those fights . . . most of the time. Even when I know she's wrong, I always try to let her think she's right, and to be totally fair, she usually is. Even so, I always try to be a gentleman with her. In the field, however, I'm completely different with Beth. She's no longer my wife—she's a crucial member of the team. Sometimes she gets upset with me when I get stern or order her to do something out on the road, but she knows I still love her. More important than that, Beth is often the reason we get our guy. I wouldn't be able to do it without her by my side.

The guy I was taunting on the phone was a client of Mary Ellen's, and Mary Ellen didn't like to lose money, so not finding him wasn't an option. Beth looked up the corresponding address to the phone number he had called from and discovered that it was a rural farmhouse in Brighton, a town just outside of Denver. We called the Brighton police to let them know we were on our way. They said they'd give us thirty minutes to get to the farm or they'd make the bust themselves. Thirty minutes was a push for us to get geared up, make the drive, and get our guy.

Beth and I jumped into my car and floored it, driving ninety-five miles per hour in order to get there on time. I was hoping and praying we didn't get pulled over on our way down. Beth, who is usually the driver, was on the floorboard the entire time, scared we were going to crash.

When we got to the property, we saw that the farm was set way back off the road. There were fields as far as the eye could see. If someone was looking out the window of the house, they'd spot us coming up the driveway because of the dust and debris our car kicked up on the dry dirt road. There was no way we could ever sneak up on them without being noticed.

By the time we arrived, the cops were already searching the trailer we suspected our fugitive to be hiding in. We waited outside until they finished up and came out empty-handed.

"Now let Dog look for him," Beth said to one of the cops.

When the cops said they couldn't find the fugitive, something inside me knew he was hiding inside the trailer. This was where he was at when his last phone call came in less than an hour earlier. Plus, it had been raining for two days and nights. There were twenty-five yards of pure mud surrounding the trailer. I took a flashlight and began circling the perimeter. I was looking for fresh footprints or some other clue that would lead me to him. There wasn't a single footprint, so I knew he had to be in there.

"He's in there. I know he is," I told the commanding officer. Beth and I went back inside the trailer with a couple of the cops on the scene. Most trailers are long and narrow. There's usually a bathroom in the center, a living room and kitchen on one side, and a bedroom on the other. When we walked through, I opened every door possible until I got to one that was locked.

"Why is this door locked?" I asked the girl who was living there. I didn't know if she was our fugitive's old lady, a relative, or a friend. It didn't matter to me. I was positive she was hiding our guy.

"I know he's in here, honey. Tell me why this door is locked."

"It's not locked, Dog. It's just stuck," she said. "I can't get it to open."

"Look. I know he's here. So let me tell you how this is going to go down. If I find him behind this door and he shoots at me or he's with one of your babies, I'm calling Social Services and they'll come take them away, got it?" I threatened the woman right in front of the cops.

"C'mon, Dog. Let's go. He's not here," one of the cops said as they all stepped out of the trailer.

And then the girl turned to Beth and asked, "Can I get my baby out of the room before you search it?"

"Absolutely, of course you can," Beth sweetly replied. If a mother asks if she can get her baby before we search a place, we know our guy's in there. Beth and I gave each other "the look," which is a particular exchange of glances that we call our "Bonnie and Clyde" look. Our eyes grow wide and we don't have to speak a word—we just know what's coming next.

No sooner did the girl have the baby in her arms than I was right there behind her searching the room. As I knelt down to look under the bed, I saw the seam of an old pair of jeans through the slat of the closet door.

"Either those are really dirty jeans and they're standing up all by themselves or we've got a real mofo hiding in the closet! FREEZE!" I yelled.

When they heard the commotion, the cops came rushing back into the room. I looked up at the three stooges standing there and said, "We got him."

Beth walked over to the sheriff, pointed her forefinger right at me, and said, "He got him!"

In the meantime, our guy refused to come out of the trailer. He began whining like a girl. "You can't let him take me. I don't want to be caught by Dog. He's going to kill me! Help! Somebody, anybody!" He was swinging his arms and kicking his feet, doing everything he could to avoid being taken by the Dog. I finally put him in a headlock and carried him out under my arm like a football.

The cops were embarrassed by their inability to find the guy. There was no way they'd ever tell the truth in their report. I handed the cuffed prisoner over to the local deputy, who put him in the back of a patrol car. One of the cops told me the guy we caught was a member of the Aryan Nations. Beth and I were stunned, because he was being such a sissy. Being stuffed into the back of a cruiser made the guy even more irate than he already was. He began calling me names, saying I was a half-breed mofo and that the Brotherhood was out to kill me. I didn't pay much attention.

When you're cuffed with your hands behind your back, the only thing you can do is move your upper body around. Suddenly, the guy started banging his head against the Plexiglas shield between the front and back seats of the police car. He hit his head so hard that he busted it open. No one did a thing except let the poor bastard bleed in the backseat.

Every now and again, I caught a glimpse of Beth, who was standing next to the patrol car and had balanced her flashlight in her cleavage, shining the bright light right in his eyes. "You're a punk-ass jerk!" she'd hiss, and then whenever the cops strolled by, she'd quickly turn her flashlight in the opposite direction, and look around, whistling. When they'd turn around again, she'd shine that light right back in his face. Eventually, an officer caught her in the act.

"Ma'am," he said. "You have your light in the prisoner's eyes. Would you kindly turn it off?"

Beth acted as though she didn't realize what she had been doing. "Oh really?" she asked innocently. She removed the flashlight and began spinning it like a baton between her fingers.

The prisoner kept yelling at Beth, "At least Dog didn't get me! Ha ha!"

"Whatever," Beth fired back. "Dog got you. He's just not taking you in. Either way you're going to jail right now in care of the Dog—signed, sealed, and delivered!"

After that capture, I went through about a year or so of guys on the run getting caught by the cops and telling them, "Thank God you got me, because I didn't want to get brought in by Dog." For whatever reason, they feared being caught by me more than the police. I never understood it because I'm the guy who will buy you a Coke, give you a smoke, and let you call your old lady or momma before taking you in. Their logic never made any sense to me.

A lot of criminals like to brag they're the one that got away from the Dog. Let me tell you something about that. No one gets away from me. Not now—not ever. In an ironic twist, a few years ago my brother Mike was in jail. He called to tell me about a guy I put in the joint who loaned him a couple of cigarettes.

"Is he mad at you because I popped him?" I asked.

Mike quickly shot back, "No! He really likes me. And everyone in here loves this guy."

"Why is that?" I was curious to know the reason.

"Because you put him in here," Mike answered. "The guys you capture, Dog, they're the coolest cats in jail. They've got bragging rights no one else has. It took the Dog to capture and put him in this hellhole and not some cop."

That was the first time it had ever occurred to me that it was prestigious to be caught by the Dog.

Our conversation got me thinking about what it would be like if I someday ran for sheriff. I'd like to find some small town that has criminals running amok. I'd be just like Sheriff Buford Pusser in *Walking Tall*, doing whatever was needed to whip that town back into shape. I'd be incorruptible and intolerant of crime, while cleaning up the streets and making the town a safer place to live.

Whenever I go to small towns or big cities, I go without fear. Whether it's Medicine Hat, Canada, with a population of fifty thousand; south central Los Angeles; or Harlem, New York—I'm not afraid to get in the trenches and meet the people in troubled places and try to help them see there's a better way.

While I was up in Canada in 2008 doing an appearance in Medicine Hat, some of the local police officers began telling me of a particularly bad area of town they named the "needle district." The officers said they didn't like to go into that area of town because the hookers and junkies were known to stick you with their dirty old needles. They asked my opinion on how to clean up the district.

"You want my thoughts, fellas? All right. Here's what I think you need to do. First, you've got to start driving through the streets. Then, you've got to get out of your patrol cars. If someone tries to stab you with a needle, break their arm. Take your billy club out of the holster, walk down the street, and use it if you have to. It's as simple as that." When you go to dangerous areas with no fear of law enforcement, you have to believe you're Superman. That fearless attitude is how I face every risky situation I'm in on a daily basis.

Bounty hunting has led me to some of the most dangerous places in the country. Although I may be unsure of my surroundings from time to time, as I search a violent neighborhood, crowded street, or dark back alley, I can never let doubt or fear creep into my mind. If I do, I know I'm a goner. I have to have supreme confidence in my ability to track a fugitive down no matter where I am. That's not to say I take any environment for granted. On the contrary, my head has to be on a swivel at all times, no matter what. But I never limit any hunt simply because a fugitive has run off and hidden in a bad area. As everyone already knows, I will go to the far ends of the earth to catch my man.

When I was twenty-five years old, I found myself hunting for a fugitive named Lupe in Compton, California. Back in the day, this was an area white boys didn't hang around if they wanted to live. I took a cab from Los Angeles International Airport to the 'hood, armed with forty copies of Lupe's mug shot. I started passing out the papers like I was the Pied Piper. Within twenty minutes I had fifteen kids behind me walking around looking for Lupe. I caught a glimpse of my guy just as he was climbing out the second-story window of his apartment building.

I cupped my hands around the sides of my mouth and screamed up, "Freeze! Don't you move! This whole place is surrounded. Come out the side door right now or I'm coming up there to get you." I looked around as if I motioned to someone and shouted, "It's OK, Lieutenant. Stand down. Don't shoot." Of course, there were no cops, but Lupe didn't know that. Within minutes, he surrendered and I got my man.

The police actually pulled up just as I was leaving.

"Hey, buddy, do you have any paperwork to take this man into custody?" one of the officers asked.

"I sure do. It's right here," I answered, handing over all of the documentation they needed to let us go. The officer looked at the papers and then glanced at me over the top of his silver aviator glasses. "Do you know where you're at?" he asked.

"Yes, of course. I'm in Compton." I wasn't sure if it was a trick question or not, so I decided to be straight in my answer and not mouth off.

"If you were smart, you would get your ass out of here . . . NOW!"

I turned to the officer to make sure it was safe for me to leave with the prisoner and said, "Can I go?"

"Go? You ought to run. Do you know how lucky you are to be alive? Take your guy and don't ever come back to this neighborhood again." The officer handed my paperwork back to me and pointed for me to beat it.

As I was driving away, a carload of Crips stopped me. I got out of my car and asked if they knew the guy I was bringing in. Most of them did.

"Do you know what this bastard is wanted for? He's a damned child molester. I hate anyone who commits crimes against babies!"

All of the guys started in on Lupe in the backseat of the car, taunting and making fun of him.

"Hey, Lupe, looks like you're going away for a while, homie," one of them said.

"And he's worth ten thousand to me for bringing him in," I told them.

Woops. I quickly realized I probably shouldn't have said that to a bunch of gangbangers. I fumbled for a moment and said, "I don't have the money on me. I need to turn him in first, so don't get any ideas, boys."

I flashed them a smile and we all had a good laugh. From the moment I started my career as a bounty hunter, I quickly realized I had more friends in the criminal realm than anywhere else. There are more people who love me there than hate me. That's a good place to be in my line of work.

Throughout the years, I've routinely found myself in neighborhoods I probably don't "belong in," at least not without chasing a fugitive. When I was in New York City for the Martin Luther King CORE dinner, in early 2008, I decided I wanted to take a ride up to Harlem one afternoon to check it out. I had never been there before, but I felt a pull to make a visit on that particular trip. My usual driver in New York hesitantly asked if I was sure I wanted to take the drive to that part of Manhattan. Considering we were still dealing with the fallout from the *National Enquirer* tapes, he thought it wouldn't be such a good idea to travel through a predominately black neighborhood. Despite his concern, I emphatically said, "Yes!"

On our way up to Harlem, I asked the driver, "Have I ever told you about my rodeo days?"

"No, Dog," he said.

When I was twenty-two years old, I rode bucking broncos at a farm in Pampa, Texas. I'd never ridden wild horses before, but I knew I could do it. The trainer told me he'd give me seventy dollars for every horse I could tame. It took me two or three days to break the horses I rode, but I did it with ease

and comfort. I got so good at it I decided to enter a local rodeo and try my hat at being a real cowboy.

I showed up with my long hair and biker boots on while
the other rodeo riders had their hair cut short and wore tra-
ditional gear. I thought that my extra tall cowboy hat would
help me fit in, but it didn't. It mostly made me stand out. One
of the guys turned to me and said, "What are you doing here,
man? You don't belong here. This is not your world, biker boy.
You're not one of us. Why don't you get the hell out of here?"

I knew I had the talent to be one of the best rodeo cowboys in the world. I didn't understand why this guy was telling
me to get out before I even had the chance to prove myself.
I've never been the type of guy to back down from a situation
just because someone else tells me I can't do it. Telling me I
shouldn't do it is the best way to get me to do something.

My driver understood what I was telling him as we made
our way up the West Side Highway along the Hudson River
toward 125th Street, the heart of Harlem. I wasn't afraid to go
someplace just because someone might not think I belonged.
I knew in my heart that the only way to make peace with the
people I'd hurt was to be among them. We drove through
the historic neighborhood with the darkened windows of our
shiny black SUV rolled down so people could see Dog was in
the 'hood. That's when our experience began.

"Dog, Dog! Hey, brother. Don't worry. We love you!" A
young black man chased after the car as we slowly moved up
the street. He began shouting to his friends that Dog was in
the car. People began walking over and circling the vehicle as
we stopped for a red light. I shook as many hands as I could
while several people snapped pictures of Beth and me on
their cell phones. Our driver was nervous, suggesting we get
out of there as soon as we could, but I never felt threatened
for one single second. As the light turned green, I heard a
woman shout out, "He's a fricken racist." I never saw her, but

I heard her loud and clear. It broke my heart. Beth could see I was upset.

"It's OK, Big Daddy. They loved you. They all knew you didn't mean to use that word . . ." She did her best to console me, but at the time, I still felt like that woman spoke for so many others. I thought about the experience the whole way back to our hotel. It felt good to see my many brothers and sisters reach out their hands, as if they had accepted my olive branch of peace by being there and loving me that day. The more I thought about it, the more I realized that Beth was right. They knew I'm not a racist. One woman's voice couldn't drown out the sound of everyone else's love and forgiveness. Mercy was alive and well and, apparently, living in Harlem!

END OF
INTERMISSION TWO

CHAPTER 17

A&E Real Life Change.   TIME WARNER CABLE THE POWER OF YOU   Date: May 5, 2011

Pay to the Order of: WINNERS' Camp

$ 10,000.00

Ten Thousand and no/100 Dollars

On Behalf of Duane & Beth Chapman
In Loving Memory of
Barbara Katie Chapman

Libby O'Connell

One of the greatest benefits of being on television is having the chance to give back to the community. One of the ways I do that is by participating in local outreach programs where I can meet and mingle with people who are searching for a reason to change their lives, and need guidance to take those steps and encouragement to get there. A&E started a program called the A&E Recovery Project. Its mission is to reach out to the more than 22 million Americans who suffer from addictions, as well as their family members, friends, and colleagues, who are all touched by the disease. The Recovery Project was "created to break the stigma of addiction, raise awareness that addiction is a treatable disease and prove that recovery is possible."

In the spring of 2009, I took part in a rally held in Honolulu to help spread the word for A&E, the network that had shown me that I was worthy of a second chance and was now telling thousands of people in my hometown that they were worthy of a second chance too. The atmosphere of this event was exceptionally different from most of my personal appearances. It wasn't quite the somber feeling of a funeral, but no one was there to celebrate. It was something in between—a situation I'll never forget. Not one fan asked for an autograph or to take a picture with me. They were there for help. For a few people, it was pretty obvious this was a last chance stop.

Some of the people who came to the event were looking for a helping hand themselves, while many others were there to plead for their children's well-being. They were all looking to me to wave some magic wand and make their pain disappear. I wish it were that easy, but it's not. Lord knows, I've seen it happen in my life over and over again. I've never been one for tough love, but I'm not a roll-over-me type of guy, either. There's always a solution—the trick is finding the right one for you.

I always tell people that God will give you answers to all of life's problems and worries. Here's the thing—He won't always give you answers that you will like. Sometimes the solution appears worse than the problem, like jail, illness, and such. If a couple of months behind bars is what it takes to get clean, then ultimately, that's the right solution. I don't want to help someone after they've been brought to their knees unless that's the only time I get the chance to. I'd rather help people fix themselves before they bottom out. I know how hard that is firsthand from my own experience getting off drugs.

Mothers, fathers, brothers, sisters, boyfriends, and girlfriends all want to know, "What would *you* do, Dog?"

I'm always brutally honest when I answer that question, because these people are seeking life-saving advice, so I'd better be right in what I have to say. I tell them to go to the police and report the user. Get him into rehab. Sit your kid down and talk to him. Sit there and tell him you were also once a teenager. Tell him about your own experiences with drinking or drugs. If you raised hell when you were a kid, you can count on your child being the same way. There's no shame in youth. Experimentation is natural.

However, if there is a predisposition to addiction in

your family, it is your obligation as a parent to help prevent your child from suffering with the disease she inherited from you. Today, more than ever, kids have access to information through the Internet where they can make dangerous drugs out of common household items and over-the-counter drugs that are easily accessible. They live with twice the amount of peer pressure I grew up with, which means they have to be twice as strong, twice as educated, and twice as secure with who they are to stay on the right side of the law.

If you struggle with addiction, chances are pretty good that your kids will too. If you got help, they'll need it, too. If you're still struggling, get help together. There's no gray area when it comes to getting sober. You can't be a little bit of an addict.

My grandpa used to say I was the greatest dreamer he ever met. He'd say, "Watch your fantasies because you're the kind of guy that can make those dreams come true." To this day I think of myself as a dreamer and totally believe that is one of my greatest gifts. I tell people all the time that I started off as an ugly caterpillar, but through a miraculous metamorphosis, I turned into a beautiful butterfly. If I can change my life with a seventh-grade education, as a convicted felon and a former drug user—*anyone* can.

I spoke to the crowd at the Recovery Project event the same way as I am writing these words to you. My message comes from the deepest part of my heart and soul because despite everything I know as a parent, all of the positive messages I tried to instill in my own kids, and all of the life experiences I've had over the years, one of my children is still so very lost.

I shared something very personal with the crowd on that special night, something that is always difficult to admit as a parent. My son Tucker was back in jail for failing his mandatory drug test. His probation officer caught him with the prosthetic penis he'd been using to pass the tests. In a show of mercy, his parole officer gave him the opportunity to come back the following week to retest. He told him to go get clean, but my son couldn't do it. If I was still a part of his day-to-day life, I would have made sure he showed up clean as a whistle the following week. Unfortunately, I was unaware of his situation until it was too late. Baby Lyssa came to me to say Tucker was so messed up on drugs. She was as worried as the rest of us. Even though my son and her brother betrayed us, he's still my baby. I thought about the story in the Bible where Jesus asks God to forgive the guys who were crucifying him, by saying, "Father, forgive them for they know not what they do." I always wondered why he didn't call upon ten thousand angels to set him free instead of asking the Lord to forgive his enemies. After the news of Tucker had broken, I received phone calls from all sorts of people offering to "take care" of Tucker for what he had done to me. That's when it occurred to me that the love Jesus had for those men was the same as the love I feel for my son. No matter what happened, I had to forgive Tucker "for he knows not what he has done." So when I heard he was back in prison, I worried someone would hurt him inside the joint. I put out the word and prayed others would understand that I had forgiven him and they should too.

Whether he wants it or not, I'm going to love him as much as I do Duane Lee, Leland, and all of my kids, for the rest of his life. The sad and ironic truth is that Tucker is back in prison for the exact reason I warned him about during our last phone call.

I'd spent too many sleepless nights worrying about Tucker in the short time we'd been estranged. Every time I heard an ambulance or siren in the middle of the night

I'd pop up in bed and beg God, "Please, help Tucker. Don't let that siren be for him." Now, when I heard a siren I could take a deep breath and know for sure it wasn't for him. He was safe in jail. Only a parent who has exhausted every other option can understand the strange sense of relief I felt knowing it was better that my child be locked up than on the street.

After I finished sharing this news with the audience that night, I looked up and saw parents putting their arms around their kids, to hold their child just a little closer. I looked into the front row and saw a bad-ass-looking, tatted up young man touch his mother's knee. And then I noticed a little boy about Gary Boy's age, certainly no older than nine or ten, lay his head on his mom's chest and begin to cry. She was gently caressing him, consoling him because even this child knew that what I was saying was real. I don't know the circumstances of that youngster's life, but I'm positive drugs have touched his family in a way that scares him to death.

When I was done speaking, I literally felt like I had given all I had to the crowd. I was mentally exhausted and physically drained. I thought about the story in the Bible where Jesus was walking along a path to speak on top of a mountain. A large crowd was following him along the way. Jesus's disciples were holding back the crowd, who were trying to reach out and touch the Savior. They believed He could create miracles if they could just have contact with Him. The Bible says there was a sick woman who touched the hem of His garment as He walked by, and when she did, Jesus stopped to ask John who had reached out to Him.

John pointed to the woman and said, "She did."

Jesus said he felt like a lot of virtue had gone out of Him. He turned to the woman and said, "You are healed," and then kept walking. I felt the exact same way when I was done speaking. All of my virtue was gone. I poured every bit of myself into the crowd. Hearing testimonials from people afterward made it all worthwhile. I can't think of any higher compliment than to hear someone tell me that something I said helped them turn their life around. I want to be the fixer for these people because they don't have anyone else to turn to. I'm the guy who is going to give them that last bit of hope. I'm not satisfied unless they are, which means I need them to leave with a changed perspective and a desire to live a better life than they had before they showed up. I derive my happiness, wholeness, and feeling of being complete from knowing the crowd left pleased. That night was exceptional in every way. If just one person heard my message that night and decided to do something about it, I would have been satisfied with the result.

Not long after that appearance, a man walked up and began telling me he'd just put his son in jail a couple days earlier. He said, "Dog, I heard your message and all you had to say a few weeks ago about losing a child. Putting my son in jail was the hardest thing I have ever done, but I realized you were right. There's nothing I won't do to help one of my children stay clean, even sending him to prison. I now know how you feel whenever I hear an ambulance or police siren late at night. I no longer wonder if it's my boy they've got. I will not love my son to death. Thank you, Dog."

I was standing with a friend from A&E at the time. I put one hand on his shoulder and the other on this man's. I looked at my buddy and said, "Here's our one."

His response was quick and to the point. "I think there will be more than one this time, Dog. Many more."

My grandpa used to tell me that the military was successful in training soldiers because they could tear a man down and build him back up to be faster, smarter, sharper, and more aware than when they started. It wasn't until I began studying with Tony Robbins that I realized you didn't have to be in the military to have those methods work for you. I once asked Tony his opinion on how to help people get off drugs. We opened up a dialogue on whether addiction was, in fact, a disease. I told him I thought that addiction was like an uncontrollable virus that spreads. Tony said he felt there are always signs of a spreading virus. In some cases it may be lesions, while in others it could be a limp. "If they've got a limp, you've got to give them a crutch," Tony said.

That's when it occurred to me that there were lots of nonthreatening crutches to offer. It could be the Bible, watching television, reading a book, or anything else that helps you relax and unwind from your stressed-out daily life. Taking a drink of alcohol, smoking a joint, or popping a pill here and there may not seem harmful, but I fully believe it's not the long-term answer.

In the spring of 2009, I got a phone call from a guy named Bobby Magnuson, asking me if I would bond out his girlfriend, who I'll refer to as Darlene. She had been arrested on drug charges. Bobby told me that she had a terrible methamphetamine problem and that he would only put up the bond for her if she promised to go to rehab and quit doing drugs. She agreed to get clean, so Bobby put up the collateral to get her out of jail.

They went to rehab together, but soon after they arrived, Darlene split in the middle of the night. Bobby left rehab to find her and bring her back. He called her over and over until she finally answered her phone. Bobby could tell she was high.

"Why do you have to be such a big pussy? Why don't you just leave me alone? I don't love you. Quit calling me!"

Darlene was lashing out at Bobby, but she was too wasted to care.

"I'm going to kill myself if you don't come back to rehab. I swear, I'll do it. I can't live without you!" I think Bobby believed that threatening her would help Darlene come to her senses. Instead, it backfired.

"Why do you keep threatening to kill yourself? Why can't you be a man and just do it already!" Those were the last words he heard from the love of his life before Bobby threw a rope over the tallest branch of the largest tree he could find and hung himself. Just before he put the noose around his neck, he called Darlene one last time and left a message on her voice mail.

"I told you not to push me. I hope you're happy now. It's over." Bobby hung himself, but his phone never disconnected, so Darlene could hear the sounds of him choking until there was dead silence except for one single bird chirping in the background. Bobby was dead.

When Beth found out about Bobby's death, she called Darlene up and told her to come in and see us. She was crying from the moment she walked through the door. I looked at Darlene and said, "You know that Bobby is dead because of you, right? You wouldn't get off the dope, you dared him to kill himself, and now he's dead. You're under arrest."

Just as I told Darlene she was going back to jail, Bobby's mother and oldest brother walked through the door. They were looking for anything they could find with his handwriting on it. She wanted something from her baby to hold. When the mother saw Darlene in my office, she started calling her every horrible name in the book. Who could blame her? I sat the mother down and told her about my daughter Barbara Katie. I assured her that I understood her pain because I had lost a child too. I wanted her to know she wasn't alone in her grief.

"He's with you now and forever." I started telling her all of the words of comfort that were said to me when I got the news about Barbara Katie, hoping they would relieve her anguish at losing her son. Bobby's mother looked up and asked Beth if she could see Darlene. She wanted to talk to her. Beth was hesitant at first, but she wasn't going to deny Bobby's mother this simple request. If the meeting became heated, we knew we could handle it.

To my surprise, they hugged each other and cried in each other's arms. Darlene was cuffed at first, but when I realized what was happening, I uncuffed her so she could hold Bobby's mother.

"When you were hungry, didn't I feed you? When you were cold, didn't I clothe you? I knew you and Bobby were doing wrong things, yet I treated you like you were my own daughter." The mother had her hands on Darlene's shoulders. "Look at what your drugs have done. Don't let your addiction kill anyone else. Get yourself clean, Darlene. If you do, I will always be there to hold you, help you, feed you, clothe you, and whatever else you need. If you do this, know you can come back to me."

I was moved to tears as Bobby's mother held Darlene that night in my office. I was stunned by her show of mercy, her generosity of heart. I could only hope and pray that Darlene heard the words that were spoken to her, that she'd somehow find her way to get sober and clean up her life so Bobby's death would not be in vain. I drove her to jail later that night with hope in my heart but doubt on my mind that she would find her way.

It's hard to know there are people in the world who, despite every chance given, will not make it. I get so discouraged and disappointed by them. It's hard for me to hear that someone I had high hopes for is back in jail . . . or worse. It's too sad to think about, so I try to avoid the "where are they now" conversations. I make it a point not to become friends with the people I bond, so I can't possibly get dragged down to where they are. I pray for all of them, but I try not to think about them after they're off the bond. It's the only way I can leave my work in the office at the end of the day. I owe it to my family to be present for them, to be there for their needs and comfort them when they need it from their dad and when Beth wants it from me as a husband.

If you're struggling with drugs or addiction, think about Bobby and Darlene's story. Don't let your situation take you down to the point of no return. Ask for help or be willing to accept it if someone you love tries to tell you it's time to make some changes. There is absolutely no reason someone has to die to understand how precious life is. When you're in the gutter, there's no place to go but up. Ask yourself, "What's the worst-case scenario? If I keep doing drugs, what will happen? If I stay in this abusive relationship, what will happen? If I keep acting recklessly, making foolish choices and hanging out with the wrong crowd, what will happen to me?" In the end, I think you'll find that none of those answers work in your favor. In fact, they all lead you toward the same result. Do something now to change your circumstances before it's too late. If you don't know how to take that first step, you can contact a local help line by calling 411. All calls are anonymous and will be held in the strictest of confidence. The help line will be able to guide you to a safe place in your community where you can get the help you want, need, and deserve. I often remind myself that writing bail means having to watch my heart. If a client jumps on me, it feels like one of my own kids is running. It hurts my feelings so bad when one of my clients jumps bail. I get mad at first, but only until I catch him.

So many of the cases I've been a part of don't have happy endings. I'll sometimes spend hours explaining to my clients all of the reasons they need to get their lives together, much like you see me do on the show after we make an arrest. Those conversations in the backseat are real—they reflect who I am. I want these men and women to know that they have it in their power to change the way things are in their lives. Most of them won't end up doing anything about it, but at least I planted the first seed toward change if they want it.

Women who jump surprise me more than men. More female clients discover the straight and narrow path than males, although there have been some memorable exceptions. When I first started bounty hunting, I pretty much worked alone. I didn't want anyone along for the ride or to share in the glory. I found it sometimes made things easier for me, especially when tracking down a female fugitive.

Back in the day, one of the most memorable women I ever went after was a girl named Susan. I was chasing her for a buddy of mine. I'd spent a couple of days looking for her around Denver, when someone tipped me off on where she was staying. When I called the number my contact provided, Susan answered the phone.

"Hey, baby. How ya doing?" I asked in my coolest, sexiest voice.

Susan didn't recognize me at all. Why would she? We had never actually met. I played like we had, though. I told her we hung out down at her favorite bar, the Blue Café. Susan suddenly realized, or thought she had, exactly who I was.

"Are you the guy with the beard and the blue eyes?" she asked.

"No, honey. That ain't me. I have the long blond hair."

"Ohhh. Right. Yes. Man, that was a couple of weeks ago. I was so hammered that night I could barely remember my own name!" And then she began shamelessly flirting. The more she talked, the less I had to. And boy, did she start to sweet talk me. That's when I knew she was mine for the taking. When I asked her out on a date for the next night, she immediately said yes.

I showed up at her door the next day looking sharp and ready for the night. I had a photo of Susan from her bondsman so I could be certain I had the right chick before arresting her. The moment she opened the front door, I knew it was her. I told her I thought we'd catch a movie at the local drive-in. It seemed like a good idea. Given the conversation we'd had the night before, I didn't think she'd mind. I was eager to get her out to the truck, but then her mother came to the front door to meet me. I had to be polite, like I was excited to be taking out her daughter. After a few minutes of small talk, I took Susan by the arm and walked her to my truck. I opened the passenger door and did all of the gentlemanly things I would have done if this had been a real date. Just as I walked around to get into my vehicle, I noticed her brother walk up to the driver's side door. He was wearing army fatigues and looked like a real killer.

"Be cool with my sister, man." I could tell he was being serious.

"I will," I said. I backed out of her driveway and headed to the drive-in. As we drove away, I asked Susan about her brother.

"Your brother sure seems protective. What was he doing at your house?"

"Yeah. I've got a little trouble with the law right now. I'm on the run and I wanted to be sure you weren't a cop."

I just about swallowed my tongue thinking she might

be on to me. About three minutes into our ride, I pulled over.

"What are you doing?" Susan asked.

"This ain't no date and you're under arrest, you bond-jumping bitch!" I yelled, quickly slapping the cuffs on her. That's when I realized where I had chosen to pull over. There's a portion along Highway 85 between Brighton and Denver that all bounty hunters and bondsmen know because it's the darkest stretch of road on the route. I've always referred to that stretch as the Brighton Triangle because so many accidents and incidents happen there. I always held my breath as I made my way through that area, hoping nothing would happen. Unfortunately, this was where I'd chosen to stop. I thought Susan was secure as I sped toward the Adams County jail, but before I knew it, that crazy bitch came right out of her cuffs! She started beating on me while I was driving seventy miles an hour down the highway, taking wild swings with her fists at my head and neck.

"What are you going to do now, you mofo?" she screamed at the top of her voice.

I started swerving in and out of traffic trying to avoid both her fists and oncoming cars at the same time. She finally connected and hit me pretty hard with the cuffs, and then she did it again, over and over. I was in trouble. Finally I thought, *Lord, I don't want to hit this woman, but what am I supposed to do?* God told me to settle her down. I pulled my truck over to the side of the road, pulled her out, subdued her like a man, and slapped the cuffs back on her wrists. This time, however, I made sure they were on good and tight. I wanted to be sure there was no way she could bust out of them until the cops themselves took them off her wrists. I was pretty sure there would be a mark when they removed them.

By the time we got to the jail, Susan was screaming to

anyone who would listen that I had beat her. She already had a black eye when I picked her up, but now she was insistent that her injuries were from me. The officers sequestered me while they tried to get the story from Susan. She was pushing for assault charges, but it was her word against mine. Thankfully, I remembered the photo her bondsman had given me that was in the glove box of my truck. She had the same black eye in the picture taken two weeks before I picked her up. Once I showed her mug shot to the cops, I was off the hook.

That was the last time I picked up a female fugitive alone. I couldn't afford to be accused of assault or worse. It wasn't long after that bust that Beth started coming with me on all my hunts, especially when I was looking for female fugitives. The first time I asked Beth to come on a bounty hunt with me, I asked her to drive me to the house of the woman I was looking for. I was partying and in no condition to drive myself. Of course, this was back in 1988, before I got clean and sober.

At first, Beth refused, but I was somehow able to convince her to drive by the address one time or I would have to do it myself. We were slowly passing by the house when I spotted the woman I was looking for in the yard. I leapt out of the still-moving car and started to chase her. She ran into the house and out the back door. She finally locked herself in a corner apartment down the block. I had her. When I kicked in the door, it accidentally hit her friend in the head. Fearing I was getting close, the woman I was chasing ran again. This time, she went out the back door and into a junkyard behind the apartment building, where she hid in a doghouse.

"I'm out of here, Duane. I don't want any part of this!" Beth was yelling at me as I went to grab the woman.

Just then the police showed up and told us to freeze.

They wouldn't let me capture my fugitive. Instead, they arrested both Beth and me.

In Colorado, the law states that anyone who enters and remains in a dwelling to commit a felonious act is guilty of first-degree burglary. Beth and I were booked and thrown in jail. I kept telling Beth, "I told you we were always going to have fun times!" I thought the whole thing was funny. Beth did not.

"You're nothing but trouble, Duane Chapman!" Beth said.

When we finally went to court over the arrest, Beth's charges were dropped to a "dog at large" offense. No joke. It amounted to walking a dog without a leash. I don't know if the district attorney was trying to be funny or was just sending me a message. Either way, all I could do was laugh. My punishment was to help the Adams County Sheriff's Department track down some of their fugitives for thirty days. I had the best time showing them how to bring in these guys. I taught them that they can lie if they have to in order to bring someone in. I showed the department some of my trade secrets, and over the course of the month we brought in two dozen fugitives.

I know there's a world of people who are confused, hurting, and need the help and guidance of a guy like me. Every time I sit next to a captured jump in the back of my Suburban, I understand that I have a captive audience of one. If I can reach that guy or girl in the few minutes we spend together on their way to jail, all of the stress, effort, and energy expended in finding them becomes worth it and far more valuable than the price of their bond.

I arrested a guy a few months back who was disappointed to find out the police were going to escort him to jail instead of me.

"Dog, why don't I get my ride?" he asked.

I was taken aback because I remembered something Tim Storey said to me while I was fighting for my freedom and feeling pretty low about myself. There were a few times I wanted to throw in the towel back then and just pack it in. After he'd used his best preacher techniques to get me to see that helping people was my true calling in life, I still wasn't convinced I had what it took to be a leader and role model.

And then Tim looked me in the eyes and said, "Who is going to give them the ride, Duane? Who will give them the cigarette and who will give them 'the talk'?" When the preacher posed those questions to me, I realized he was right. If not me, then who? Whether I realized it or not, I was leading a backseat ministry, one ride at a time.

I looked at my fugitive for a minute without saying a word. I wanted to be certain of his intentions. Was he trying to split? Was he avoiding the inevitable, or was he genuinely interested in what this old Dog had to say? I ran my hand across my chin and said, "You want to ride with me?"

Handcuffed and shackled, the guy looked up and said, "I've been waiting two weeks for that, Dog."

A ride with the Dog was all he wanted.

"Load him up," I said. "You've got your ride, son."

I lit a cigarette and placed it in his mouth so he could grab a smoke before we took him in. We talked nonstop all the way to the county jail. He shook his head as I spoke about getting off drugs and manning up for his wife and baby. I told him he had to quit making stupid choices so he could start living as the smart man I could spot inside of him. This guy wasn't a stupid fool. He was just making stupid foolish choices. As we spoke, I didn't judge him or instill any false hope in him for his future. I assured him he'd be cooked if he didn't stop the crap and get himself together—now. Not tomorrow, or the next day, but right now.

"I've been there, boy. I know what you're going through. It's a lame excuse to say you 'can't' do something when you have your health and a family that loves you no matter what. It's lazy behavior, for sure, but you're not handicapped by anything other than yourself. This is your wake-up call. You either answer it now or pay for it later and for the rest of your life. You're being given another shot at things, but only if you take the risk to make the right decision. The choice is yours. What's it going to be, brotha?"

As we approached the jailhouse, I could tell he was scared and feeling sick from coming down off the drugs. "Remember this feeling, son. Hold on to it so you never find yourself here again," I said.

As the outer steel door slammed shut and the young man was no longer in my sight, all I could do was hope and pray he heard the calling. The second I've got them in the back-seat, they're no longer a fugitive, jump, or the poor bastard who thought he'd be the hero to outrun the Dog—they're my children. I just want what's best for them. I'm the "fix it" guy. My true calling is to inspire those who don't believe in themselves that they are worthy of a second, third, fourth, or even fifth chance in life. I want to give them the hope and inspiration that it is never too late to turn things around.

CHAPTER

There's a famous saying, "The difference between a wise man and a fool is a wise man learns his lessons from other people's mistakes and a fool only learns from his own." One of my goals in writing this book is to help you avoid living as a fool by listening to someone who used to be one. I've been there, done that. There's not much I haven't been through over the years that hasn't made me stronger, smarter, and wiser.

Thankfully, my life has gotten progressively better every year since I went to prison in Huntsville. I still have pitfalls and stumbles, but despite all I have been through, I am a really happy and fortunate man. I am grateful for my family, career, friends, and last but certainly not least, I am most appreciative for the opportunity I have that allows me to reach so many other people. I am humbled by how many fans we have. Looking back, there have been some trying times. I find comfort in knowing the Lord has a plan and that He would never give me more than I could handle. Even so, he has laid a load on my back over the years. Whenever things aren't going my way, I take that as a sign that it is time to make a change.

Perhaps you've been wondering about your own life—you know, like whether or not it's time to make some important personal decisions to help you live at your very best. Maybe you've been thinking about moving, changing jobs, getting out of a bad relationship, or quitting drugs. These decisions are never easy, but they're worth the pain to get to the next level of freedom in your life where you can thrive, grow, and become a healthier, happier person.

As parents, we have to show our children love and patience and provide clear boundaries on what is acceptable and what is not. Beth and I have an abundance of overflowing forgiveness in our hearts when it comes to our children. The Bible says that if you bring children up in the ways of the Lord, they will never depart thereof. I once heard a story about a defiant young boy who refused to listen to his mother's pleas to follow the Lord. His mother was dying in the hospital when she begged her son to be with the Lord so she could go in peace. She uttered that wish with her last dying breath. She never saw her son grow up to become Billy Graham.

The Bible doesn't promise we will see the final plan, but it assures us it exists. I've spent numerous nights dreaming of my life twenty years from now and beyond. I've seen my son Tucker standing over my grave crying and saying he is sorry for the mistakes he made. Someday I hope he comes to realize that what he did was wrong, that what he did hurt me almost as much as dying. Even if he doesn't come around before I'm six feet under, I have forgiven him in my heart. I want him to know I still love him. In fact, I was finally able to say those words to him on his birthday this year. A police officer inside the prison allowed me to say three important words to my son over the phone.

"I love you," I said. I passed the phone away before I could hear Tucker respond. I didn't need to hear him. I only wanted him to know that he is loved.

When our children fall off their path, they're still our

children—our babies. You have to forgive them and hope they do better.

No matter how bad you think things are in your life, know this: There is *always* someone else out there who has it worse than you do. You can't sit around and make excuses for not implementing changes once you know there are options. We have a young man who works for us named Justin. He was my personal assistant for a couple of years and has looked after Gary Boy since the first season of *Dog the Bounty Hunter.* Our family grew very fond of Justin. He wasn't just an employee, he had become a member of our family. I even referred to him as my nephew. We even invited him to be on a couple of episodes of the show during our first season on the air. After a while, Justin's ego grew a little bigger than his role. He began acting pretty cocky with all of us and was getting a little too big for his britches.

One day, Beth found a burn hole from one of Justin's cigarettes in one of the cup holders in her car. When Beth went off on him, Justin decided to fight back by very aggressively mouthing off.

Mouthing off to Beth is *never* a good idea.

Justin started calling Beth all sorts of names before storming off and punching a wall right in front of Leland. As a trained boxer, Leland knows better than to show his temper by hitting a wall, so he confronted Justin. He told him how immature and destructive Justin's behavior was, reminding him that Beth had told him not to smoke in her car countless times. When Beth came outside and saw Justin's swollen broken hand, she essentially told him he was no longer useful to us on bounty hunts. She explained that he wouldn't be able to drive a car, make a fist, or grab his can of Mace on a hunt until he was fully healed. He hurt himself, which meant he was off the show.

Leland drove Justin to the hospital to get his hand fixed. We thought he'd get it set in a cast and hopefully be on the road to recovery so he could quickly rejoin the team. Several hours later, Beth noticed that Justin still hadn't come back from the hospital. She began calling around to find him, but none of the hospitals had had a patient with his name come through their doors. Finally, the last place Beth called told her Justin had checked himself out hours ago. They had given him some pain pills and let him go without any other medical attention to his hand.

We didn't see Justin again for quite some time and didn't hear from him for weeks, and then months. This was devastating to Gary Boy because Justin had become his confidant, friend, swimming partner, surfing pal, and all-around buddy. We called Justin's mom, Moon, who had worked for our family for years but wasn't employed by us at the time. We asked if she had heard from him, but she said she hadn't. We all knew Justin had done something really dumb—he relapsed back into his old life of getting high and hanging out with the wrong friends who were enabling him further by encouraging him to do more drugs. The second the hospital gave him the dope, he was back to his old addict ways.

Many addicts slip back into their addictions after something happens in their lives that causes them to take painkillers. They get that old familiar feeling again and slip right back. I've seen it a thousand times. And that's exactly what happened with Justin.

It turns out he went to visit some relatives in upstate New York. Unfortunately, those relatives weren't the stable influence on Justin that Beth and I had been. They were enabling Justin's habit. Worse yet, they began filling up his head with stories of how he should have been getting paid a lot more money to be on my show. They told him our ratings would plummet without him and the show would inevitably fail if we didn't bring him back for season two, because he was the "real star" of the show.

If enough people start telling you something, even if it isn't true, chances are you're eventually going to believe whatever it is they're saying. So Justin bought into their rhetoric—hook, line, and sinker. He started playing the money game with our producers. When they asked him where he thought the show could take him professionally, he said he wanted to do BVD underwear commercials, become a model, or become a singer.

Wrong answer.

You see, when the producers asked each of us the same question, Leland, Duane Lee, Beth, and I all answered exactly the same way. If the television show went away tomorrow, we'd all still be writing bail, bounty hunting, catching fugitives, and keeping our family business alive. We don't want to be models or actors or pursue any other claim to fame. We are bounty hunters.

The producers decided not to bring Justin back to the show. His family and their bad advice had basically talked him out of the greatest opportunity this young man had ever had. He wasn't getting paid a lot of money—hell, none of us were back then—but at least he belonged to something. He was successful and blew it all over greed, jealousy, and what other people thought he should be doing.

We let him come visit us on occasion, but it was difficult for all of us because we could physically see he was having a hard time letting go. He had been on the show, had built a fan base, and suddenly it was all gone.

Eventually, we had to distance ourselves from Justin because he was continuously making bad choices. I heard that he had moved to the Big Island and begun partying all the time. He was doing drugs and excessively drinking night after night. Although it hurt my heart to hear he had fallen so far off his path, I didn't give it much mind because even though I still loved him, he was no longer any of our business. He was on an uncontrollable downward spiral that would eventually bring this young man to his knees—literally.

Three years had gone by since we spoke to Justin or his mother. One night in 2008, Justin's grandfather called to say his grandson had been in a pretty bad drunk driving accident. His car flipped over several times before he was thrown from it. Because he was driving late at night on a road that isn't well traveled or well lit, he lay on the side of the road for a long time before coming to. The grandfather said he was being airlifted to Honolulu and asked if Beth and I would go to the hospital to make sure they didn't cut off his grandson's legs.

Shortly thereafter, Justin's mother, Moon, called crying and screaming for her son's safety. Although we hadn't spoken to her in some time, it didn't matter. We were family, and family comes together in times of need. Beth immediately bought Moon a plane ticket to fly from Denver to Honolulu so she could be with her son and see him through this tragic situation.

When we got to the hospital, Justin told me the last thing he remembered from that fateful night was jamming to some music and dancing in his seat. The next thing he recalled was waking up, hearing the sound of croaking coqui frogs all around him, and then being put on a stretcher and placed in a helicopter that was airlifting him to the nearest hospital.

When Justin was in high school, he'd become well known because he had a sixty-four-inch vertical leap in basketball. He was the shining star of the Hilo High School basketball team. He was in every state championship and always made the all-star team. He was a terrifically funny kid, always making everyone laugh. He was Moon's pride and joy because he was her child who had the potential to go the furthest in his life. Sadly, it had all been wiped out in that one night. He suffered massive damage to his legs. His ankle was severed from the bone and the rest of his leg. They had to reattach his foot and leg below the knee. His face had been severely cut, with stitches going all across his eyelid. He was lucky to still have his eye, as it had almost been pulled from its socket. His hand was also very badly damaged.

We begged Moon to leave Justin with us in Hawaii while he recuperated, but he chose to go back to Denver to be with his family. Beth instinctively knew Denver would end tragically for Justin. Unfortunately, she was right. He slipped into a depression and began using drugs as a mode of escape. This time he wasn't just overindulging in painkillers—he was smoking crack too. The drugs were dumping all sorts of impurities and toxic chemicals into his body, which wasn't helping his healing process. In fact, it was poisoning his body, causing infection after infection, until he finally developed a huge hole in his ankle that went straight down to the bone. The wounds were green and full of pus.

One day, Moon went over to Justin's house and smelled a really awful odor when she walked into his bedroom. When she ripped the blanket back off his body, Justin's leg was completely black. Moon knew what that smell was because she had taken care of Beth's father several years ago when he became ill. Beth's dad had developed gangrene twice. The first time, the doctors had to cut off his pinky toe, and the second time it was his big toe. Eventually, her father died from the infections. Moon instantly and quickly realized that Justin had a big problem. He had developed a bad case of gangrene.

After several weeks in the hospital and doses of various antibiotics, doctors told him they'd have to amputate his leg below his knee. The news was devastating to all of us. Justin was a really handsome, tall, blond-haired, blue-eyed boy who had his entire future ahead of him. Since the accident, he had completely lost his smile, his boisterous laugh. As he lay in his hospital bed thinking about all of this, it was clear that Justin knew his whole life had been changed by choosing to get behind the wheel after drinking and the bad choices he'd made that led him there. It was a difficult realization that those choices had sent him spiraling into unbelievable negativity that would be extremely challenging to come back from.

When Justin got out of the hospital he moved in with this girl who was still living at home with her parents. Everyone was using Justin as the trash guy—they made him take out the garbage, do the dishes, run a few errands here and there, but nobody made him go out and get a real job. He started using his leg as an excuse to avoid having to face reality. He'd say things like "I can't work because of my leg." And for a while, everyone bought into it, placating him and pretending he was incapable of doing much more than he was doing because of his prosthetic leg.

His relationship started deteriorating as fast as his self-esteem. Eventually, Justin's girlfriend kicked him out of her house. Beth somehow convinced him to come back to Hawaii and live with us so he could heal and get stronger. However, she was clear that he had to promise to stay close, work hard, and not go back to taking drugs. He promised us he wanted to change his ways, so we allowed him to come back.

It didn't take long for Justin to break his promises. Shortly after he arrived, he ran off again in the middle of the night, without saying good-bye to Gary Boy. That was

it. We had to wash our hands of Justin because he'd broken our son's heart again, leaving us to pick up the pieces
when Gary Boy asked questions about why he left. Gary
thought he'd done something wrong to upset Justin. It's
hard to explain to a six-year-old that it wasn't his fault, that
Justin had adult problems that a little boy couldn't possibly
comprehend. Beth and I had a hard time coping whenever
the subject came up, because we never had the right words
to comfort our son or ourselves.

A year went by without any contact from Justin. He
sent messages through Moon and other people we knew in
common, but we wouldn't even let him have our new
phone numbers, because he wasn't in a stable place in his
life. We heard he was in another tumultuous relationship,
and this time his girlfriend had called the cops on him over
a money issue. That's when Beth asked Moon to bring him
to our house so we could talk to him. She was afraid that if
we didn't step in and help Justin do something with his
life, we'd lose him once and for all. He'd either end up in
prison or worse. It was clear he was lost, and would have
no hope, no love, and no future unless we extended a hand.

When Justin showed up, he was a broken, ruined boy.
His color was ashy, he'd lost a lot of weight, and he was
missing the spark that made him Justin. No smile, no
warmth. His years of constant disappointment, one after
another, had taken a toll. He'd spent years running away
from us after he wasn't asked to come back to the show,
but now it appeared he wanted to return to the fold. Beth
warned Justin that we would give him another chance, but
if he left Gary Boy like he had in the past ever again, the
door would be closed forever. She explained to Justin that
in life, time passes quickly, and if he didn't seize opportunity when it presented itself, it wouldn't be there for the
taking later on.

I sat Justin down and told him he couldn't give up on life. He needed to find a way to turn his physical challenge into an asset. "This is your chance. Jump on board while it is moving, Justin. Start shoveling coal and do whatever it takes to keep the train in motion. We don't know if it'll last two more months or two more years. You have to ride the train while you can or the train will pass you by."

Someone once told me "What you compromise to keep, you lose." And that was exactly where Justin was in his life. He'd compromised his job with us and lost it. He'd compromised his life and almost lost it. He'd compromised his leg by smoking dope and lost it. If you had asked him if it was worth it, I think he'd have said, "Hell no."

Before the accident, Justin would often accompany our crew on bounty hunts. I asked him if he still had his badge. He said he did. I told him there would always be a place in the car next to me when he was ready to come back to work, but first he had to get healthy.

By the summer of 2009, Justin had gained fifteen pounds, got some healthy color back in his skin, and found his laughter again. He never hesitates to do whatever it takes to get the job done. He doesn't complain or grumble about anything. He doesn't ask for time off and, frankly, doesn't want it. He is willing to be by my side twenty-four hours a day, seven days a week, taking care of anything and everything. His answer is always "Yes, Uncle." There's nothing he'd do today that would jeopardize the relationship we've all built.

Justin is a kid who needed a second, third, fourth, and fifth chance before waking up and realizing he had to do something to change his life or he'd live as a broken-down addict the rest of his days.

Justin returned to the team with great pride and humility. He shows up at the office dressed to hunt. He had to learn how to walk all over again, mostly by hopping on one leg or by using his prosthetic leg. He can jump as high as a kangaroo. He is as fast as a sprinter. He can move like a gazelle, quickly and with great agility. I can't really think of Justin as disabled, because he hasn't let his circumstances slow him down one bit. He's been through a tremendous amount of physical therapy since losing his leg and has learned to walk without a noticeable limp when using his prosthetic leg. When he removes the leg, he'll jokingly shout out, "Periscope down."

Beth and I have made it a point to keep Justin close to us wherever we go. We are determined to make sure he stays on the path he's now on. I love him like a son. We are always encouraging him to keep fit and take care of himself so he'll never have to worry about his health again. Even though he is still self-conscious about it, he has started using his disability in a positive way. Through the show, he now has a platform to show people that having a disability doesn't have to handicap you. Sitting around moping about his challenges is what handicaps a person. Being a one-legged bounty hunter is a huge step in educating people about that. God gave Justin back everything he ever wanted, but with a twist. He now has life lessons and a story he can share to be a blessing to somebody else.

A few weeks after Justin came back to us, a little boy from the Make-a-Wish Foundation came to see me. Beth and I were so busy with work she couldn't come with me for the meet-and-greet with the young boy, so she asked Justin to accompany me. The little boy began telling Justin about how bad it hurts when his doctors and nurses poke him with needles. He said the shots make him very sick and that he doesn't want any more treatments. His mother had told him that if he could just endure a few more treatments he'd get to meet Dog the Bounty Hunter, which is how he ended up there that day. Justin was so moved by his story that he spontaneously lifted up his pant leg and popped off his leg to show the little boy. He let him touch his nub and play with his prosthetic leg like he was Captain Hook. The boy and Justin laughed together for several minutes before Justin turned to the little boy and said, "You see? Even I have disabilities, but you can't let that stop you. You have to move on." He showed that little boy that his problems weren't as bad as he'd thought. Being poked with a needle was minor compared to having your leg sawed off. The boy drew so much strength and positive energy from Justin, something Justin had barely had himself a few months prior. I knew in that moment that Justin was well on his way to becoming strong and full of self-respect. It was clear to me he would never leave us again.

Later that day, when Justin returned to the set of the show, he was full of energy, love, and laughter and had finally gotten back to his old adorable self. All it took was for him to be a blessing for somebody else, to show Justin that life is hardly ever as bad as it seems. Justin, who has had his fair share of second chances, is now teaching other people how to get theirs. It's so good to have him back. I'm very proud of the man he's becoming and I take great pride in once again calling him one of "us."

The lesson here is to understand that everybody has problems, handicaps, stigmas, and challenges in their life. How we deal with them is what truly matters. There is hope. If you've been laid off or fired, you can go out there and get another job. You may not get the same job you had, but there is work available if you need to make money. If someone said you're not talented, smart, or educated enough, you can go back to school to study your craft to become the very best at what you do. I'm positive you can overcome most anything life throws your way, because I have done it over and over again. I've gone from a zero to a hero—from a first-degree murder convict to a best-selling author, television star, and advocate for change. If I can do it, you can too.

And just in case you thought my troubles were all behind me, think again. As I write this book, I am faced with the challenge of having to start all over again financially, because I am deeply in debt to the IRS. The truth of the matter is I've never been very good at keeping up with my taxes or other financial obligations because someone else has always taken care of those matters for me. I spent years not knowing where my bank accounts were or how much money was in those accounts, because my mother did my bookkeeping until the day she died. Because I am a convicted felon, my career choices were limited from the very day I was released from prison. It's hard to get a job with a felony conviction on your record. Many people never get the chance to make something out of their lives when they get out of the joint, because society won't give them the opportunity.

When I started writing bail, I made sure my mother kept me current on my bills, taxes, and every other financial obligation I had as a businessman and a parent. I'm not terribly realistic about money and never have been, because I know the Lord will always inevitably provide for me. All I've ever been was the breadwinner—and I'm very good at bringing home the bacon. I've always done whatever it took to make sure I could provide for my family. I did all sorts of odd jobs to supplement the lean years—I sold vacuums, took on private investigation jobs, and anything else that would add a few hundred bucks to my pocket so I could make sure the bills were getting paid. If my bills were two grand a month, I made $1,198—just enough to stay almost even and always two dollars behind.

I've never had large assets, so there were never any real large expenses for homes, boats, cars, and such. I've always rented the houses I've lived in because I never had enough money for a large down payment. Even the cars you see me drive on the show are paid for by the network. With twelve kids, most of my money over the years went to keeping them clothed and fed. After that, my first priority has always been to provide a good education for them. The younger kids all attend private school so they can, at the very least, get a good education. My older kids never had the option of private school because I didn't have the finances to pay for it back then. Since I didn't appreciate school growing up, I always wanted to be certain my kids didn't make the same mistake I did by dropping out. I've always encouraged all of my children to pursue an education before joining the family business.

My mother always told me the love of money was the root of all evil. Having money isn't a bad thing, but *loving* it can be very damaging. I've never had a love of money. If I had gotten the reward money for Luster, I would have given a portion of it to the victims because I feel they were just as deserving of it as I was. At the end of the day, the real reward for me is seeing justice served, not the money I put in my pockets. I guess that's why I am usually without money. I like to share it.

I'm not a fancy guy and my needs have always been basic and simple. One of the reasons I have such an understanding for the people who watch my show is because I am that person. I struggle with bills. I've been a single dad with five kids who each wanted a pair of fifty-dollar jeans. I was never the type of father to tell my kids that they couldn't have something, so I always found a way they got whatever they needed.

After my mother passed away in 1995, my life took a

downward turn. I spiraled out of control until I was no longer able to make my own way. I was on welfare for three months before I finally flew back to Colorado to straighten out my life, get off the drugs I had turned to in my darkest moment, build up my strength, and yes, start all over again. Things were never easy, but I always found a way to get by, and for the most part, despite our limited resources, we were usually pretty happy.

In 2000, I started bounty hunting again after recovering from my battle with drugs and health issues. I was finally on my way back financially. For the first time in five years, money began coming in and I could actually catch up and meet my bills.

At the time, Beth and I had six children under the age of eighteen living at home, plus Moon and her three children were living with us too. Even though I was climbing the ladder again in business, I decided I didn't want to stay in Colorado. I wanted to return to Hawaii. Since my license had been revoked and I could no longer write bail there, I needed to get Beth licensed so she could write bail in Hawaii for us. We were flat broke at the time, so we went to San Diego, where she could get licensed, because it was cheaper than flying all the way to Hawaii.

By late 2001 we were beginning to make a little bit of money, writing one bond at a time. We might have had close to a total of ten thousand dollars in the bank when I got the lead on Andrew Luster. Since I had to fund the hunt for him all on my own, I spent every last dollar I earned in 2002 chasing him down. Once I caught Luster, I thought everything was going to be OK, because I was certain the judge would award us the cost of apprehending him, which totaled more than $300,000 out of my own pocket. The law in California clearly stated that I had 180 days to capture a fugitive to make the claim. We captured

Luster in 166 days. Upon Luster's return to the States, the court was supposed to return the $1 million bail to the person who put it up, less the cost of apprehending the fugitive. In this case, it was Luster who'd posted his own bail, so he was entitled to the balance of the $1 million after our expenses were paid.

At the time, I figured I'd have the reward money from capturing Luster to put a small down payment on a house for my family and catch up with the IRS, which I had fallen behind on during that hunt. Several times during the course of my search for Luster, reporters would ask what I intended to do with the reward money when I found our guy. My response was always the same: "Write my check to the government." But I never got that chance.

We finally started making a little money when we began filming the show, although a lot of it went to paying for my legal defense. I filed my back tax returns and tried to catch up. I paid whatever the accountant told me to pay. By 2005, my tax returns from 2001 to 2004 had all been prepared and filed. Even though I wasn't making any money from 2001 to 2003, the IRS estimated my income to be somewhere in the neighborhood of $800,000 a year. There was significant money coming into the bail bonds businesses I owned in Colorado and Hawaii, but the income wasn't flowing to me personally. It was paid to whatever agent wrote the bond, so I never made the money the IRS was taxing me on. Bail bonds is one of the most heavily audited industries because it is such a high-cash business. The IRS has its own special manual just to audit bail bondsmen. A lot of the time, I don't charge people for picking up a fugitive, so it's hard to prove when I've had to pay a snitch fee or money to informants. Of course, these people don't want to give up their Social Security numbers so I can 1099 them at the end of the year for giving me a little information. Doing that would leave a trail of who my anonymous contacts are. Over the course of my career, I've captured well over six thousand wanted fugitives at no cost to the taxpayers. I am not now, nor have I ever been, out to screw Uncle Sam. The government should have been able to give me the benefit of the doubt, but they didn't.

The IRS decided to audit me in 2006. I had been audited numerous times in the past, so I knew what to expect. For years, I spent countless hours accounting for every dime and deduction on my past tax returns. I even helped a group of auditors in Denver learn about the bail bonds business so they would understand what they were looking at when they examined my accounts. Every single time they audited me, they never found anything unaccounted for. My final bills were always zero. But this time was different. This time around the government based their assessment on inaccurate information, and it was up to me to prove they were wrong. Until I did, I was on the hook.

While they scrutinized every last detail of my financial life, I sat in limbo, unable to make any payments until they came to me with their findings and a final tally of what they believed I owed. I started saving money in a special account marked just for my taxes, so I could settle up with them as quickly as possible once they were done. I received notice in 2008 that I owed the government for back taxes, penalties, and interest from the past several years. I nearly fell out of my chair when my accountants called with the horrifying news and numbers. How could I possibly owe more than I made? I was confused, shocked, and nearly paralyzed by the daunting task of paying off this debt.

Within sixty days of receiving their notice, I paid the government a substantial part of the sum they said I owed, as a gesture of good faith that we would be able to come to some understanding and agreement for a payment plan on the rest of the balance. When my tax attorney asked the IRS for some type of a payment plan and deal, the response was "No deal for the Dog." The IRS told my lawyer that I had the ability to earn money, so there would be no deal for me.

Hmmm. I had to think about this reasoning for a moment because I was well aware that the Senate had just confirmed Timothy Geithner as treasury secretary only days after the fact surfaced that he had only belatedly paid $34,000 in income taxes. Tom Daschle withdrew as President Barack Obama's nominee to be health and human services secretary, even though a day earlier, Obama had said he "absolutely" stood by Daschle in the face of problems over back taxes and potential conflicts of interest. Nancy Killefer, nominated by Obama to be the government's first chief performance officer, ultimately declined the post because she didn't want her bungling of payroll taxes on her household help to be an issue. The list of heavyweight politicians and Hollywood heavy hitters who have had tax issues is long and significant, and yet almost all of them are cut deals so they can settle their debts and move on. Why doesn't this apply to everyone? How is it the government can cherry-pick who they give deals to and who they don't? What exactly are their criteria? I keep thinking this has to be a bad dream, except it's not. It has become my living nightmare. I know the Bible says that sometimes we ought to turn the other cheek, and so far I have, but I've hit my limit when it comes to the Internal Revenue Service.

In the meantime, I am back to where I started so many times in the past. Flat broke—Willie Nelson–style broke. I can barely pay my bills again and am struggling to keep my office doors open. Yet I have an obligation to be a fugitive-catching machine for A&E or I'll be in breach of my contract, which means I won't be able to pay the government because they get 100 percent of my paycheck, leaving me virtually nothing to pay my other bills until my entire debt to them is paid in full.

I could have laid down at any time over the years, allowed my twelve kids to go on state assistance, collected unemployment, and let the government pay me for a while, but I didn't. Even when I did file for welfare several years back after Amwest shut me down, I could only bring myself to stay on it for three short weeks. My pride was too great and my talent too big to waste doing nothing. I manned up for my family, went back to work, and persevered. I picked myself up and rebuilt our business, with Beth by my side, over and over again, until we had built back everything we lost.

Just when I thought I had made it through this last storm with the *Enquirer* and was about to get up on my feet yet again, along came the IRS, like a speeding freight train headed straight for me, saying, "Not so fast, Chapman."

Life is funny like that because whatever it is you're running from, whether it is the IRS or the Dog, you can be sure we'll come back to get you when you least expect it, when you finally think you're safe. Most people don't have the stamina to undergo challenge after challenge, let alone become bankrupt and then make it again, only to repeat that cycle over and over, living life without any sense of stability.

When I got the news about the IRS, I turned to Beth and said, "Let them take it all, honey. I don't care. I've started over before and we can do it again." A few weeks after the accountants delivered the blow, Beth and I anxiously awaited the decision of two $50,000 bonds that were up in the air. Judge Hiatt, the same judge who gave me back my bond license after Amwest took it away, was at lunch pondering his decision. I knew he was never going to give me a break, but he will always rule with dignity in justice. He is one of the most honorable judges I have come across. I turned to Beth and told her he was going to rule in our favor. I was certain of it.

"He can't, Duane. It's impossible." If the judge ruled against us, we'd be on the hook for a hundred thousand dollars. For the first time in years, I heard a defeatist tone in Beth's voice. Her doubt shook me to the core.

"Don't you give up on me, Beth. I know things are going to turn around for us. Judge Hiatt will rule our way and everything will be all right." I took off my black wrap sunglasses and looked at my wife dead in the eyes so she would know I was being very serious. "You believe me, don't you, honey?"

"Yes," she said, but I still wasn't convinced.

"Look at me," I said. "Believe me. It will happen."

"OK, Big Daddy. I'm with you all the way."

I had to smile because inside her doubt, she found her faith. A half hour later the judge called to say he was all set to rule against us, but sometime during his lunch, for reasons he couldn't or wouldn't explain, he changed his mind. I think it was the Lord who spoke to him that afternoon. He must have said, "Be fair to Dog," or something like that, because the judge ruled in our favor.

With Beth on my side, there is an undeniable power between us that makes us impenetrable and unstoppable. We are much stronger together than we are apart. Beth is my rock, my voice of reason, and my almighty protector.

I know I will survive this round of starting over, but it's harder than it used to be. My heartburn is so bad and constant. I have trouble sleeping at night and can barely keep my eyes open during the day. Even so, I keep on going like the Energizer bunny because I have to. In a way, the IRS is nothing more than a federal money detective agency, so as

I would any other detective, I've got to respect them, be nice, and cooperate. This too shall pass.

I won't get beaten down. But I do find it a bit ironic that the very same country that fought to extradite me to Mexico for capturing one of its most wanted fugitives is now standing in front of me, gun to my head, with their hand out saying, "Pay us or else . . ."

The greatest feeling in the world for a bounty hunter—especially this bounty hunter—is knowing justice will be served right after he's caught a fugitive and put him in the backseat of the car. Something about that experience juices up my batteries and gives me the motivation to do it all over again day after day. If it weren't fulfilling, I wouldn't keep risking my life to do it. Not everyone is blessed with the opportunity to do work that they're passionate about. I've always made sure that I had that chance, even when the risks outweighed the reward. As long as I am able to physically keep up the hunt, I will be in the field chasing down criminals and helping to make our communities and country a safer place to live.

It wasn't until a recent fishing trip in the Colorado Rockies that I realized there are alternative ways to keep my batteries charged, without all the adrenaline-pumping risk and danger of bounty hunting.

Beth and I decided to take the kids on a two-day fishing trip during a short break we had from filming our sixth season of *Dog the Bounty Hunter*. We camped out, fished for our food, and cooked over an open campfire every night. We shared a couple of unforgettable days of family bonding and getting back to the basics. It is so easy to get caught up in the hustle and bustle of everyday life, especially when you're juggling family, career, and looming financial obligations. I'm the type of guy who doesn't like to slow down, because I fear I may not want to gear back up again. This trip was different though. I needed some downtime. I wanted to spend a couple of nights with my family, out of cellular range from the rest of the world. I told my manager, lawyers, accountants, and producers I was checking out for a few days.

"If you need to reach me, it better be an emergency." With that message clearly conveyed, I knew I would have the peace, quiet, and quality time with Beth and the kids that I so desperately wanted and needed. With everything that has transpired over the years since capturing Luster, I hadn't taken any significant time off to enjoy being with my family. I missed the days of all of us being together.

On the last day of our trip, we anchored our rented pontoon boat toward the center of the lake. I sat back, stretched out my legs, and breathed in the clean, pure Rocky Mountain air. I could feel the crispness in my chest as it filled up my lungs. The pine trees were fragrant as the cool light breeze and warm sun skimmed my weathered face. My body began to relax as I thought about all of the years that had passed by, my many blessings and, even more so, the numerous life lessons I'd gathered along the way.

For a few minutes it was just me and God.

For the first time in years, I was calm. I didn't have a care in the world. I wasn't concerned about the IRS, getting back into production for season six of the show, or any of the drama from my past. Nope. It was all just flecks of dust in the scheme of what was truly important in life. I realized how absolutely blessed I was.

I must have drifted off, as my mind began playing back the story of my life, like it was an old-time silent movie. I couldn't hear any sound, but I could vividly see all that I held dear, with so much clarity that it felt real. The first person I saw was my mother, who was looking down at me from heaven, her eyes filled with light as she smiled with pride for the decent man I had become.

Barbara Katie was there too. The first thing I noticed was that she wasn't wearing her glasses. My God, she looked so radiant and beautiful. She said, "Daddy, my eyesight is perfect now. I no longer need to wear my glasses." I could feel tears welling up and a giant lump growing in my throat because I was so glad to see her again. She was genuinely happy and finally at peace. I realized I could now rest easy, knowing she was safe because she was now in God's hands.

Unexpectedly, Jerry Lee Oliver, the man I was convicted of murdering, appeared too. He looked exactly the same as the last day I saw him in Pampa, young and full of life. I was a bit startled as he turned to me and said, "I know you weren't the triggerman. But you did your time and I want you to know that I forgive you. Now I am asking you to forgive yourself, Dog." Those were the words I've spent the past thirty-five years waiting to hear. Even if it was only my dream, I felt a sense of relief and a strange feeling of freedom from Jerry's acknowledgment.

Seeing Jerry Lee brought back thoughts of Boss Ironhorn, Warden Curly Horton, and all of the other guys I knew from back in Huntsville, who inspired me to go out and make something of my life. I smiled as I thought back on those eighteen months I spent behind bars. Nothing in my life could have prepared me for my future better than my time in Huntsville. It taught me how to survive, endure, and thrive in the face of hardship, challenge, and adversity and—most important—to face those things with courage and integrity. Without those eighteen months in prison, I am not sure I would have found my way to living on the right side of the law.

The movie in my mind began to speed up as visions of my twelve children and all of their children filled my heart with the greatest joy I have ever known. Even though I have a little anger toward some of my ex-wives, I can't help but feel completely grateful for the children we share.

I could feel the boat gently rocking in the calm lake. The splash of a jumping fish coming out of the water startled me and woke me up. My eyes shot wide open. I had to focus for a moment, but then I noticed a bald eagle perched on the branch of a tree that hung about twenty feet above the water. I quietly pointed the eagle out to Beth and the kids. We all sat quiet and motionless as we took in the unforgettable, once-in-a-lifetime moment. I slowly got up and reached for our bucket of fish. I grabbed the biggest trout I could put my hand on without making any abrupt moves and then tossed it into the water. I never took my eyes off the eagle. I wanted him to know it was safe—that we wouldn't hurt him.

The eagle took flight, majestic and proud. He soared through the sky, circling above our heads until suddenly he dove headfirst toward the lake.

Swoosh!

He grabbed the fish in his talons and, in a single motion, took off toward the west and into the sun. We were mesmerized by his grace and beauty, yet touched by the trust and faith he and we gave to one another.

Bonnie Jo has a natural instinct when it comes to her love of nature and animals. "Throw another fish into the lake, Dad. Maybe you can get him to come back for more!" she squealed with delight.

Even though I tossed another fish into the water, I knew he was not coming back.

In Native American culture, the eagle is a symbol of power and perfection. It is also a witness, a sign, that everything is as it should be. In an instant, I felt as if I had no more secrets and that my life was finally on the right path. In that second, I felt as if mercy had ultimately been shown.

The thing about moments like this is that you can't re-live them because they cannot be re-created. That's why it is so important to cherish every minute of bliss each and every day. Life can change quickly. You never really know where, when, how, or what to expect, so you may as well embrace all of your experiences, good and bad, with gusto.

There is no greater gift or blessing in this world for me than spending quality time with my family. Wherever I go, people always ask me about my children. Some of you have watched my kids grow up in front of your eyes, week after week, as each season of the show passes by. As a father, I often wonder which of my kids is destined to do greater things in his or her life than I have done.

Duane Lee has the brains to be a doctor or lawyer. He has the smarts to do and be anything he wants in his life. When I look at Duane Lee today, I see a lot of my father and quite a bit of me. Duane Lee isn't abusive like my dad was, but he knows how to put up a good fight, stand his ground, and isn't about to back down from anyone or anything, including his old man. Whenever he and I have some sort of disagreement, I have to remind myself that I may as well be standing there arguing with myself. I thought about an analogy I once heard where someone held up a mirror and began arguing with the face in the reflection. Who's going to win that fight?

Even though Duane Lee is six two, I still see my baby boy in his eyes, the one that always reached his hands out to me and said, "I want to go with my daddy." Today, of course, I stand behind Duane Lee as we crash through closed doors and into the unknown when we're on chases, because he's grown into such a fine man and excellent bounty hunter. He and I communicate with a single look. He never has to ask me what I mean when I give an order. He gets it, and does whatever I say without hesitation. He's tough, smart, and fearless, and I'm so proud of who he has become in his life.

Baby Lyssa loves to write and has the potential to become a great author someday, but in the meantime she has turned into quite the bounty hunter. She studied with the best woman role model I can think of—Beth. Baby Lyssa is as tough and sharp as Beth in every way. I'll never forget the first hunt we took her on. We were chasing down a fugitive who was giving us a pretty good run, when Baby Lyssa spotted him across a parking lot. She called it in on her walkie-talkie, but was on the ground with the guy before any of us could get to her. She's got great spunk and spirit.

At twenty-two years old, Baby Lyssa has experienced so many of life's ups and downs. She's been through a lot of trauma, having survived a rape, drug addiction, the death of her older sister, becoming a teenage single mom, and the betrayal of her brother. It is a relief to see that she's found herself after so many painful years of struggling. I watched happily as she married her sweetheart in the spring of 2009 in the most beautiful ceremony on the north shore of Oahu. She was radiant in her gown, glowing with joy. We were surrounded by two hundred of our closest family and friends, who were there to help us celebrate the marriage of my oldest living daughter. I was moved by the realization that she would now hold her husband in higher esteem than me, and yet I was so relieved to see my baby finally happy and content. Baby Lyssa gave birth to her second child, Madalynn, on August 7, 2009. Even pregnancy couldn't stop her from being in the field with her old man and brothers, helping us find fugitives. She proves to me every day that women can do it all.

There is no greater joy for a parent than knowing you've done all you can to prepare your children to go out into the world and seeing your influence and inspiration come to life as they mature and find their own way as adults. I have watched Baby Lyssa accept the responsibilities of becoming a parent in a different way than she did with her first child, whom she had when she was only fourteen years old, just a child herself. The attachment she has to her newborn baby is nothing short of a miracle.

Leland is the child I think has the greatest chance to follow in his old man's footsteps. When Leland was born, I only had one son—that I knew about anyway. I didn't yet know about my oldest boy, Christopher, whom I would discover was mine twenty-nine years after he was born.

There was something about Leland as my baby boy that made him extraordinary in my eyes. I'm sure most fathers feel that way about their sons, just as they carry a special place in their heart for their firstborn too. It takes a man to make a boy, and at the time, I had two boys whom I loved with all my heart.

Leland and Duane Lee moved to Colorado Springs with their mother after I went to prison. Leland was a baby, barely nine months old, when I went in. Duane Lee was a toddler. I missed out on so many moments of their lives, special times that I'll never get back. I take the blame for that. Even so, I hoped they would welcome me back into their lives when we finally reconnected.

I spent five years fighting their mother, LaFonda, in court before I was awarded visitation rights to see the boys on weekends. I had waited seven years for the chance to get my boys back. As excited as I was at the idea of seeing them again, they didn't share my enthusiasm. My boys were scared to be alone with me because I was a stranger to them, especially Leland, who was now nine years old.

It took time for the three of us to get to know one another again. Although the process was sometimes very frustrating and heartbreaking, eventually we began to bond. I showed them affection, gave them lots of hugs and kisses, and tried to be the best father I knew how to be.

I had finally begun to connect with Leland when I almost blew us back to square one when he came to show me a loose tooth one day. When I was a boy, my grandpa used to tie one end of a string around a doorknob and the other to my tooth. When the tooth was good and loose, he'd yank it out by slamming the door! I thought that was how all teeth got pulled, so when Leland came to me, I did what Grandpa had done. The problem was that Leland's tooth wasn't quite ready to come out. He went flying off the stool I had him sitting on and tumbled onto the floor. Duane Lee cracked up watching this disaster unfold, as his brother lay there crying, more from fear than pain. I felt awful, but it turned out to be a breakthrough moment for us.

From that day on, Leland has stuck it out with me through some pretty rough times. And for as long as I can remember, he has shown more interest in bounty hunting than any of my other kids. All of my children have grown up in the family business, but Leland was a natural-born bloodhound.

As my kids got older, I didn't feel comfortable being away from them all the time, so I began taking them to work with me. By the time Duane Lee was fifteen, an age where young boys need more attention so they stay out of trouble, I really knew I couldn't leave him unsupervised, so I kept a watchful eye on my boys as often as I could.

As close as we were, I had to be careful not to be just friends with my kids. They needed a parent who was willing to be present. It's important to be a part of their lives so you know what's going on with them outside the home, and then stay there until it is time for you to go off to the old folks' home. Being with them gives you gigantic purpose and meaning in life. I'm happiest when I'm surrounded by my wife, children, and grandchildren. There's nothing more precious in the world to me than family. As a dad, I feel it is my responsibility to make sure the children are taken care of in every way. Although I encouraged them to have friends growing up, as a large family we always had one another. I wanted to include my kids in every aspect of my life, so I made sure they learned the family business from an early age.

Some people think it's unusual that our family is so close. We work together, spend free time with one another, and have built a television dynasty based on our strong family foundation. It's natural that as parents, we worry about losing our babies, even when they are no longer children. After the tragic loss of Barbara Katie, I swore I'd never let any of them out of my grip again.

As hard as we try as parents, though, our kids still have the gift of free will and therefore the ability to make their own decisions along the way. You hope and pray you've done everything you can to prepare them to be out on their own, but there are no guarantees. I read an article about two boys riding ATVs without helmets who decided to have a chicken fight. They crashed into each other going forty miles per hour. They didn't stand a chance of survival. Worse, one of the guys had his girlfriend on the back of his vehicle. She survived, but ended up in a coma. After hearing that story, I thought about those parents and how they felt when they heard the news. I have no doubt those boys knew about helmets and safety—that their parents taught them what was right when it came to riding their ATVs, and yet, sadly, they chose to ignore all that they knew was for their own well-being, and in the end, they paid the ultimate price for their stupidity. In the process, they left their parents behind to grieve and wonder for the rest of their lives what they could have done to prevent their children's deaths.

As a parent, I spend lots of time questioning whether I am being the best role model for my kids. Do I set the standard I want them to live up to, or am I somehow showing them it's OK to be less than your very best? I've made a lot of decisions along the way that I probably wouldn't have made if I'd had the knowledge then that I have now. Of course, experience is born out of necessity, and I know there's no way to gain it before its time.

I spent years trying to prove to my kids that I wasn't the bad guy their various mothers made me out to be. All of my ex-wives told our kids I was a no-good criminal, a biker, and a deadbeat dad. It was important to show them who I really was and what I did for a living. I wanted them to see firsthand that their dad wasn't any of those things.

There were times I took the kids on bounty hunts when I probably shouldn't have because they were too young or the situation was too dangerous. I'll confess that on more than one occasion I even ended up taking my work home with me.

One morning, the kids woke up to find a fugitive handcuffed to the fifty-five-gallon fish tank in our living room. I'd warned the guy that if he broke my fish tank and hurt my fish or my kids, I'd beat the crap out of him. The kids got up to get dressed for school and asked the poor fool if he wanted a piece of toast. To them, he was nothing but another bad guy Daddy caught who'd spent the night at their house. They each waved good-bye to him as they left for school like it was an everyday occurrence and just another morning in the Chapman household.

Sometimes the kids would be in the car when I caught

my guy. I'd warn him he'd better be civil and polite in front of my babies or he'd be roadkill. The kids never thought much of the day-to-day adventure that was our life. They'd start up a conversation with the captured fugitive like an old family friend had gotten into the car.

"Hi. You going to jail? What did you do wrong?" they'd ask him.

On a few rare occasions, I even used the kids as decoys. Leland once carried Baby Lyssa up to the front door of a suspect's house and asked if they had seen her missing puppy. Baby Lyssa was crying like she had really lost her best friend. We sprayed a little milk on her face to make it look like real tears, messed up her hair and clothes so it would look like she was distraught. When they answered their door, Leland looked in the house to see if our guy was there. Blam. He was.

I spent years trying to instill a solid work ethic into each of my children. I taught them to strive for excellence at whatever they did. I wanted them to seek out things they were interested in and become the best at them. Some have followed that route, while others . . . not so much.

Leland had shown an interest in my work from the day he came to live with me. As he got older, I began taking him with me whenever I had to fly from Hawaii to Denver for a job. Leland was no more than twenty-one or twenty-two years old, but he was quickly becoming a very good bounty hunter. On one particular trip, I picked up a jump from a local bondsman that said we were looking for a guy named Mad Max Valez. We made a quick stop at Radio Shack to pick up batteries for our walkie-talkies. As we were pulling out, a cop car blocked us from leaving.

The cop got out and started walking toward us. I guess I looked like a bounty hunter to him. "I can see *what* you are, but *who* the hell are you?" he asked.

"I'm Dog Chapman, the bounty hunter from TV." At that point, I had only been on a show called *The Secret World of Bounty Hunters*. This was a couple of years before I had my own show.

"I don't watch much television. Sorry, pal. Who you looking for?" he asked.

"A guy named Mad Max Valez. You ever heard of him?"

"Yeah. He used to be around all the time, but he ain't been here for a while."

"Really?" I was intrigued.

He continued. "Yeah, he and his kooky old lady are gone."

I glanced over at Leland, hoping he was picking up on all of the clues the cop was unaware he was feeding us. "Are you sure his old lady is gone too?" I asked after a moment.

"Naw. She still may be around. Just Mad Max is gone. We searched the house three or four times and came up with nothing." The cop instinctively knew we were legit, so he didn't detain us much longer. After he drove away, I turned to Leland and asked him if he'd caught all the clues.

"Yeah. The guy said, 'We searched the house and came up with nothing' was the first one, Dad," Leland told me.

"Good boy. Any others?"

"Yeah. His old lady is a whacko."

"Good boy. Anything else?"

"No."

Leland got them all.

I beamed with pride as Leland and I drove to the local library to pull Max's library card, something I used to do before the Internet. You'd be amazed at how much information you can gather at your local library. It turned out he had a different address listed with the library than we had on the bond. We drove to the house, knocked on the door, and asked if Max was home.

An elderly couple answered. They could have been his parents. "Oh no. We haven't seen him in weeks," they told us.

As we made our way back toward our car, I turned to Leland and asked if the report listed what type of cigarettes Max smoked. Most fugitives are smokers, so a lot of bondsmen will ask them for those types of details when filling out the paperwork. Sure enough, Leland said, "Salems."

We had some searching to do. Leland pulled a pair of rubber gloves from his pocket and began picking through the trash cans in the back of the house. I call this technique "garbology" because we're like archaeologists sifting through the ruins looking for any sign of civilization. We go through the layers of trash trying to piece together any clue that will help lead us to our man. When you've done this as much as we have, you can pinpoint dates, times, and all sorts of other helpful information. At the very bottom of the bin we found an empty pack of Salem cigarettes. We knew the pack hadn't been in there very long because we found a recent newspaper right on top of it. I was proud to see that Leland was growing into a seasoned bounty hunter and was learning all the tricks of the trade. I had taught him well.

After finding the cigarette pack in the trash, we walked back around the house and knocked on the door again. However, this time no one answered. Something wasn't right. Before Leland and I knew it, two pit bulls came tearing out of the backyard and began chasing us. I quickly reached for the Mace can on my belt and blasted one of them in the face. I soaked that son of a bitch from head to tail, being extra careful not to get any in his eyes. The dumb dog actually stood there and let me spray him down. I hit him with as much Mace as I could, hoping he'd run back into the house through the dog door I spotted. If there was someone hiding in that house, they were in for a burning surprise when that dog came bolting in. I didn't intend to hurt the animal, but we had to be absolutely sure no one was home.

Then, Leland and I put our ears up to the front door to listen. One sneeze or cough was all I needed. But there was nothing. Still, I was convinced someone was home. While being very careful not to be seen, Leland peeked into one of the windows that was wide open with the screen down, so we could take a look inside the house. Nada. Zip. Zilch. Yet I couldn't shake the feeling they were there.

Leland was convinced they were listening to us. We were talking out loud, saying what our next move was going to be, so maybe that was the case. It was time to regroup, assess the situation, and make a plan.

We decided to head to a diner on the corner to get some lunch. It's important to nourish the body when you can when you're on a hunt, because you never know how long it'll be before your next meal. We used that time to brainstorm and gather our thoughts on where Max could be hiding. We rehashed everything we'd seen and decided Max was definitely at that house.

When we went back, Leland peered in the same window as before. Only this time he spotted two plates and a pizza box.

I asked Leland if he was positive there wasn't a box there before.

"I'm not positive, Dad," he said, going back over it in his mind. "I didn't do my job right, because I'm not absolutely one hundred percent sure."

"Close your eyes, son, and visualize what you saw. Think hard. Was there a pizza box there when you looked inside the house the first time?"

"I don't know!" he snapped. I could tell Leland was getting flustered. The only way we'd be able to know if the pizza was fresh was to touch it. If it was old, it would be cold, but if it was fresh, it would still be hot.

"You've got to go in, son," I told him. "That's the only way we'll know for sure."

"But, Dad, isn't that breaking and entering?" Leland asked.

"Yes, but it's a misdemeanor. If you get caught, I'll bail you out."

Luckily, Leland was able to slip through the open window. Once he'd climbed into the house, he crouched down on the floor like a soldier and shimmied his way over to the pizza box. He reached his hand up to touch it and then jumped up and through the window in one fluid motion.

"It's hot, Dad. The pizza is hot," he said quietly.

"We're going through the front door, Leland. That's probable cause and we're going in right now," I whispered back.

Boom! We booted the door in. Immediately, a woman came running into the room screaming her head off.

"Help me. Police!" She was yelling into her mobile phone. "They're here right now. They're breaking in. Can you hear them?" And then she held the phone up so the police could hear the ruckus.

I began to worry that Leland was right, we shouldn't have broken in, but then I remembered that in Colorado, you had to have the intent to commit a felony and remain in the house or it is considered a misdemeanor.

Before either of us knew it, there was a cop at the front door. Not just any cop, the same one who had pulled us over earlier in the Radio Shack parking lot. He was soon flanked by two of his deputies. Leland and I were in a tight spot, so I did the only thing that popped into my head in the heat of the moment. I bolted through the house like greased lightning and hit the back door going forty miles an hour. I ripped the screen and took the door right off its hinges.

"Tell the cops I'm on his ass!" I yelled back at Leland.

Leland knew I was lying, but he did it anyway. "My dad saw the guy tear out the back door. He's chasing Max Valez!" he shouted.

The cops bought into the story hook, line, and sinker. As I was running I could hear dogs barking and see the flashing lights in the distance behind me. The dogs were sniffing, looking for a scent. A moment later, the sheriff yelled out, "You got him, Dog?"

"No, but he's out here somewhere," I answered back.

In the meantime, Leland went to work on the woman back at the house. He told her she better tell him where Max was hiding or she was going to jail for harboring a fugitive. Still, she refused to cooperate.

"Let me see your cell phone," Leland demanded. When he paged through the recent calls, sure enough Max's number was on her phone. They had spoken an hour after we got to her house the first time. She had tipped him off that we were hot on his trail.

By then, I had the cops with me searching a nearby field. I knew there was no one hiding in the area we were in, but I had to go through the motions or we were going to go to jail for breaking and entering. Just as I started to tell the sheriff, "It doesn't look like he's out here," Leland radioed me. It was the first time he'd ever used the radio on a hunt.

"Dad, Dad, come in," he called.

"What is it, son? Do you have him?" I turned around and started running back toward the house. The cops also heard the call on the radio and hightailed it back as fast as they could.

"I got him, Dad. There's a cave dug under the basement and there's a bunch of dead animal carcasses in there. I think he's hiding in the cave. Hurry, Dad, hurry!"

I got back to the house and saw the dead animal remains all over the basement. He must have been feeding the dogs with the meat. Leland and I locked arms and made our way into the darkness of the cave. It was so dark that I couldn't see my hand in front of my face. We began patting down the walls and every other surface, feeling mostly rocks and dirt, and then we felt a body. I immediately jumped on him and put him into a headlock.

"You son of a bitch. What's your name?" I shouted.

"Max Valez."

"Gotcha."

I told Max to follow me out of the hole or I'd be back down to get him, and next time I wasn't going to be as gentle. I pulled myself out of the hole so the cops would know I was coming out without Mad Max but he was in there. I wanted to watch the dramatic ending to this hunt myself.

I yelled down and said, "You coming or am I coming back for you?"

Max emerged bloody and a little tattered. The cops got most of the glory for the capture that day, but I'd gotten the man we were all looking for. Actually, check that. Leland had gotten our man that day. That's my boy.

A film crew once asked three of my children what they thought my secret to success was. Duane Lee told the reporter that I have a way of just figuring things out. Baby Lyssa told him I have always been able to find who I am looking for. And finally, Leland answered, "I know it's God." I think all three had the right answer. Those kids sure do make their old man proud.

When I was a young boy, my mother used to tell me she had eyes in the back of her head. She could see everything I did, so I'd better behave or else. I once looked at the back of her head while Mom was getting her hair done, to see if I could spot an extra set of eyes, but there wasn't one. It took me years to figure out those eyes were just a mother's intuition. And I suppose fathers have that special talent too.

Leland would follow me to the ends of the earth. In many ways, he always has. Our journey to Mexico to find Andrew Luster was as close to hell as I ever want to lead my pack. Whenever we find ourselves in some type of confrontation, Leland is right there with me, ready to pounce. He's a trigger just waiting to go off. He's not rash or uncontrolled. Quite the contrary. Leland assesses everything he sees and is ready for whatever comes his way. If Beth or I find ourselves being confronted by someone, Leland is already circling like a hawk waiting for its prey. He's patient, smart, loyal, dedicated, and very cautious not to make a move until he absolutely has to.

While shooting an episode for our fifth season, I was surprised when one of the fugitives we caught slapped me right across the face. I hadn't even bounced back from the shock, when Leland grabbed the punk's hand and beat him down. I always tell people I never worry about not carrying a gun. When someone asks if I carry a weapon, I always respond by saying, "Yup. A double-barreled shotgun . . . and her name is Beth." Beth's better than any firearm, and Leland is a lethal weapon.

My youngest son, Gary Boy, is just like Leland. He's got bloodhound running through his veins. He wants to be a cop when he gets older, but I think he'll grow up to be the best bounty hunter this family has ever produced. While most kids spend their childhood playing cops and robbers, cowboys and Indians, Gary Boy plays bounty hunter and fugitive. He has watched his old man catch bad guys on television his whole life.

I had taken my daughter Bonnie Jo and Gary Boy Christmas shopping a few years ago, when I noticed a tweaker walk by us at the local mall. I could tell he was a criminal bastard from the moment I saw him. He had a backpack slung over his shoulder and was out boosting stuff from all the stores. As soon as he spotted me, he began to freak out. He was twitching, shaking, and clearly avoiding eye contact with me.

Gary Boy noticed almost as quickly as I did. He turned to me and said, "Dad, did you see that guy? He's a bad guy! He's stealing things."

I had to laugh, because he was right. For fun I said, "Let's tail him, Gary."

The three of us slowly turned around to follow him. When he saw us, he took off running. As soon as Gary saw him bolt, he started chasing after him. I followed after Gary, who was outpacing me by two strides. Bonnie Jo was bringing up the rear. I worried about losing her behind us so I yelled the same commands out to Gary as I do when I'm out on a real hunt.

"Stand down. Stop, Gary. Freeze!" Gary spent the next twenty minutes begging me to let him go after the guy, who was now long gone.

"What are you going to do if you catch him, son?" I asked.

"Give me your cuffs, Dad. I'll grab him and cuff him."

I was humored by the exchange yet proud too. I said, "Gary, he's twice as big as you are. He'll clobber you if you try to catch him."

"No, he won't, Dad. I'll use my martial arts on him that Master Lee taught me." Gary Boy had been taking self-defense classes for some time. Even though he was only seven years old, he was confident in his ability to protect himself.

Gary Boy's interest in bounty hunting only seems to grow stronger as time goes on. He loves to be on the lookout wherever we go. Seven months after the incident at the mall, our family was in Colorado celebrating the Fourth of July at a large event in Denver. I gave Gary a radio just in case he got lost. A short time later, I heard him call me over the speaker.

"Dad, come in, Dad. This is Gary."

"Go ahead, son. Where are you at?" I asked.

"I'm following a criminal. The police are coming with me too." Gary had found a police officer and told him he had a suspect in his sight and needed backup! I'm very proud that Gary's got the hunter in him. He's a natural and a chip off the old block.

And if Gary Boy decides not to pursue bounty hunting, I believe he'll grow up to become a professional baseball player like Beth's dad. He's got an extraordinary natural talent for the game. He surely doesn't get that from his old man!

My daughter Cecily celebrated her sweet sixteen in 2009. That's a real milestone in our home because that's the age our children are allowed to sit with the older kids, Beth, and me around the patio table at night when we hold Chapman Family Powwows. That's where we discuss everything happening in our lives as a family. On the night of her sixteenth birthday, I invited Cecily to join in. Since that night, I feel our relationship has grown closer. I am extremely proud of Cecily. She is the first in our family who will attend college. As a seventh-grade dropout, that makes me very happy. Education was never a priority to me when I was younger, so I've gone out of my way to see to it that my younger children don't follow in my footsteps. Cecily recently witnessed the birth of Baby Lyssa's daughter. She was in the room with her sister when the baby was born. A couple of days later, I asked Cecily what she thought about witnessing the miracle of life coming into this world. Her response was unforgettable.

"I've taken all of the boys' names and numbers out of my cell phone for now!"

I had to laugh. "You didn't like the experience?" I asked.

"Not for at least another ten years!"

Right answer, sweetheart!

The Chapmans are like a pack of wolves. We want to be bondsmen and bounty hunters. We chase human beings for a living. That is what we do, who we are, and all we want to be.

Because I'm the leader of the pack, my children are reflections of the way I am. If we go home without a capture, everyone is pretty down about it. When we walk through the front door after a long day and night of bounty hunting, we're annoyed, hungry, tired, and pissed off we didn't get our jump. The first thing Bonnie Jo and Gary Boy ask is if we caught the bad guy. When I tell them no, they get sad too. But when we capture the fugitive, we're like the Waltons. There are hugs, high fives, and "I love you's" all the way around. Beth starts singing "Hallelujah" and we're all bonded as one chord. So if any of us were ever to walk away from our show, there's no doubt what we'd do with our lives. It's in our blood.

ACKNOWLEDGMENTS

I must first thank my wife, Beth, for all of the time, effort, insight, and intelligence she offered to this book. Without you, I would never be able to accomplish the things I do every day as a husband, father, businessman, and leader. I love you for all you do to protect me and for helping make all of my dreams come true.

Next, I want to thank my fans. Your never-ending support and understanding keeps me going, especially when times are tough. I commit to being a better role model so that my actions inspire each of you to lead with pride in your own lives.

I want to thank my family at A&E for sticking with me. They knew my heart even though they were sometimes offended by my words. I need to give a special thank you to Nancy Dubuc. Nancy, you gave me life at the network. I know I must have offended you with my carelessness or, worse, embarrassed you. I am truly sorry. I owe you so much and will do my best to never let you down again.

And to Doug Jacobs, who has been a great champion of mine throughout our years working together on my never-ending legal entanglements. I will always remain grateful to you for giving me the green light to make some hard decisions and then sticking by me when I pulled the trigger.

I need to thank my legal team, who finally put an end to the Luster case and gave me back my freedom. James Quadra, Alberto Zinser, Eduardo Amerena, and Brook Hart. Jim, you took the reins and led our team to victory with the authority and mastery we needed. Alberto and Eduardo, you handled the situation in Mexico with grace and finesse. My only regret is not meeting the three of you sooner! Brook, your precedent-setting legal maneuvers freed me from jail. I'm forever grateful.

To Bob DiBietta and Rob Sharenow, for your support and for standing up for us and doing all you can to help us through the tough times. We know you are our strongest supporters through the toughest times.

I want to thank my manager and literary agent, Alan Nevins. Alan stayed when most managers would have fled. Thank you for having enough respect for me to ask the hard questions. I knew for sure that you understood how I felt in my heart. You've put countless hours of your own blood, sweat, and tears into helping me shape my career and making the right choices along the way. Don't think for a moment that I don't know what you give up to be there for me. I will be forever appreciative of the day you stepped into my life and for remaining a large part of my success.

Anthony Mattero at Renaissance. You are an important and valuable member of our team. There are simply no words to thank you enough for everything you do on a daily basis for me.

Thank you to my co-author, Laura Morton, for coming on board for our second book together. You once again captured my voice in a way that garners my utmost respect. Your patience, understanding, and commitment mean the world to me.

Adam Mitchell. You make the process enjoyable for all of us.

I want to thank my family at Hyperion, starting with my publisher, Ellen Archer, who didn't flinch at the idea of a second book when she took over. Thank you also to my wonderfully patient editor, Brendan Duffy, and to Kristin Kiser. I have to give a special thank you to Muriel Tebid— my most beloved nemesis. I know you were looking out for me and always had my back and Hyperion's back, but that doesn't mean we don't want to argue about it! You have great patience and a wonderful calm about you that helped us navigate the sometimes rough water. I know there are many others at Hyperion who I've not met but who have played a role in helping me create my book. I want to thank you all for the countless hours I know you've put into the process.

Finally, I want to thank the Lord for His love and for blessing me with my wonderful family. I try to keep all of my babies close to me, as it's my family that keeps a smile on my face and has given me my greatest purpose in life. It is my sincerest hope that my children understand the life lessons I am passing on to them and that they learn from Dad's mistakes rather than making them on their own. I love each of you and pray we stand strong and remain united as a family for the rest of my days. May God be with you and your families long after I am gone.

DUANE "DOG" CHAPMAN
DECEMBER 2009